"What are the main issues psychoanalysts face while working in their institutions: training institutes, societies, international associations? Are they the same as in any institution with regard to the conflicts between individual requests for more freedom and the need to have institutional structures and rules? Or do psychoanalytical institutions have some specific problems and solutions? These questions are studied in a very precise and profound way in this book by many experienced psychoanalysts and authors. It is well known that conflicts in psychoanalytic institutions are linked to the specificity of the psychoanalytic experience and of its transmission to candidates within training institutes. Most splittings in psychoanalytic Societies have been caused by differences in training philosophies and practices. One reason could be the differences between the analytic experience which concerns psychic reality and involves no restrictions of time, and the requirements of training by psychoanalytic institutes with educational tasks, especially the evaluation of candidates, implying time limits. This is a paradoxical situation: it is necessary to evaluate an internal process which is not observable or quantifiable. But at the same time this evaluation involves a judgement whose aim is to take an institutional decision, involving issues of power and authority. This very stimulating book rightly shows that psychoanalysts are exposed to narcissistic and identity-related problems because of the pluralism in training models and in psychoanalytical theories and practices. A solution to these paradoxical situations, which is stressed by many authors, would be to promote the development of work groups and to always rely on a third-party position, which would contribute at different levels, to overcome dual and conflictual issues. This book should be of great help to psychoanalysts and psychoanalytical institutions in reflecting on extremely important issues for the future of psychoanalysis in these times of scientific, political and social challenges."

Alain Gibeault is a training analyst and president of the Education Committee of the Paris Psychoanalytical Society, past president of the European Psychoanalytical Federation and past secretary general of the International Psychoanalytical Association

I0091846

Living and Containing Psychoanalysis in Institutions

Encompassing diverse perspectives on the psychoanalyst as individual, social being, and member of psychoanalytic institutions, this book provides practical and informed answers to the question of how psychoanalysts can take care of their psychoanalytic institutions.

The book draws urgent attention to concerns about how the field of psychoanalysis can be sustained into the future, and sets out several studies in institutional dynamics as a form of provocation for psychoanalysts to reflect on their position as members of the institution and to act courageously in their collective efforts. Correlations between institutional dynamics and familial relationships are emphasized, alongside varied and detailed accounts of the styles of leadership required to facilitate improved cooperation in psychoanalytic institutions. The authors draw on their experiences as group participants, leaders, and observers at both local and supranational levels, to investigate the historical context underpinning the disillusion among psychoanalysts, offering readers richly informed perspectives on how to nurture collegial ethics.

With an emphasis on a shared ethics of responsibility, and the work involved in building secure professional relationships among psychoanalytic groups of all kinds, this book will prove essential to those engaged in understanding the work involved in psychoanalysis, whether in training or in practice.

Gabriele Junkers, PhD, is a psychologist, analyst and training analyst of the German Psychoanalytic Association (DPV). She can look back on 40 years as analyst and 25 years as training analyst in private practice. She has experience of institutional counselling in various clinical settings, in addition to ethics and gerontology, having worked with psychiatric in-/outpatients and in private practice for 35 years. She was previously a member of the EPF Executive for 15 years and has worked for IPA as a sponsor for developing a new group. She has published books and papers in the field of psychoanalysis, gerontology, and institutional matters.

Leading and Containing Psychoanalysis in Institutions

Psychoanalysts Working Together

Edited by Gabriele Junkers

Routledge
Taylor & Francis Group

LONDON AND NEW YORK

Cover image: photo by John Churcher, Annalisa Ferretti de Montalcini, and Gabriele Junkers

First published 2023
by Routledge
4 Park Square, Milton Park, Abingdon, Oxon OX14 4RN

and by Routledge
605 Third Avenue, New York, NY 10158

Routledge is an imprint of the Taylor & Francis Group, an informa business

British Library Cataloguing-in-Publication Data
A catalogue record for this book is available from the British Library

Library of Congress Cataloging-in-Publication Data
A catalog record has been requested for this book

ISBN: 9781032295121 (hbk)
ISBN: 9781032295138 (pbk)
ISBN: 9781003301936 (ebk)

DOI: 10.4324/9781003301936

Typeset in Garamond
by Newgen Publishing UK

Contents

Contributors

Stefano Bolognini, MD, is a psychiatrist and works in Psychiatric Services as a supervisor. He is training and supervising analyst of the Italian Psychoanalytic Society (SPI) and IPA, has served as honorary secretary (1997–2001) as well as president of SPI (2009–2013). He was IPA Board Member (2002–2012), IPA president (2013–2017), and member of the European Editorial Board of the *International Journal of Psychoanalysis* (2002–2012). He has been the founder and chair of the IPA Inter-Regional Encyclopedic Dictionary of Psychoanalysis (IRED) since 2016, as well as honorary member of the New York Contemporary Freudian Society (CFS) and of the Los Angeles Institute and Society for Psychoanalytic Studies (LAISPS), and member of the Advisory Board of the International Psychoanalytic University of Berlin (IPU). His main theoretical interests are Empathy, Inter-Psychic Dimension, and Institutional Issues. He has published numerous papers and volumes, translated to several languages.

Cláudio Laks Eizirik is a psychiatrist, training, and supervising analyst, Porto Alegre Psychoanalytic Society; he was dean of the Medical School, chair of the MsC and PhD Program of Psychiatry and is professor emeritus of Psychiatry, Federal University of Rio Grande do Sul, Brazil. He was IPA Board Member (2001–2004) and president of the IPA from 2005 to 2009; president of the Latin American Psychoanalytic Federation (1998–2000); recipient of the Sigourney Award, 2011; He is currently chair of the IPA International Committee on New Groups. He is also author of psychoanalytic papers, book chapters, and books with special interest in psychoanalytic training and technique, the process of aging, institutional issues, and the relationship of psychoanalysis, psychiatry, and culture.

Serge Frisch, MD, is a psychiatrist, and training and supervising analyst of the Belgian (SBP) and German Psychoanalytic Society (DPG). Former general secretary (2006–2008) and president (2008–2011) of the Belgian Psychoanalytic Society. He was president of the European Psychoanalytic

Federation (2012–2016), chair of the Working Party on the Specificity o
Psychoanalytic Treatment Today (WP SPTT) (2009–2012), member of the
IPA Board (2017–2019), the Excom (2019–2021), and of the Sponsoring
Committee to Beirut (2009–2021). He had advisory function within the
Ministry of Health, Luxembourg. He was active member of several sci
entific committees of psychoanalytic journals, and has been lecturing a
Brussels University.

Gabriele Junkers, PhD, is a psychologist, analyst and training analyst of the
German Psychoanalytic Association (DPV). She can look back on 40 years
as analyst, and 25 years as training analyst in private practice. For 10 year
she was coordinator of the DPV's ethics council and for 10 years a member
of the mediation committee of the DPV's ethics commission. She has
treated patients in psychiatric hospitals on an inpatient and outpatient
basis, and acted as an organizational counselor in various (clinical) settings
and social institutions. She has taught psychology at the University of
Bremen. With her special interest in the problems of aging, she treated
elderly people in clinical, in- and outpatient, as well as in private-practice
contexts, published studies on the psychic problems of the elderly, on
older analysands and aging psychoanalysts, and included these topics in
the training for budding psychoanalysts. For approximately 15 years, she
was a member of the executive board of the EPF as editor of the EPF bulletin "Psychoanalysis in Europe," honorary secretary of the EPF, and chair
of the EPF work-group on training. She initiated the EPF Forum on the
subject of aging, founded and headed the IPA committee "Psychoanalytic
Perspectives on Aging," dealing with the subject of aging in patients and
psychoanalysts. She was the initial editor of the German yearbooks of the
International Journal of Psychoanalysis. For seven years she was involved in
the inception of a new IPA society. She has published readers, monographs,
and articles on psychoanalysis and gerontology.

B. Miguel Leivi is a psychiatrist, MD, psychoanalyst, training-analyst,
and has been for 15 years, with a specialization in Psychoanalysis, at the
University Institute of Mental Health (IUSAM). He is also professor of the
Psychoanalytic Training Institute of APdeBA, and full member of Buenos
Aires Psychoanalytical Association (APdeBA) and of the IPA. He has been
president, vice-president, and scientific secretary of APdeBA, former director of *Psicoanálisis*, a scientific journal edited by APdeBA, and is current
director of the Master degree in Culture and Mental Health of IUSAM, and
current member of the Sponsoring Committee of the IPA for the Korean
Psychoanalytic Study Group (KPSG). He has published numerous psychoanalytic papers.

Philip Stokoe is a psychoanalyst and fellow of the British Psychoanalytical
Society, IPA. Working in private practice with adults and couples, he is

also organizational consultant to a wide range of organizations. He has been a senior manager in a range of health and social care settings since 1978, including St Charles Youth Treatment Centre; Family Welfare Association; Kensington and Chelsea Social Service Department; Brent Adolescent Centre; and finally working in the adult department of the Tavistock & Portman NHS Foundation Trust between 1994 and 2012, where he was appointed clinical director in 2007.

He has been responsible for the creation of innovative services; developing a model for understanding organizations called the Healthy Organisation Model, from which he created an innovative intervention for teams and organizations, the short course intervention, which combines teaching and consultation; he designed the Primary Care Psychotherapy Consultation Service (PCPCS), and these ideas have led to a radically different approach to training psychiatric nurses, which has been running at City University. He designed two Masters courses and was the co-designer of the Couple Psychotherapy Training at the Tavistock Clinic. He is a member of the European Psychoanalytic Federation Forum on Institutional Matters, which studies the nature of psychoanalytic institutions.

Martin Teising, MD, PhD, is a psychiatrist and training analyst of the German Psychoanalytic Association (DPV). He was professor at the Frankfurt University of Applied Sciences (1994–2012), chair of the Alexander Mitscherlich Institute, Kassel (1998–2002), member of the executive board of the DPV (2008–2014) and chair of DPV (2010–2012). He has been president of the International Psychoanalytic University Berlin (2012–2018), and since 2018 member of the Scientific Advisory Board of the International Psychoanalytic University Berlin as well as being member of the working group European Psychoanalytic Conference for University Students of the European Psychoanalytic Federation (EPCUS). He was European Representative on the Board of the International Psychoanalytic Association (IPA) (2013–2017), member of the Committee on Budget and Finance of the International Psychoanalytical Association (2015–2019), and since 2021, member of the Committee on Confidentiaality of the International Psychoanalytical Association.

David Tuckett is fellow and training analyst of the British Psychoanalytic Society and emeritus professor of decision-making and director of the Centre for the Study of Decision-Making Uncertainty at University College London (UCL). He founded the New Library of Psychoanalysis (1987), was editor-in-chief of the *International Journal of Psychoanalysis* (1988–2001), and president of the European Psychoanalytic Federation (1999–2004). The author of books and journal articles in psychoanalysis, economics, finance, and sociology, he received the IPA Training Award (2004) and the Sigourney Award for distinguished contributions to the field of psychoanalysis once in 2007 and again (as a CEO of Psychoanalytic

Electronic Publishing, PEP) in 2018. As well as working in private practice, with colleagues, he researches psychoanalytic practice and training as well as how to apply the fruits of psychoanalytic understanding to strategic decision-making and economic and finance understanding and policy. He has spoken at the Davos meetings and other occasions and is the author *of Minding the Markets: An Emotional Finance View of Financial Instability* as well as many academic papers. He is currently involved in advising the Bank of England and UK central and local government on how to improve economic life and wellbeing in disadvantaged areas of the UK.

Harriet L. Wolfe, MD, is a training and supervising analyst at the San Francisco Center for Psychoanalysis, clinical professor of Psychiatry and Behavioral Sciences at the University of California San Francisco School of Medicine, president-elect of the International Psychoanalytical Association, and past president of the American Psychoanalytic Association. Her scholarly interests include clinical applications of psychoanalytic research, organizational processes, female development, and therapeutic action. She has a longstanding commitment to psychoanalytic public health intervention. She has co-authored a number of guided activity workbooks for children, parents, and teachers to help children cope with natural and man-made disasters. She teaches analysts-in-training, psychiatric residents, and junior faculty psychodynamic understandings of severely ill patients and the value of listening in the clinical setting. She has a private practice of psychoanalysis, and individual and couple's psychoanalytic psychotherapy in San Francisco.

How this book came about ...

Gabriele Junkers

Wherever we happen to be, the global crisis triggered by the Covid-19 pandemic has confronted us with an unprecedented situation. It is hardly surprising that the idea for this volume should have taken shape under the impact of drastic personal and professional contact deprivation. The impossibility of face-to-face exchange in our analytic organizations has forced us into social isolation for months and left us no choice but to carry on without seeing our colleagues. This situation has proved to be a powerful spur to reflect on the things we have had to do without.

The fact that we have painfully missed the opportunity to meet may appear to contradict the discontent rampant for so long in our analytic institutions, many members of which deplore the absence of genuine containment. How can psychoanalysts cooperate more effectively in their institutions, where unlike other organizations the items on the agenda are not merely unfinished business but questions pertaining to human existence, impaired physical integrity, psychic suffering, and mental distress?

This was a question that I had carried around with me for a long time, and I asked myself whether the crisis we were going through together might not also be an opportunity. In many walks of life, the pandemic has mercilessly revealed failures and obstinate weaknesses, it has speeded development and engendered a courageous willingness to square up to issues never broached before. The question that imposed itself was: Is dissatisfaction with our institutions something perennial that we have learned to live with, or can we seize this chance to open up new perspectives and change the situation for the better?

In this situation I was reminded of the productive euphoria that reigned during the restructuring of the European Psychoanalytic Federation (EPF) as a platform for European psychoanalytic conventions assembling international colleagues. At the time, I worked very constructively with a number of psychoanalysts who have contributed articles to this volume. To my surprise and intense gratitude, all these colleagues were not only pleased to support the project of a book on psychoanalytic organizations with new articles of their own, they also recommended other colleagues I might approach for the

DOI: 10.4324/9781003301936-1

purpose. And this is how the present volume came about. It contains a wide range of ideas, some reassuring, others highly disturbing or even distressing, assembled from different perspectives and thus reflecting the diversity of the institutions we belong to. I trust that experienced analytic readers will be able to deal professionally with the defenses that can be expected to arise against the discomfiture some of these articles are likely to provoke.

What all these authors have in common is not only their extensive practical experience with institutional work and psychoanalysis itself but also their relatively advanced age. To say anything cogent about life in institutions we need to have had years of experience in dealing with them, which necessarily means that all the contributors to this volume are fairly well stricken in years. This perspective has advantages and disadvantages. We cannot expect the elderly to have the same degree of openness, informed and involved interest in the near and more distant future as younger people will have. From older colleagues we expect the common sense born of experience that tells them how stimulating it can be to free themselves from the restrictions of an exclusively analytic perspective on analytic organizations. Greater tolerance brings with it the scope required for the essential and creative incorporation of research findings from other spheres.

All our authors draw upon their experience as participants in groups, sometimes as observers from the margins, sometimes as members exposed to the maelstrom of group dynamics, among colleagues and yet alone, solitary leaders, birds of a feather. We would gladly have come together to discuss the subject of the book and all our different perspectives on it, but the pandemic and various other circumstances ruled that it was not to be. All the greater is our hope that intensive discussion in a larger group will be possible sometime in the future.

The volume assembles chapters that for interested members of analytic organizations can function as something like a helpful third party providing a basis for discussions on the topic "Psychoanalysts in and with their Institutions." Its aim is to draw attention to approaches often overlooked amid the din of mainstream thinking and in the ideal case acting as a stimulus for thinking about and discussing things we have never thought about before. Above all, or so I believe, the book may offer material for discussion between the generations. None of the contributors has come up with propose pat recipes for satisfaction in/with organizations. Many of the critical voices raised in the literature on this topic argue from a position of impregnable self-assurance; with their accusations they hope to obtain a clear-cut verdict in favor of the prosecution. This is precisely *not* what we are out to achieve.

One important conviction that informs this book may serve as a connecting thread. There is no right to, nor guarantee for, happiness and satisfaction, neither in life nor in our analytic institutions. Life and our professional work confront us permanently with anxiety and discontent. Much as we may regret the fact, a psychoanalytic institution is not a bountiful breast finally bestowing on us what we have so painfully missed. But as a place where we can share the difficulties in our work and the problems we encounter in achieving the aims we have set ourselves, especially the complex task of training upcoming generations, it can give us support and solace and help us to see things more clearly.

Each chapter in its own way is characterized by the specific and uniquely subjective fit between the authors and their attitude to psychoanalytic institutions. Common to all is the ambition to treat the topic of the book with respect, optimism, and perhaps even a degree of audacity. I am grateful to a number of international colleagues for intensive exchanges during the writing of my chapter, especially John Churcher, Annalisa Ferretti, and Maria Teresa Hooke.

Gabriele Junkers, August 2021

Chapter 1

The Institutionalisation of Psychoanalysis[1]

Martin Teising

In autumn of 1902, the Vienna Wednesday Society met. Wilhelm Stekel, Alfred Adler, Rudolf Reitler and Max Kahane discussed psychoanalytic topics with Sigmund Freud in his practice. These meetings were the starting point of psychoanalytic organisation. The Wednesday Society was the forerunner of the Vienna Psychoanalytic Association, founded in 1908 by 14 members, the first psychoanalytic institution in history (Bronner, 2011).

At that time, there were also considerations to found an International Psychoanalytical Association, which was completed in Nuremberg in 1910. One of the aims of the association was to counteract the isolation from the academic world of the universities. Although international professional societies exist today in all scientific disciplines independently from the university context, this founding motive continues to have an effect in such a way that the relationship between the international and national professional societies on the one hand and universities on the other is marked by tension. I will come back to this.

At the International Psychoanalytic Congress in Budapest in 1918, Freud spoke about "Lines of Advance in Psycho-Analytic Therapy", using the well-known metaphor of gold for analytical therapy that had to be alloyed for other forms of application. He remarked that it is therapy "into which, indeed, we owe our place in human society- and to take a survey of the new directions in which it may develop" (Freud, 1919, p. 159) but that we must be on the lookout "and to take a survey of the new directions in which it (*psychoanalysis*, MT) may develop" (op. cit., 159). Today, it is rather the humanities that value psychoanalysis "as the most modern of all humanities"[2]. In psychology, on the other hand, which is increasingly oriented towards the natural sciences and nomothetics, psychoanalysis is considered outdated.

In his lecture, Freud first compares the work of the analyst with that of the chemist but then emphasises that the work with transference has recently become of great importance. He describes the principle of abstinence as a further innovation. He warns that the sick person can find substitutive satisfaction in the cure, but admits that the abstinence principle was developed

DOI: 10.4324/9781003301936-2

in work with hysterical patients, and that this principle can also be restricted "more or less, according to the nature of the case and the patient's individuality" (op. cit., 163). By name, he mentions the treatment of phobic and obsessive compulsive patients who require a different technique. In the case of "unstable" patients and those "unfit for existence", the analytical aspect must be united with the educational. Not all forms of illness can be treated with one technique; different approaches are required of the psychoanalyst.

The few analysts available, Freud continued, could only treat a small number of patients:

> At present we can do nothing for the wider social strata who suffer extremely seriously from neuroses...Now, let us assume that through some kind of organization we succeeded in increasing our numbers to an extent sufficient for treating a considerable mass of the population. On the other hand, it is possible to foresee that at some time or other the conscience of society will awake and remind it that the poor man should have just as much right to assistance for his mind as he now has to the life-saving help offered by surgery; and that neuroses threaten public health no less than tuberculosis...When this happens, institutions or out-patient clinics will be started to which analytically-trained physicians will be appointed, so that men who would otherwise give way to drink, women who have nearly succumbed under their burden of privations, children for whom there is no choice but between running wild or neuroses, maybe made capable, by analysis, of resistance and of efficient work. Such treatments will be free. It may be a long time before the State comes to see these duties as urgent...We shall then be faced by the task of adapting our technique to the new conditions...It is very probable, too, that the large-scale application of our therapy will compel us to alloy the pure gold of analysis freely with the copper of direct suggestion; and hypnotic influence, too, might find a place in it again, as it has in the treatment of war neuroses. But, whatever form this psychotherapy for the people may take, whatever elements out of which it is compounded, its most effective and most important ingredients will assuredly remain those borrowed from strict and untendentious psycho-analysis.

(166)

In 1920, Max Eitingon founded the first training institute in Berlin, a historically important step towards the institutionalisation of psychoanalysis. It was here that Edith Jacobson developed the structure of psychoanalytic training still used today, whose elements of training analysis, theoretical seminars and treatment under supervision are found in all recognised training models worldwide.

Freud's dream of "treating a considerable mass of the population" was fulfilled in this institute by treating poor patients free of charge. Today, this dream has been fulfilled in Germany in that analytical psychotherapy and the psychodynamic psychotherapy derived from it were approved at the end of the 1960s for the treatment of patients with statutory health insurance, which is the vast majority of the population. Psychoanalysis thus gained social recognition, for which it paid a price. Integration into the social insurance system requires external control of treatments, influences the training system and is, today, still the subject of fierce disputes conducted by the umbrella organisation of psychoanalytic associations, the German Society for Psychoanalysis, Psychotherapy, Psychosomatics and Depth Psychology (DGPT).

Institutions and Their Functions

Institutions in general give interpersonal relations a form suitable for the public sphere. Institutional arrangements enable a "superiority over all groups that are so 'free' that no promise binds them and no project holds them together" (Arendt, 1957, p. 313). They de-privatise and de-individualise interpersonal relations. Institutions are shaped by acting players and they shape the persons acting within them. They regulate human interaction and are necessary for the survival of human groups.

Institutions enable an expansion of the ego into a "we". The sense of belonging goes hand in hand with the experience of expanded ego boundaries. Elias Canetti described in "Mass and Power" (2010 [1960]) that the individual loses his body boundaries in the mass and gets a new body. Behavioral biologists, referring to the marking of territory and territoriality, speak of an expansion of the body into the immediate outside world.

Institutions make a social body schema possible. "The boundaries of this body schema are continually established through a process of demarcation brought about by interaction with others in a space that is at once corporeal and cultural" (Churcher, 2016, p. 67). They mark and demark, include but also exclude people, and confer the privilege of belonging through the possibility of identification with others who have certain similar characteristics. In many institutions, there is a fierce struggle for belonging and not belonging, for subordination, superordination and classification. Belonging provides security and serves to reduce fear, but it also excludes, hurts, offends and isolates those who are excluded.

We are all inevitably members of various institutional formations such as the family, the school. In an institutionalised partnership, in a club, in a religious community, in the military, in a psychoanalytical society, we have experienced belonging, uniformity and recognition, but also many a bitter disappointment and conflict, certainly also shame, humiliation, confinement and coercion.

Bourdieu's sociological theory of institutions characterises institutions as organised trust, whereas Foucault's theory emphasises the structural violence that emanates from institutions. According to Bourdieu (1984), an institution can provide and strengthen collectively secure self-esteem.

Institutions promote the generativity of human groups and their ideas. Their functionaries are given authority with which they secure and limit the freedom space of the individual member, ultimately (Arendt, 1957, p. 162) ensuring a survival of the individual as well as of the group and the institution.

The consolidation of institutions requires standardisation and codification of knowledge and action orientation, the formalisation of informal relations, as well as leadership selection, a regulation of succession and a control of group growth (see Zienert-Eilts, 2017).

Also as a late consequence of the 1968 movement which freed us from many constraints and from manifold abuses of authority, and in which the anti-institutional critique shaped by Foucault had a strong influence, the willingness today to compulsory and thus binding commitment in social groupings, with long-term assumption of responsibility such as in parties and trade unions, is clearly declining. In the German Psychoanalytic Association there is a shortage in some institutes of training analysts younger than 70. In some places, this shortage is also caused through a number of colleagues who are now around 65 years old and who decline the "rituals of submission" demanded by the institution. At the same time, it also seems to me that psychoanalysis seemed to many to be the method "that granted them the fulfilment of their longing for unrestricted and domination-free communication" (according to Jürgen Habermas, 1970, cited in Wolfgang Loch, 1974), a longing that of course could not be satisfied.

The refusal to take responsibility and exercise power oneself affects generativity, there are fewer offspring, thus the danger of encrusted structures grows.

Fundamentals of Authority in Institutions

An authority is not one without a recipient who follows its lead. Authority is characteristic of interpersonal relationships from the beginning. The expulsion from paradise, and thus the incarnation, occurred because of a violation of the commandment of divine authority. Already in the second generation of humanity, Cain slays his brother Abel. For the survival of humanity, the authority of the law is needed, an instance that is the basis of institutional organisation.

In individual development, the newborn is existentially dependent on a caregiver who exercises authority. Flooded with beta elements, to use Wilfred Bion's (1962) metaphor, the newborn is absolutely dependent on the literacy function of a knowledgeable and rule-abiding "authority" and seeks it in its existential need, with an "incredible need to believe" as Julia Kristeva (2014) so beautifully puts it. The child literally courts the attention of this authority, whose demands it wants to fulfil. Or as Freud says: "The credulity of love becomes an important, if not the most fundamental, source of authority" (Freud, 1905, p. 150).

Hermann Beland has described "the imperious desire of the newborn to be understood, the fulfilment of which makes their sociality possible. This desire is associated with the greatest fear but also with the psychic exercise of power (crying)" (2016, p. 424). The newborn is thus extremely helpless and existentially dependent, but at the same time possesses anti-authoritarian power itself. Her Majesty the Baby is able to force its counterpart to act, which is sometimes perceived by parents as quite tyrannical.

The subject, as the term implies, brings with him the willingness to submit and at the same time strives to break away from it, to be able to act independently, and somewhat less kindly, to subjugate others. This conflict, which is repeatedly fought out interpersonally during the course of life, and of course also in psychoanalytic institutions, becomes a central intrapsychic conflict within the experience of one's own efficacy and responsibility as well.

After the experiences of the Holocaust, Hannah Arendt (1957) distinguished a pre-political "authority in general" from authoritarianism. The task of authority is to limit freedom in order to secure it (1957, p. 162). Authority and freedom are not opposites, "authority at all" secures life in limited freedom.

Authoritarianism and authoritarian rule, on the other hand, limit freedom in institutions by abusing power. They invoke a higher, often allegedly God-given, power, proclaim eternal duration ("1000 Year Empire"), demand blind submission and promote equally blind hatred of opponents. Authoritarian structures that abuse power suppress aspirations for independence and increase subjugation tendencies. Some psychoanalysts tend to use a borrowed authority, namely the authorship of their founding father, in an authoritarian manner, believing in its evidential value. Something is so, because Freud wrote it.

Arendt's definition of "authority in general" follows the recognition of facts of life, such as that an individual's life is founded on the authorship of two others who are responsible for the child who is unable to survive on his or her own, from which derives a commitment to "authority" in which the young child must necessarily be able to trust. Responsibly exercised parental authority expresses itself in age- and environmentally appropriate supportive, nurturing and demanding ways.

Long before the anti-authoritarian movement, Arendt remarkably diagnosed a:

> kind of abdication of contemporaries...who, as parents and educators, refuse, as it were, to take over one of the most elementary functions in any polity, the guiding of those who have newly entered the world by birth and are therefore necessarily strangers in it, and thus to ensure the

continuity of this common world. It is as if parents no longer wanted to assume responsibility towards their children for the world into which they had conceived and born them.

(op. cit., p. 164)

Alexander Mitscherlich famously saw us on the way to a fatherless society after the ideal of an omnipotent leader had proved to be a narcissistically destructive fiction.

Renouncing the exercise of authority, wrote Krainz (1988, p. 15), corresponds to "using children for one's own purposes, an attempt to strengthen one's own position, to gain power, seduction of minors, fornication with dependents, so to speak; in any case a failure to respect generational boundaries".

The self-determination of the individual has meanwhile developed into the highest moral value of the Western world, the responsibility of solidarity for one another is lost, authority and benevolent paternalism have become obsolete.

Rachel Blass (2016) also identifies a development following this zeitgeist in psychoanalysis, whose mainstream increasingly seems to be concerned with not making the patient responsible for their suffering, but to attribute it to their limited abilities and to let it rest, as having been "caused through an early deficient environment or other early traumas" (p. 114). She sees a tendency "to resist the recognition of difference and to deny privileged knowledge and the associated exclusion from the circle of those who know, preferring instead to regard everyone equally as a victim of their circumstances or life circumstances" (p. 129). There is a great sensitivity today to the possibility of knowledge for control and the exercise of power, but little confidence in the possibility that knowledge will also be applied in the sense of loving one's neighbor.

According to Rachel Blass, one forgets that it is the feeling of guilt, ultimately resulting from the fantasy of patricide or matricide, that fundamentally shapes and determines our existence as human beings (cf. Blass, 2016, p. 118). In many psychoanalyses it is a long way until this insight is reached, an insight which frees us from the exclusive victim position and opens up the experience of self-determined and self-responsible decisions.

The reciprocal bonding of generations of parents and children, a central feature of human civilisation, also manifests itself in institutions as the assumption of responsible authority, first by parents towards their children, and later by adult children and grandchildren towards their parents and grandparents. Subsidiary maturity is characterised by the fact that authority can be assumed in the well-meaning interest towards one's own needy parents. Slotterdijk (1996) speaks of a procreative debt and a creative debt of children, of a gestational debt, a breastfeeding debt, nutritional debt and educational debt. This debt and gratitude weave the bond "by which the descendants...

are bound to the previous achievements of the older generations" (Slotterdijk, 1996, p. 11). Bonds are increasingly perceived as bondage, not bonding is misunderstood as an expression of autonomy.

In training analyses, bonding and binding relationships that promote the desired regression are established. By means of transference, the willingness of candidates to bind to the previous achievements of the older generation is promoted.

The authority of the training analyst, whom the candidate trusts, is based on a "body of knowledge that exerts its effect in the background, ceaselessly inspiring, permeating and influencing the practical work of the analyst, and on his emotional grounding in this body of knowledge as a result of the personal training analysis" (Davids, 2016, p. 255).

The regressive character of the transference to the training analyst is described dramatically by Bernard Chervet:

> The candidate's aspiration for growth turns to that "power", even implores it, confers on it the ability to realize the path of "becoming" and also grants it the authority to make it a reality....But it also becomes the target of murderous hatred.
>
> (Chervet, 2016, 282)

Those who embody authority inevitably become the object of hatred, in a moderate form of derision. However, older colleagues sometimes also complain of being overly idealised by younger colleagues.

Peculiarities of Psychoanalytic Institutions

In psychoanalytic institutions, structures of order are repeatedly destabilised, especially by the entanglement and lack of separation of personal-emotional and factual-formal levels (cf. Zienert-Eilts, 2017).

Like other institutions, they serve to maintain and cultivate certain goals and to convey them to younger people. What is specific is that psychoanalysis deals with psychic areas in which we are not masters in our own house, i.e. negativity and primary-process-dreaming.

Psychoanalysts are always looking for the uniquely paradoxical position of not knowing. For this stance to be developed and to flourish, there must be a protected free space that has to be secured again and again. This is why psychoanalysis places so much emphasis on its treatment, training and initiation rites, which is often interpreted as rigidity.

The need for protective institutions seems to me to be particularly pronounced among psychoanalysts because they encounter deep patient helplessness and their own fear, powerlessness and insecurity on a daily basis. This could explain why many colleagues remain attached to their institutes throughout their lives.

The inclusion-exclusion theme of the primal scene has a specific meaning for institutionalised psychoanalysis. The treatment situation itself is one in which the patient's inner psychic world becomes a shared and thus social one in the relationship with the analyst. This is only possible if the exclusion of third parties is safely guaranteed. This core of the psychoanalytic relationship, with the painful experience of inaccessibility to outsiders, is enacted in many variants in the institutes and is a central problem for any serious psychotherapy process researcher because it must lift the basic condition of exclusivity.

Precisely because colleagues believe they know something about the unconscious, they sometimes disregard the framework conditions of their institution that actually apply to others, I am thinking here of the abstinence rule, and claim for themselves that they can relativise them – they authorise themselves and thus no longer take the effectiveness of the unconscious quite so seriously. They think they are ready for self-determined legislation, sometimes with fatal consequences.

In Germany, one becomes a psychoanalyst not only according to the rules of a professional society, but also through training at privately organised institutes that are recognised by the state and the social insurance funds. State authority confers privileges for which we pay a high price, some think too high, and which can become a curse. In the process of recognising this institutional authority, for example in the form of social insurance, some colleagues have not moved beyond an adolescent protest attitude of enjoying the privileges while not taking the duties seriously.

Much time is needed to develop a psychoanalytic identity which encourages dependence on authority. Idealising and authority-submissive transferences to training analysts are difficult to dissolve. They influence the life of the institute and thus the organisation of psychoanalysis.

It is often said with a glorifying undertone that the profession of psychoanalyst is incomparable. The psychoanalyst and with him/her the institutions of psychoanalysis are not infrequently marked by such exaggerated idealization. It becomes all the more significant to belong to it.

Disappointment and the anger stemming from it, together with massive devaluation inevitably arise from idealistic visions with omnipotence conceptions. The anger is directed towards the institutions representing psychoanalysis and their officials. This dynamic is, in my experience, an important basis of many institutional difficulties. It is certainly also effective in other institutions. What seems characteristic to me is a particularly strong idealisation and the correspondingly violent reaction formation.

A psychoanalytically trained view of group dynamic processes in psychoanalytic institutions is helpful in principle. However, it also leads to interpretative attributions that are not infrequently used. The behavior of colleagues is interpreted without them having been asked. Because of their own interests in the group and the difficult requirement to tolerate opposing interests and the otherness expressed in them, destructive intentions are attributed to the other person. This creates a division, the cause of which is seen in the other person. The leader's task is to maintain the integrity of both sides, which not infrequently earns him/her the reproach of not sufficiently counteracting destructive tendencies or coming to terms with them.

Good psychoanalysts, however, are characterised by reflection and analysis of their own initially unconscious countertransference reactions within themselves, and not so much by projective attributions and unsolicited interpretations. Anyone who works as a manager in a leading position in an organisation knows the dilemma that arises when one thinks to understand the psychodynamic of interaction phenomena, but has to refrain from interpretation. If interpretive abstinence is not observed, the authority conferred is abused.

Personal interviews seem most likely to identify unsuitable candidates for psychoanalytic training at an early stage. Admission interviews allow for preliminary decisions regarding subsequent membership in the Psychoanalytic Society. Rejections can cause deep grievances which can lead people to act against psychoanalysis and its institutions decades later, sometimes with deep hatred.

Admission, on the other hand, can be linked to the fantasy of now being chosen, a vision that can be nurtured after each subsequent examination passed, such as the preliminary colloquium, the colloquium and the examination to become a training analyst.

The personal development in psychoanalytic institutes is accompanied by initiation rites, which, in the sense of Mario Erdheim (1982), can be understood as organising principles to strengthen the incest taboo and reinforce generational barriers. However, such rites also promote conformist thinking.

Among psychoanalysts, one can repeatedly observe the need to distinguish "true" from "untrue" psychoanalysis, thereby denying others their belonging and professional identity. Sometimes one has the impression that this involves fantasies of purity and impurity with an idealisation of one's own position.

Psychoanalysis faces persecution. There are real threats, but also threat scenarios fomented within its own ranks. It is not always easy to differentiate between real and self-generated fears of a paranoid quality.

Among some functionaries in psychoanalytic institutions, a seemingly masochistic self-sacrifice and self-exploitation can be observed which reminds Pollak (2013) of one common in monasteries. This "masochistic-narcissistic sacrifice" takes place with a high libidinous cast, but is found in many forms of organisation, for example when talking about a manager's working hours and workload. The observation may be no less true because of this, but it may also have non-religious motives.

Besides the desire for narcissistic affirmation, the great commitment of our members could also stem from the need to gratefully give back something of what one has received oneself.

Personally, I owe a great debt of gratitude to many colleagues who hold or have held positions in psychoanalytic institutions. They have created forums in which lively discussion is possible on how insight into unconscious processes can be gained. We are looking for ways to apply this insight in cultural and therapeutic contexts. We cooperate in the national and international sphere with other psychoanalytic societies that differ from us and we endeavor not to lay claim to any truth. Psychoanalysis gained social recognition in Germany with the introduction of psychoanalytically based procedures as a health insurance benefit. Our institutes are authorised to provide training and further education, at the end of which there is a state-protected title that ensures privileges. We all benefit from this recognition. Probably no candidates during recent decades have been trained in pure psychoanalysis, all of them have been trained in analytical psychotherapy within the framework of health insurance funding. When we treat sick people within the framework of the health insurance system, it is not compatible with a strict lack of tendency. Restricted contingencies and frequencies have an impact on the psychoanalytic process, on the density of transference and on the rhythm of interaction. The sting of psychoanalysis becomes less hurtful due to our social inclusion.

Psychoanalysis and the University

The International Psychoanalytic Association (IPA) was founded with the aim of promoting and maintaining psychoanalysis as a science. It had not yet found its way into the universities, so the IPA was to be the alternative institution in which psychoanalysis as a science was promoted.

After World War 2, psychoanalysts were appointed to university chairs in many places in Germany until the 1980s. They were appointed not as clinically active psychoanalysts, but on the basis of special knowledge in the diverse fields of applied psychoanalysis, such as clinical psychology, psychiatry, psychotherapy, psychosomatics, educational science or pedagogy, history, literature, cultural studies, sociology, philosophy, gerontology, law, nursing sciences, etc.

Applied psychoanalysis is taught in universities which secures an important place in society. Professors gain their students' interest in psychoanalysis, and by so doing, indirectly generate psychoanalytic candidates. Most of them teach and research in universities and manage a balancing act between their work in private practice and in psychoanalytic institutes, some even work as training analysts.

In 1959, the Sigmund Freud Institute was founded in Frankfurt initially as a training and research institute, then as a pure research institute financed by the Federal State of Hesse. A similar foundation in Berlin, the Berlin Kulturplaninstitut, failed in 1963 due to quarrels between the

German Psychoanalytic Association and the German Psychoanalytic Society (Lacher, 2013).

During the past 25 years, many university chairs have once again not been filled by psychoanalysts. It is well known that the development in psychological and medical disciplines follows an increasingly nomothetic understanding of science that neglects the uniqueness of the individual. This development is also a reaction to the critical sting of psychoanalysis, but is largely attributable to the inability of psychoanalysts themselves to secure a lasting interdisciplinary connection to the university. The development of psychoanalysis as a science cannot be achieved from the consulting room alone, as significant as clinical findings are for the further development of psychoanalysis.

The question of what science is and who a scientist is, one of inclusion and exclusion, preoccupies psychoanalysis at the university as well as in the institutes. Colleagues who sit behind the couch claim their activity is scientific and, according to the impression of empirically active colleagues, ignore their efforts to connect with the university world. These colleagues do not consider psychoanalytic treatment to be scientific research as long as an investigative element is missing.

The researchers, in turn, are denied being "really" psychoanalytically active. Psychoanalysts who are committed to research, not only behind the couch, perform, as I said, a balancing act between the treatment room, the laboratory and the lecture hall. They do not feel sufficiently recognised and appreciated by the psychoanalytic community.

What is needed is mutual respect without devaluing the other on the basis of the narcissism of small difference that flourishes in this field.

The Importance of the Psychoanalytic Institutes for the Transmission of Psychoanalysis

The generative function of the institutes, education and training in psychoanalysis is seen as their most important task and serves to ensure survival.

The lecturers impart a valuable wealth of experience of psychoanalytic forms of application, primarily in the clinical as well as in the psychosocial and cultural-theoretical field in a non-university setting, not infected by the "Studium Bolognese"[3].

Analytic training offers and demands the deepest possible self-knowledge and aims at identification with the method of psychoanalysis, which can promote dependency processes if the training analysts do not sufficiently process idealising transferences. At this point, I would like to recall the work of Wolfgang Loch (1974) entitled "The analyst as legislator and teacher", which states:

> The therapeutic process is characterized by the paradox that, on the one hand, the therapist must confront the patient who has become immature

as a result of the neurotic illness, as a teacher and giver of potentially binding linguistic interpretations, but on the other hand, at the end of the process, the power imbalance thus established is to be abolished and the patient is to come into the open.

(op. cit., 431)

In training analyses, the act of liberation is particularly necessary and particularly difficult.

The quality of our clinical understanding is based on the psychoanalysis of micro-processes that manifest themselves in unconscious transference and countertransference phenomena. As early as 1993, Henseler and Wegener presented the volume "Psychoanalyses that need their time". The occasion for this was a discussion in the German social insurance system about the payment of long-term and high-frequency psychoanalyses. Twelve case histories impressively demonstrate the effectiveness of long psychoanalyses. Regarding the frequency, it says:

> The hours in which she (the patient) had felt well-understood in her anxiety had awakened in her the desire to continue to turn to me... But with each suspension of the analysis, even if only by a day, I had interrupted this movement, worse still rejected her... A shell grew around her; she no longer sought an exchange.
>
> (Henseler and Wegener, 1993, p. 157)

Elsewhere it says:

> It was also only with the start of the four-hour analysis that the disturbed thought processes could be perceived and also analyzed within the framework of the treatment, because it was only through the close succession of treatment hours that they could be observed more clearly by me, as well as made understandable to the patient. The attacks, but especially the analysis of the attacks on my thought processes, could only find the necessary attention and resolution in this framework.
>
> (Henseler and Wegener, 1993, p. 211)

In our experience, access to the unconscious is most likely to be achieved in high-frequency treatment, without guaranteeing that psychoanalytic processes will actually unfold in this setting and also without denying that they are also possible in low-frequency settings. In order to be able to perceive and interpret unconscious phenomena even in low-frequency treatments, in short-term therapies, in crisis interventions and even in counselling, a particularly thorough training is required, especially intensive psychoanalysis of one's own.

The Board of the International Psychoanalytic Association agreed on this during the discussion on changing the training guidelines of the Eitingon model. There was also agreement that it is problematic to make quantifying regulations for a qualification that, as the term implies, is supposed to ensure "quality". Nevertheless, regulations that quantify seem indispensable to limit possible arbitrariness of subjective assessment. Perhaps we do not really trust genuine psychoanalytical methods in the formulation of training guidelines? Otherwise we could dispense with measurement figures and limit ourselves to assessing whether the candidate is capable of initiating a sufficiently good psychoanalytic process and adopting an appropriate attitude. We would have to trust the expert judgment of those we empower more than we would trust measurements. However, the now modern, and in many cases certainly justified, mistrust of paternal authority was so great that no one in the IPA seriously wanted to eliminate quantitative data. Psychoanalysts are thus certainly also subject to a trend of the zeitgeist. In my opinion, not deleting the figures but relaxing them, not only for control cases but also for one's own training analysis, is the wrong signal at a time when studies, training and further education, including psychoanalytic self-awareness, as promoted by the Bologna process, are not primarily phases in life of personal orientation and search for meaning, but are a preparation for earning a living.

In times of uncertain volatility, much more attention is paid to formal and pecuniary aspects, which I regularly observe at information events. Psychoanalysis must respond to the social conditions that have caused potential candidates to perceive aspects of the world today in a different way to those who were socialised in the 1960s and 1970s.

Members of that generation had the feeling that the future was reasonably secure, and they also had the possibility of being able to decisively change social structures at quite short notice and with the help of psychoanalytical insights, in order to participate in the shaping of a humane world. Concern about securing their future existence did not move them much; it was largely denied with a consciousness fed by the economic miracle. The question of whether candidates qualify in behavior therapy, depth psychology or psychoanalysis, for example, is frequently not decided on the basis of content. Nevertheless, there are still many young people today who seek a personal development process through their training.

If they want to secure the existence of their institutes and thus the preservation of psychoanalysis, psychoanalysts must nowadays take note of the fact that manageable and well-structured training and further education programs that offer factually based authority while promoting self-determination are in demand, above all from young potential candidates. In a flexible society, it is particularly important to offer a safe framework to engage in working through unconscious processes in their own training analysis. Of course, candidates are not to be treated like customers, and psychoanalytic training is not a commodity. But in a society where capital permeates everything, any institutionalised training is also permeated by it, even if it seems offensive to us.

Psychoanalysis as a science of the inner world of the human being positions itself in the outer world with the help of its institutionalisation. This helps to secure its position in society. Institutionalisation inevitably goes hand in hand with a formalisation of relationships, with standardisation and codification, leadership selection, authority and the exercise of power (cf. Zienert-Eilts, 2017). In many respects, these processes contradict elementary principles of psychoanalytic thinking and the psychoanalytic stance. For:

> the central term of psychoanalysis, Freud's dynamic unconscious, describes as a basic category of psychoanalytic experience a missing point. The "un-" of the unconscious marks a negative constitutive of psychoanalysis. What consciousness cannot know and grasp, what remains intangible due to the drive of the human being, precisely determines subjectivity which, as such, cannot be grasped directly, but only through omissions, through absence and through privation. As a science of the unconscious, psychoanalysis deals with the negativity of experience in an understanding way. (Küchenhoff & Warsitz, 2017, p. 204)

It is characterised by the hypothetical, the provisional and the fluid, which inevitably coagulates in the institution. Institutionalisation processes therefore trigger unease in many psychoanalysts. This unease makes them highly ambivalent towards their own institutions. On the one hand, they strongly identify with them; on the other hand, they criticise them fiercely again and again, while still remaining attached to them.

The cause of this discomfort and the need to endure it must be made conscious. Psychoanalysis needs the institutional space as a platform for action and protection in society in order to be able to apply the outlined attitude in the treatment of the sick and in the training of psychoanalysts who are also psychotherapists. Therefore, the psychoanalytic organisation, despite its contradiction with essentials of psychoanalysis, must be cultivated. That we psychoanalysts, as specialists for the inner world, also have to move, position and assert ourselves in the outer world with the manners that apply there in order to be able to survive, is something we should always bear in mind. Psychoanalysts who are involved institutionally should not be devalued for their balancing act between psychoanalytic stance and action in democratically legitimised and socially integrated organisations, associations, committees, etc., but should be respected and supported.

Notes

1 Enlarged edited version of a lecture on the occasion of the 40th anniversary of the Alexander Mitscherlich Institute Kassel, Germany, 28.4.2018 and a lecture at the Swiss Society for Psychoanalysis (SGPsa), Basel, 1.9.2018.

2 Peter-André Alt, former President of the FU Berlin and now President of the German Rectors' Conference, at the opening of the lecture series jointly organised by Freie Universität Berlin and the International Psychoanalytic University in the winter semester, 2013/14, "Who is Afraid of Sigmund Freud? Perspectives on Psychoanalysis Today".

3 Designation for Europe-wide standardised study programs with Bachelor's and Master's degrees, which were modularised according to the resolution of the European Ministers of Education and Cultural Affairs in Bologna in 1999.

Literature

Arendt, H. (1957): *Fragwürdige Traditionsbestände im politischen Denken der Gegenwart. Vier Essays*. Frankfurt/M.: Europäische Verlagsanstalt.

Beland, H. (2016): Lehranalyse und Institution. Die Progression des Verstehens ist im Rahmen des organisierten Vertrauens möglich. *Forum Psychoanal* 32, 413–430.

Bion, W. R. (1962): *Learning From Experience*. London: Heinemann.

Blass, R. B. (2016): Bedeutung und Aktualität des freudianisch-kleinianischen Verständnisses von Autorität und Verantwortlichkeit: Implikationen für die analytische Situation. *Psychoanalyse in Europa, Bulletin* 70, 111–129.

Bourdieu, P. (1984): *Homo academicus*. Paris (Éditions de Minuits).

Bronner, A. (2011): The three histories of the Vienna Psychoanalytic Society. In: Loewenberg, P., Thompson N. L. (eds.): *100 Years of the IPA*. London: Karnac, pp. 9–24.

Canetti, E. (2010 [1960]): *Masse und Macht*. Frankfurt/M.: Fischer.

Chervet, B. (2016): Wege und Stimmen der Autorität oder wie können die Psychoanalytiker ohne Werturteil auskommen? *Psychoanalysis in Europa, Bulletin* 70, 280–282.

Churcher, J. (2016): Der psychoanalytische Rahmen, das Körperschema, Telekommunikation und Telepräsenz. Implikationen von José Blegers Konzept des »encuadre«. *Psyche – Z Psychoanal*, 60–81.

Davids, M. F. (2016): Discussion des Beitrags von Aydan Özdaglar. *Psychoanalyse in Europa, Bulletin* 70, 254–260.

Erdheim, M. (1982): Die gesellschaftliche Produktion von Unbewusstheit: eine Einführung in den ethnopsychoanalytischen Prozess. Frankfurt/M.: Suhrkamp.

Freud, S. (1905): Three essays on the theory of sexuality (1905). *SE* 17: 135–241.

Freud, S. (1919): Lines of advance in psycho-analytic therapy. *SE* 17: 157–168.

Henseler, H., Wegener, P. (Ed.) (1993): *Psychoanalyse, die ihre Zeit brauchen*. Opladen: Westdeutscher Verlag.

Krainz, E. E. (1988): Vom Individuum zum System – und zurück. In D. von Ritter-Röhr (Hrsg.), *Gruppenanalytische Exkurse* (S. 1–23). Berlin: Springer.

Kristeva, J. (2014): *Dieses unglaubliche Bedürfnis zu glauben*. Giessen: Psychosozial.

Küchenhoff, J., Warsitz, R. (2017): Von der Eigenständigkeit psychoanalytischer Erfahrung. *Jahrb. Psychoanal.* 75: 197–218.

Lacher, M. (2013): Das gescheiterte Kulturplaninstitut in Berlin auf dem Boden der Beziehungen zwischen DPV und DPG. *Psyche – Z Psychoanal.* 67: 770–793.

Loch, W. (1974): Der Analytiker als Gesetzgeber und Lehrer: Legitime oder illegitime Rollen? *Psyche – Z Psychoanal.* 28: 431–460.

Pollak, T. (2013): Psychoanalyse als Religion? Zur Kritik des Dogmatismus in psychoanalytischen Institutionen. In: Berrouchot, S. a.o. (Ed.): *Der Andere im Prozess psychischen Wachsens*. Gießen: Psychosozial.

Slotterdijk, P. (1996): Alte Leute und letzte Menschen. Notiz zur Kritik der Generationenvernunft. In: Tews, H.P. a.o. (Ed.): *Altern und Politik*. Melsungen: Bibliomed.

Zienert-Eilts, K. J. (2017): *Destruktive Gruppenprozesse. Entwicklungslinien in der Geschichte der psychoanalytischen Bewegung und Erkenntnisse für gegenwärtige gesellschaftliche Konflikte*. Giessen: Psychosozial.

Chapter 2

The psychoanalyst and his society

Serge Frisch

The history of psychoanalysis is rich in schisms, exclusions and self-exclusions of members. Analytical institutions and their history have increasingly become an object of scientific investigation, a new institutional clinic.

In *On the History of the Psychoanalytic Movement* (1957[1914], SE v. XIV pp. 7–65), Freud expresses his regrets as regards the first psychoanalysts:

> I could not succeed in establishing among its members the friendly relations that ought to obtain between men who are all engaged upon the same difficult work; nor was I able to stifle the disputes about priority for which there were so many opportunities under these conditions of work in common.

The same disillusionment returns several years later, when Freud writes in *Group Psychology and the Analysis of the Ego* (1921, p. 79) that "When individuals come together in a group all the cruel, brutal and destructive instincts, which lie dormant in individuals as relics of a primitive epoch, are stirred up to find free gratification." And according to van der Leeuw who cites him (1968, p. 160), Freud actually said that "doing analysis spoils one's character" ("Das Analysieren verdirbt den Charakter"). If we add to this the fact that psychoanalysis is the third impossible profession, we may well be surprised to see that analytical societies still continue to exist and to function, albeit not always in a satisfying manner.

Is this unease inherent to the institutions and identical among them, or does it differ from one analytical institution to another? What might be the specific factors that confer upon it its quite particular characteristics?

Institutional training of analysts

The transmission of psychoanalysis with its various facets, such as deepening practice, continuous theoretical development and above all the teaching and training of analyst candidates, are the principal functions of any psycho-analytical society. In creating the International Psychoanalytic Association

DOI: 10.4324/9781003301936-3

(IPA), Freud bequeathed the societies with the *obligation to transmit* that binds members together in an unconscious pact, a pact that we adhere to, no matter what, once we become members of the IPA. The discovery of the unconscious is Freud's essential discovery and it determines our identity as analysts. It is up to our institutions to transmit the exploration of this discovery from one generation to the next. To do so, in the course of a candidate's training, the societies take into account the norms or standards of training as prescribed by the IPA, in combination with the modalities specific to each society.

The IPA recognizes three models of training: The Eitingon model, which is the original model; the French model, very widespread in Europe; and the Uruguayan model, which is used only in Latin America. I was trained in the French model[1] which I shall discuss as regards to certain important differences that it has with the Eitingon model. In the latter, the candidate pursues her theoretical training and supervisions in parallel to analysis. The candidates often have had only very little personal analysis before being accepted for training. Their selection, based first and foremost on psychopathological criteria, represents a gamble on the future.

In the French model, personal analysis precedes training, and it is only towards the end of their analysis that applicants ask to begin their apprenticeship. The analysis is therefore not strictly speaking part of training, but rather it is called "extraterritorial" in that it takes place outside of the training institution. According to this model, it is important that the analytical institution abstains from any and all interference in the treatment of future candidates. In the French model, selection of candidates takes into account the way in which they are able to speak about their desire to become analysts via the personal experience of treatment.

Let us note that the presence of the analytical institution in each of these models of training is very different: the Eitingon model has treatment take place within the training institution, whereas in the French model, the institution should remain as far removed from training as possible.

This major difference between the two training models indicates a difficulty inherent to the very essence of analytical training. A comparison with classic academic training might allow us to better understand this difficulty.

In order to register for university, students must respond to certain objective criteria such as marks from pre-university training programs. Students who fulfill these criteria are automatically accepted. Following their academic training, the young graduates will seek employment outside of their universities, with no obligation to remain in touch with their teachers and professors. If their training requires internships, these will be completed in organizations external to the university. The graduate's professional life takes place outside the walls in which they studied.

As far as the future psychoanalyst is concerned, the procedure is completely different: Once his training is completed, he will become a member of the society that trained him and typically will remain with it for the entirety of his professional life. His analysis and supervisions take place with elders who become colleagues and whom he will frequent throughout his institutional life. "Student" life and professional life take place within the same walls and with the same people, whose statuses change. The place of training and the place of scientific exchange merge into one. Additionally, the admission of a student-analyst is based on criteria that are not always objectifiable and which have to do with his psychic functioning or ability to come into proximity of his unconscious. Such criteria are hardly quantifiable and incur a significant margin of error. Potentially strong candidates may not be accepted, and the inverse is equally true.

A certain unsolvable dilemma exists in the training of analysts, seeing as the training model is such that candidates never leave their analytic family. Quite the opposite: They are encouraged to establish themselves as part of it. It is as if children were encouraged to stay with their origin family for their entire life, whereas the academic discourse addressed to students says "free yourselves from university and seek your happiness elsewhere." It is impossible to reflect upon the lives of our analytical institutions without taking into account this unsolvable dilemma, a veritable common thread in the examination of our institutions. There is no magic solution and the only way out is to talk about it, to create specific, institutional spaces where we may talk about it.

As Freud pointed out, we find barbary in all groups, but in psychoanalytical societies this barbary is complicated by the fact that analysts are, in a certain sense, captives of their "family".

Let us examine the training of analysts: "The evaluation of candidates is at the very core of the psychoanalytic institution" (Dejours 2016, p. 271). In accepting certain postulates and rejecting others, psychoanalytic societies demarcate an institutional interior that delineates limits, boundaries, a separation from the exterior. This limit determines individuation, identity, a space for analytic reflection. This capacity to say no is in the service of Eros, as part of his separative function.

The admission of a candidate takes place on the basis of "psychic" criteria more so than on academic transcripts, and this selection introduces a very particular kind of asymmetry. Indeed, for some psychoanalysis societies, this selection process turns out to be more and more difficult given the fact that the number of applicants is diminishing: The societies begrudgingly find themselves accepting candidates that might all too often not (yet?) possess all the qualities of an analyst. This is the result of decades of a dispiriting decrease in the amount of candidates. Erlich (2017) highlights the fact that these negative choices always provoke "the fear of authoritarianism and therefore a resistance to authority which seems intrinsic to institutional psychoanalytic life" (p. 2). He indicates two reasons for this: "The role that institutional life plays in our lives according to our sensitivity to unconscious, hidden and latent motivations" (p. 2) and the difficulty that analysts have with authority. The problem is that in not authorizing the other, one remains non-authorized oneself.

Whereas Freud did not consider psychoanalysis as a profession, it has become one over time. For Kirsner (2000, p. 238), "psychoanalytical training has developed rather rigid and formalized demands (…)," a state of affairs that leads to a contradiction between the very nature of the analytical field, which tends to explore non-knowledge with a sense of risk and adventure, and a theoretical teaching that has often become quite formalized and academic. As Wallerstein (1972) has said, the dilemma lies in the choice of training toward knowledge or towards a profession. This raises the fundamental question of how to train and to what end. The corollary of this professionalization is progressive institutionalization and the risk of creating a "bureaucratic corps" (Castoriadis-Aulagnier 2008, p. 30). The conflicts surrounding the contents and purposes of training find themselves ineluctably heightened, as do the power struggles between training analysts. One might see how such professionalization implies selecting rather conformist candidates. I think this is the tendency in Germany, where one has to pass a state-recognized examination to obtain recognition as a psychoanalyst with everything that implies in terms of standardization.

A certain independence is inherent to our training institutions, which claim a certain extraterritoriality as regards the classic academic teaching they try to avoid. At the same time, a paradox arises: Analysts strive for social and professional recognition. How are this independence and this paradox examined as part of a candidate's studies, and by the candidates themselves?

These selection procedures, over which postulating analysts have no control and which depend on the desires of others, immediately trigger strong transferential movements towards the analysts and authorities in play, leading either to idealizations or to rejections. These often quite passionate sentiments will go on to infiltrate all layers of institutional relations and may provoke turbulent debates. Becoming a training analyst therefore means accepting the fact that you will become an object of transference, with its share of drives, of love, idealization, hate and destructivity.

In the society that trained me, candidates are placed under the responsibility of a training commission for the duration of their training period, during which they do not bear the title of "members" of the society. This training period might be seen as an intermediate space, and constitutes a veritable transformational mechanism for the candidate. This reminds me of Bologninis metaphor (2018), who speaks of 40 km of pavements under the arcades of Bologna. The space is neither within the house nor out in the street, but constitutes an intermediate space that is propitious for encounters and exchanges, and which evokes a flurry of fantasies. The inside of the house remains hidden and often becomes the container for various projections: What kind of dramas or love scenes might take place there?

The candidate who works towards becoming a member of the psychoanalytical society that trained him confronts not only the society's institutional bodies but also the entirety of its members around the issue of passing from one generation to the next, of transmitting life and psychic death.

The analytical institution should not have as its only function the selection of candidates and their accompaniment towards becoming analysts, but rather, and this is possibly a harder goal to attain, it should allow the candidate to remain an active member who endows his society and feels endowed by it. Let us take stock of the fact that over the years many members leave their society or indeed stay but feel increasingly isolated. Few are the societies that try to understand this aspect of things and to find some kind of remedy. Why is this so? Is the goal to train analysts and then lose interest in their future, with the hopes that they continue to pay their dues? What does this symptom, to be found in the history of every psychoanalysis society, represent? We might imagine a "clinic" of those left on the sidelines, to ponder along with them their disappointment, their isolation, their wounds, their feeling of rejection, or even their effective sidelining by the very institution they had worked so hard to become part of. Why were they admitted in the first place? Did the admissions committee make a mistake? An "institutional clinic" would take stock of such potential institutional dysfunctions.

Authority and power in analytical institutions

The functions of a president are varied: Maintaining a dynamic tension between the objectives and the functions of a psychoanalytical society, being the guardian of psychoanalysis in the promotion of scientific and theoretical activities. To these well-known functions one must add another one, essential to institutional well-being: Creating a space where people speak without taboo, where discussion takes place in such a way as to avoid creating secretive niches.

In some societies, members also ask the president to take a stand in the defense of the profession, that is, to act as a sort of union representative. This raises a fundamental question: Is the society's primary task to protect psychoanalytic science, or is there an insidious risk of turning into a union that is preoccupied with matters such as, for example, the reimbursement of sessions carried out by analysts?

For the past few years, quite a particular unease has been cropping up in societies that find fewer and fewer members willing to serve as presidents. The solitary exercise of psychoanalysis and the very particular verbal exchange between analyst and patient does not prepare one to develop the skills required to take up the post of a director. "Managing" a psychoanalytical society means being able to facilitate collaboration among colleagues and to permit other parts of the society, such as the teaching commission or the ethics committee, to work efficiently while respecting the autonomy of their space. Promoting the freedom of thought required to create new ideas means that a president must be able to set aside, without renouncing, the founding myths of the institution, in order for it not to reproduce itself identically.

A president must obviously manage people with quite different characters and social statuses. Even if there is no such thing as presidency without criticism, the hardest thing to bear are the envious projections that are experienced as all the more destructive when they come from long-time colleagues.

President and institutional bodies exercise an authority clearly defined by the laws governing non-profit associations. Nevertheless, reproaches concerning abuses of power regularly arise and produce concern, for example, certain training analysts, who monopolize supervision, their attempts to hold (also sexual) sway over candidates or who try to influence the latter to adhere to their theoretical orientation. These abuses reflect a general dysfunction of institutional democracy and should be easy to correct if the silence is broken.

In my experience, "power" can exist on a completely different level and concerns a very specific kind of institutional knowledge. The president's position brings him/her into contact with fellow presidents of other European societies and with the "upper echelons" of the European Psychoanalytic Federation (EPF) and IPA. The less the president shares this information with his members, the more he creates the feeling that he wants to keep this "power" to himself, that secrets exist there. It is surprising to note how so few societies hold a meeting at least once a year to pass on the issues that are being discussed at the IPA or regional level. How much time is there at general meetings for an in-depth discussion of the policies of international organizations that involve fundamental questions of training and many other areas of the life of each analytical society?

Integrating the institutional past

We may say: An analyst alone does not exist … outside of his national analytical institutional, which itself is part of an international network of institutions. The psychoanalyst is in need of her psychoanalytical institution and her colleagues in order to survive. We all know analysts who have distanced themselves from institutional life, whose psychoanalytical thinking has become all the poorer for it, due to the fact that it no longer takes place as part of the life-giving space of institutional interaction. At the risk of sounding provocative, should we not fear that *any* analyst who strays too far away from the orthodoxy of his institution is undermining psychoanalysis itself? Psychoanalytical societies are the firewall that protects their members from becoming isolated. But we also know that an analytical society that does not regularly reinvent itself might suffocate the individual and the unique under its formal, administrative aspects. Could we not say that the health of a psychoanalytical society is measured by its ability to create a dynamic dialogue between a certain tradition and indispensable change?

No analyst chooses his inheritance since the analytical institution, along with its rules, preexists the admission of any new member. Becoming a member, becoming an analyst in one society rather than another, is a dynamic process of appropriating the very institutional frame that the analyst is joining. The society's entire past concerns him, becomes his and at the same time eludes him.

The modalities of transmission and introjection of this "institutional topic" and of origin fantasies must be elaborated during one's own personal analytic treatment, one's training and throughout one's professional life within a psychoanalytical society. This is the endless task of re-elaborating and interrogating the institution's life-giving aspects, alongside its death-bearing ones, at both a personal and a group level. In this sense, "history is understood as the active laboratory of our present, and not only as its background" (Rosanvallon 2018, p. 363). Unconscious transmission of this heritage spreads throughout the complex network of our institutional origins and relations, since both psychogenesis and intersubjectivity make up the unconscious.

Too few societies provide candidates with a space to reflect and to think about this history, their history that precedes them. During training, it would be useful for the candidates to be able to come to grips with a critical and analytical reflection on the oft tumultuous history of their society.

Psychoanalytical societies habitually refuse to reveal their family secrets, despite the fact that the corridors bristle with stories of incest and other abuses. It is clearly difficult to evoke certain secrets publicly when it may be the case that some of our colleagues were around during the time of the facts, and without the whole matter turning into personal payback. These questions are sometimes elaborated in the secrecy of individual treatment, but are rarely ever aired in the public space of the analytical institution. We notice here this insoluble aspect (or this paradox?) that is inherent to the functioning of analytical societies.

In his book Les alliances inconscientes (Unconscious alliances) Kaës (2009), developed the importance of the analytical institution, since analysts possess an experience and a knowledge of the unconscious gained through stemming from their own analysis and a knowledge of the unconscious that is transmitted by the psychoanalytical institution. It is therefore likely that a certain understanding of the unconscious and therefore of psychoanalysis has infiltrated the fundamental understanding of any psychoanalytical society. All training is thus charged with the basic understandings that are transmitted, mostly unconsciously, to every analyst in a given society.

We may also become bearers of elements of an institutional unconscious, or of certain elements, that have not yet been metabolized by members, that remain embedded, and that are passed along as "brut objects" from one generation to another (Frisch 2010). In the *après-coup*, each one of us, in each generation, must ponder and refashion these unconscious impregnations, and reconstruct generational succession. Psychoanalysis and analytical institutions are in permanent transformation for both the individual analysts and the entire analytical community.

One might say that the institutional frame, a potential space, constitutes a reassuring environment where the candidate, enveloped in the institutional words, feels secure. Typically, the frame is silent, as if it did not exist, and exercises a protective function. This institutional frame opens the path towards formal regression, which allows analysts to contemplate and to dream their institution, as well as psychoanalysis itself. The frame provides its member with a facilitating environment thanks to which fruitful and level-headed scientific exchanges take place in the process of working on the symbolization of psychoanalysis, of one's society, of one's place in relation to colleagues. This dynamic frame creates a real and an imaginary space in which a multitude of partial conceptions of psychoanalysis meet, borne by each of the members.

Following Jean-Luc Donnet, we might ideally speak of a "well-tempered" psychoanalytical society, where exchanges and discussions take place under optimal conditions, where a process of analytical thinking takes places.

Along with Bleger (1979 [1967]), we might imagine that the members of a psychoanalytical society deposit their craziest conceptions and analytical theories into the institutional frame, as well as the violence of the transferential, counter-transferential and inter-transferential remains, unanalyzed or unanalyzable. Freud has shown that barbary is related to the unconscious organization of the individual, and this is the reason why analytical institutions set limits, derivations, sublimations, in order for their members to be able to live and work together, despite the barbary. In a sense, institutions exorcize the "originary violence" (Enriquez 2006).

Unease within the institutions

Every analyst has experienced our institutions not only as spaces for personal growth, but also as difficult, conflictual, even completely insane places. When an analytical society suffers, all of its members suffer too.

These sometimes exceedingly violent conflicts undermine team spirit and solidarity among members. Even if an analytical institution allows for the diffraction of transference, we nevertheless see that all of its spaces, including administrative, are charged with passions and a multitude of active transferences, since, by definition, transference never resolves itself completely. The causes for conflict may be varied when the same group of analysts has taken hold of executive functions over a long period of time thus crushing the following generation, and the slighted younger generation then tries to overthrow the old order. Often, however, the causes have to do with unconscious, unanalyzed conflictual aspects that are still active and that can be traced back to the very origins of a given society.

Let us recall that Freud created the IPA in the hopes of convening analysts and providing stability and cohesion to the nascent analytical movement. He allied institution and analytical theory against the centrifugal tendencies of his closest colleagues, against wild psychoanalysis, against external attacks, for example from the medical profession back then. He writes in 1914 (p. 85): "[…] I felt that there must be someone at the head," and speaking of the IPA says, "there should be some headquarters whose business it would be to declare: 'All this nonsense is nothing to do with analysis; this is not psychoanalysis'." He establishes a clear boundary between what is psychoanalysis and what is not. Indeed, all analytical societies stem from the psychotherapeutic grounds from which they had to withdraw themselves, sometimes with great difficulty. In difficult periods, such as the Covid-19 pandemic we are currently living through, with the decrease in candidates in training, these old wounds are scratched open again. Our own members take up old criticisms against analysis: that it is too far removed from people, not empathetic enough … in other words, not psychotherapeutic enough. We see how the boundaries between psychoanalysis and psychotherapy are blurred for some analysts, become porous and inconsistent, which in turn affects the orientation of their respective societies. In excessively wishing to open up, the vital substance of a society runs the risk of leaking out, and with it the society's identity. The symbolic and stabilizing value of the institutional frame is diminished, including its capacity to exclude, to be able to say "no" to certain heterogeneous elements. The analytical identity is diluted and goes astray.

Destructive result: An unease, a feeling of powerlessness, of despondency, of annoyance, of anger, of devitalization, a rampant melancholia spreads among analysts. The credo becomes: Psychoanalysis has no future. One must demonstrate how eclectic one is, or admit any which candidate to fill up the ranks, or open up to yet still more forms of therapy, which further contributes to the widening of the chasm of institutional life. At the origin of this unease is the fact that analysts feel and perceive, clearly or not, that they are busy hawking off the family jewels of psychoanalysis. And quite often analysts belonging to troubled societies are blind to their own difficulties and are themselves incapable of resolving the problems which they cannot see. They require the help of a third party. One may wonder why the majority of long dysfunctional societies do not turn to third-party institutional consultations (Erlich, 2013; Tuckett et al. 2020) in order to overcome their difficulties.

Straying too far from the fundamentals of psychoanalysis adds to a vicious cycle of despair for the future. "Outreach," the occasional bastard child of this melancholic disposition, is surely indispensable, but to what extent and with what kind of negative consequences, not only practical but also symbolic? Some training institutions, in an effort to fight against the dwindling number of candidates, have proposed different psychotherapy training modules without realizing the confusion that this causes, by giving the impression of equivalence between these different kinds of training: All are equal, none better than others. The boundaries blur, and the result: The complete disappearance of candidates for analytical training. Might it not be reasonable to give priority to "inreach," to that internal space, the beating heart of our societies?

Psychoanalysis has always sought to separate itself from the pack by virtue of its strict selection criteria and its long and rigorous training. Giving up on this rigorous position is an attack perpetrated by psychoanalysts against psychoanalysis, a loss of the ethical value of analytical work, a loss of love for psychoanalysis and the hastening of its devitalization.

No analytical society can exempt itself from reevaluation if it does not wish to turn into a hermetic ivory tower. A psychoanalysis society is a "continual story without an end ... A work of exploration and experimentation, of comprehension and elaboration of itself" (Rosanvallon 2018, p. 363). An analytical institution reinvents itself daily, or perishes otherwise. By definition, this work cannot be prescribed from the outside: It is up to the society's members to be inventive and creative.

Creating spaces for reflection on the essence of psychoanalysis, on the definition and preservation of psychoanalytical identity, on the institutional structures and on cultural insertion into society should be at the top of the list of priorities of each and every psychoanalytical society. Such work helps to define what is part of analysis, what is within the psychoanalytical society and what is outside of it.

The insidious impact of neoliberalism on our analytical institutions

As a cultural and scientific phenomenon, psychoanalysis is influenced by the world in which it operates. To ponder the unease experienced by our analytical societies also means taking into account the evolution that has taken place in our society and that exerts a certain constraint on each of us. In the following passage, I shall recall some ideas developed elsewhere (Frisch 2021).

Psychoanalysis was born in a society or a set of institutions and traditions (such as family, village, group of affiliation, political party, religion, etc.), that linked people together through different forms of collective incorporation, which were indexed in turn on solidarity. The relation to others was governed by respect for traditions, customs and ethical principles (Rosanvallon 2018). Neoliberalism has profoundly changed the ties between individuals and the relationships that tie individuals to institutions. The modalities of social ties have changed and we are now witnessing a mutation in the way in which the individual perceives herself and is perceived as part of society.

Dejours (2014) notes that this change in our relations to others means a thinning of solidarity, of collective feeling, of coexistence, as well as the growing primacy of the notion of "It's every man for himself." He argues that mutual help and solidarity disappear, that we are left with the feeling of being alone among the multitude.

In the 1990s, the American political scientist Benjamin R. Barber theorized the political horizon of societies that are saturated with globalized capitalism. According to him, economic globalization would transform the planet into an immense theme park where, in this uniform, "McWorld" world, we would all be subject to the rules of standardized consumption and hypnotized by mercantile logic.

Of these briefly outlined societal changes, what are the consequences for psychoanalysis and its institutions? Psychoanalytical societies provided a social structure for individuals and generated a collective consciousness in which the analyst saw himself channeled, framed by and articulated through the collective sphere in his society. Today, demands of individual autonomy from the collective are becoming commonplace, and many analysts are reluctant to join psychoanalytical societies. If they do become members of institutional structures, it is only after much resistance. The illusion of an analytical life without institutions, without common scientific policies, is on the ascendant. By eliminating oppositions, sexuality is eliminated. Our psychoanalytical societies are fragmenting, and individualism is replacing the desire or the need to live together. In other terms, the individual analyst is ever more becoming a consumer, rather than an active member, of her society.

Some analysts call for the leveling of the institutional structure, for the plain and simple suppression of any and all differences among members of a psychoanalytical society, and by way of consequence the suppression of full-member training analysts. And in treatment, the dissymmetry of the analytical relationship is erased and becomes instead a "dialog" between equals. Such psychoanalytical societies would be reduced to a collective administration, a technical or regulatory body overseeing training and science programs. This is the very definition of neoliberalism, where there are no ties to any form of collective and "which prescribes attitudes and characterizes a mode of interaction between people that lacks any vision of togetherness [...], which is the mark and the effect of a void in social imagination" (Rosanvallon 2018, p. 380).

Not only the tie between an individual and his psychoanalytical society, but also his tie to psychoanalysis itself is under threat. Our mode of coexistence, of each working together to construct the institution, its training, its ethics, is in danger of disintegrating.

The Covid-19 pandemic imposed its lockdowns and restrictions, and the reunions of our analytical institutions have become virtual. Institutional life has been disrupted and individualism runs rampant. We still do not know today what will be the medium- and long-term consequences of the changes that analysts have had to implement to treatment and its frame. Will these adaptations survive, and impose themselves after the return to a pre-Covidian normalcy? The answer to this question will determine what kind of new tensions might arise within our societies.

The (partially) unconscious alliances in the analytical institution

Living in a relationship, in a family, associating with other humans or creating institutions requires being able to identify consciously and unconsciously with one another, and to have projects together in which we support each other. The same goes for psychoanalytical associations. Their members must be able to identify not only with one another but also to strike up alliances and conscious and unconscious pacts among themselves. These alliances create ties among members, provide them with shared goals to realize and to defend together over time. These pacts link psychoanalysts who commit to one another and for one another, for example in the project of raising awareness for psychoanalysis or of creating a psychoanalytical society, where they might develop an ethics, or come up with analytical training of a specific kind, that differs from those created by other colleagues in other societies.

In this sense, unconscious alliances only develop in relation to others who share the same interests. We see how these unconscious alliances tie individual aspirations to those of the group. Individual and group are inseparable. The more we are invested in our psychoanalytical institutes or societies, the more we participate in the development of unconscious alliances, and the more they hold sway over us. These alliances, through which we belong to the group, also grant us with a feeling of security as regards our internal place and our individuality. If treatment is governed by the fundamental rule, by abstinence and by the analytical setting, the institution is governed in turn by other alliances, pacts and contracts that strive to assure the transmission of psychoanalysis. Whereas this goal is a conscious one, nevertheless the space of the analytical institution is infiltrated by the unconscious. If we belong to an institution, it is because we identify with both its goals and its members.

According to Kaës (2009, pp. 4–6),

> the principal function of these alliances is to maintain and strengthen these ties (between members), to determine their stakes and terms and to guarantee their duration [...] Unconscious alliances are the cement of psychic material that ties us to one another.

In the analytical institution, "the effects of transference between the properly analytic situation and the institution of transmitting psychoanalysis are part of the institution's structure." The fact that these alliances manifest themselves in analytical situations does not represent a problem, to the extent that they are acknowledged.

The Oedipus complex versus the fraternal complex

In becoming an analyst, one lives through a passionate love story with one's analyst or analysts, and to a lesser extent, with one's supervisors. We choose this analyst and not another. The Oedipus complex is primed. Our training takes place in parallel to other analysands and other candidates who were or still remain with our analyst, or with a competing colleague of theirs, who we may dislike or with whom we would have so wished to be in analysis but were not able to. "Couch genealogies" are thus created, and we find ourselves belonging to theoretical lineages, with everything that entails in terms of transference onto theories and those who incarnate them.

In order to understand the complexity of relations between psychoanalysts, it is important to refer not only to the Oedipus complex but also to the fraternal one. These two complexes cannot be dissociated and must be considered one alongside the other, or in complement of one another. The Oedipus complex is a vertical structure whereas the fraternal one is structured horizontally. Freud, if he ever spoke of brothers and sisters, would always situate them on the vertical axis.

In psychoanalytical societies, the reference to the Oedipus complex, with its vertical structure, is often used to muffle criticism and maintain the status quo. It is not uncommon to hear that analysts who may have something to say about the workings of their society have been poorly analyzed, are jealous, indeed envious of their seniors (=parents) and of training analysts, and that they require another slice of analysis. Such relations are clearly situated within a generational perspective, comprised of know-it-all parent-analysts and children-candidates who wish to take over but who still have so much to learn before reaching adulthood. I refer the reader to the excellent articles of Dirckx (2016) and Franckx and Faoro-Kreit (2016) on *The Fraternal* in the Revue Belge de Psychanalyse.

Kaës (2008, p. 5) defines the fraternal complex as "a fundamental (partially unconscious) organization of amorous, narcissistic and object desires of hate and aggression towards the 'other' that the subject recognizes as brother or as sister." As objects of reciprocal identification, brothers and sisters can support each other and construct themselves by relying on one another. Siblings are not confronted with generational differences, and their infantile sexuality is not experienced as sexual immaturity. Powerlessness is experienced as having less power. It is less crushing than in relation to the preceding generation.

The Oedipus complex (father-mother-child) and the fraternal complex (parents-siblings-subject) are both of triangular structure (Franckx and Faoro-Kreit 2016). Each person entertains a dynamic relationship with each and both of the two other protagonists. She may have a relationship with one of them while excluding the other, just as she may also be excluded or feel so. These two complexes are nourished by first relationships with father, mother or siblings as well as by the fantasmatic relationships that they mobilize.

The candidates of psychoanalytical institutions ask themselves a certain number of unsettling questions as regards the training committee that selected them, as opposed to others that deferred or even rejected them. Tustin has described this as the fantasy of the "baby nest." In analytical institutions, every new candidate may be immediately exposed to a precocious rivalry before even having had the time to make a place for himself in the nest.

A double movement operates within the candidate group: They identify with one another and rely on one another in order to feel more secure in this psychoanalysis society, where they still feel slightly apart. In this domestication stage, they tend to band together, all for one and one for all. But, in parallel and with ever more urgency, they feel the need to exhibit their differences and particularities, thereupon hatching rivalries. Some seem to be more drawn by theory, others have more clinical experience, some feel at ease as a group whereas others not at all.

According to van der Leeuw (1968), a difficult moment arises once the candidates, after a period of idealization, realize the powerlessness of their analyst and of psychoanalysis. This awakens strong, destructive drives of a sadomasochistic nature, as well as deep-seated anxieties. Feelings of omnipotence may thereupon serve as a protective shield against this depressive lived experience and the anxiety of being destroyed.

As long as the candidates are in analysis, their transferences are channeled, but as soon as they are no longer contained in the frame of analysis, the transferential remains that were insufficiently (or even not at all) treated burst onto the scene of institutional life. The question of the place accorded to candidates within their institution is at the forefront of discussions these days. In many societies, candidates are encouraged to take on elective duties. Is this not a case of analysts and societies resorting to seduction, whereas the goal should be that candidates devote this time to their training and to working on themselves? Candidates who are too soon involved in the arcana of their societies may unwittingly find a loophole to escape the pain of transference.

The fraternal complex further complicates due to the fact that training analysts are also caught up not only in their own Oedipus complexes, but also in their own fraternal complexes. In the face of the unconscious, the Oedipus complex and the fraternal complex, there is no difference between candidate and member!

Siblings experience intense feelings of hate, envy, jealousy and murderous desires since the more of us there are, the more divided must our parents' love be. We may refer to the violent biblical story of Cain and Abel at the very dawn of humanity; to the return of the prodigal son into the welcoming arms of his father and under the hateful gaze of his brother; or indeed to the story of Remus and Romulus at the origins of the Roman Empire. Nevertheless, these violent feelings among siblings are also very structuring, due to the fact that they are less stifling than those aimed against our parents. We can imagine killing a brother or a sister since we are capable of it, being of the same generation, whereas a child would be annihilated by parental force.

Fantasmatically, the birth of a child should guarantee the reproduction of the parents' duplicate. But once a second child is born, we notice a difference. And this difference grows with every subsequent birth. It is the same with psychoanalysis societies. Each new candidate accentuates the difference with the preceding generations. This is probably the reason why there sometimes are candidates who disappoint their supervisors, which is why the latter as well as the training institution must be able to mourn the ideal candidate who would otherwise assume the form of an exact copy of themselves.

One outcome of the fraternal complex is that the young analysts integrate the generational difference in order to forge for themselves a (sexuated) identity, in healthy rivalry with members of their generation, which thereby allows them to rival their elders and to become in turn recognized analysts in their own right. But each new generation of psychoanalysts is also involved in unconscious alliances of their own that contribute to the creation of their group identity. They would have to differentiate themselves from the "same" of their siblings, an often painful process, sometimes accompanied by some violence, in order to obtain their own veritable identity. Not all manage to do so.

The Oedipus complex and the fraternal complex are intimately intertwined and cannot unfold independently from one another. But, as Franckx and Faoro-Kreit (2016) have shown following Kaës (2009), the two complexes can also be used defensively one against the other. Thus, when Freud addressed his jealousy and his murderous desires towards his brother Julius, he analyzed them in respect to the Oedipus complex and not at all in reference to the fraternal complex. The tender feelings he had towards his mother had allowed Freud to mask his archaic, murderous fraternal feelings towards Julius (Houzel 2000 pp. 352–353). In Freudian theory, the place reserved for siblings is modest, and rivalry between brothers and sisters is downplayed, just as are amorous feelings and fantasies of fraternal incest, in the face of Oedipal jealousy and love.

The verticality of the Oedipus complex is interlaced with the horizontality of the fraternal complex. We might say that these interlacings create knots and stitches in the institutional weft and give it not only its strength and cohesion, but also, one may hope, its flexibility. Understood from this angle, we can see how fragile a society may be when these stitches are lacking, where the vertical and the horizontal are insufficiently intertwined. I have seen the extreme fragility of several societies, let us call them older ones, in which, for example, someone had autocratically occupied the presidency for some twenty years, and other younger societies which having hardly been created had already gone through schisms. The institutional fabric had been weakened by excessive verticality in the first case and too much horizontality in the second.

The analyst can understand and interpret everything through the lenses of Oedipus without ever perceiving the fraternal, and conversely, the analysand can see everything through the fraternal in order to avoid the Oedipus complex and all matters to do with castration.

Member analysts can interpret the actions of young analysts through the bias of the Oedipus complex, and young analysts can barricade themselves defensively in sterile quarrels among themselves in the effort to avoid entering into rivalry with the preceding generation. Detaching from the fraternal complex and acquiring otherness can only happen by using the crutch of the Oedipus complex.

In conclusion

If the profession of analyst is one of the impossible professions, then analytical societies are impossible organizations. Freud had underlined the barbary that exists in all human groups, but our societies are characterized in addition by the particular fact that we pursue our professional life while remaining in the institution which had trained us, alongside our trainers, analysts and supervisors, our brothers and sisters in training as well as future generations.

We must understand that our institutions are rather more fragile than we may like them to be, and that in order to strengthen them we must think of ways of taking care of them. Indeed our societies are all too rarely discussed as clinical facts by us members. The difficulties related to their origins and histories, with all the human conflicts, various abuses and other secrets involved remain neatly hidden and slowly poison institutional life. We might say that the oldest members tell candidates the story of their society as it was told to them and as they lived through it, reconstructed it and fantasized it. Part of this rich history contains those who were excluded and those who were isolated and that the young do not know and yet who nevertheless bear part of their history.

All too often do these "unsolvable" difficulties remain hidden, swept under the rug, whereas any solution must consist of continuously addressing them, of speaking of them and of the profession time and again. We might apply the analytical rule of saying "telling all" in spaces that the societies might reserve for dealing with institutional matters. The candidates, and the future of our societies that they represent, would likely be grateful to us.

Note

1   Belgian Psychoanalytical Society.

Bibliography

Bleger J (1979 [1967]): *Psychanalyse du cadre analytique, in Crise, rupture et dépassement*, Paris: Dunod.

Bolognini S (2018): In between sameness and otherness: The analyst's words in interpsychic dialogue. In: Joyce, Angela (Ed) *Donald W. Winnicott and the History of the Present*. London: Routledge.

Castoriadis-Aulagnier P (2008): Sociétés de psychanalyse et psychanalyste de société. *Topique* 100: 21–60.

Dejours C (2014): La sublimation entre clinique du travail et psychanalyse. *Rev. Franç. Psychosomatique* 46: 21–37.

Dejours C (2016): *Situations du travail*. Paris: PUF.

Dirckx L (2016): *Introduction au colloque sur le « complexe fraternel »*. Revue Belge de Psychanalyse.

Enriquez E (2006): Institutions humaines et organisations. *RFP LXX* 901.

Erlich S (2017): Between Scylla and Charybdis in psychoanalytic training: Unconscious and group dynamic factors in saying "yes" or "no". Invited address for the EPF Forum on Education. Brussels, December 1.

Erlich S (2013): *Psychoanalytic Societies on the Couch. In: The Couch in the Marketplace*. London: Karnac.

Franckx C, Faoro-Kreit B (2016): *De Narcisse à Œdipe, ou comment penser le fraternel*. Revue Belge de Psychanalyse.

Freud S (1921): *Group Psychology and the Analysis of the Ego*. The Standard Edition of the Complete Psychological Works of Sigmund Freud, Volume XVIII.

Freud S (1920–1922): *Beyond the pleasure principle*. Group Psychology and Other Works, pp. 65–144.

Freud S (1957 [1914]): *On the History of the Psychoanalytic Movement*, SE XIV, pp. 7–66.

Freud S (1961 [1927]): *The Future of an Illusion*, SE XXI, pp. 5–58.

Frisch S (2010): *What if Freud had stopped over in Brussels? In 100 Years of the IPA*. Karnac, pp. 25–37.

Frisch S (2021): *Psychoanalysis and Covidian Life: Common Distress, Individual Experience*. Paris: Phoenix Ithaque.

Gauchet M (2016): *Comprendre le malheur français*. Paris: Stock, pp. 323–324.

Houzel D (2000): *Le fantasme du nid-aux-bébés in L'Enfant, ses parents et le psychanalyste*. Paris: Bayard.

Joyce, Angela (Ed) (2017): *Donald W. Winnicott and the History of the Present*. London: Routledge.

Kaës R (1993): *Le groupe et le sujet du groupe. Éléments pour une théorie psychanalytique des groupes*. Paris: Dunod.

Kaës R (1999): *Le psychodrame analytique de groupe*. Paris: Dunod.

Kaës R (2008): *Le deuil des fondateurs dans les institutions: travail de l'originaire et passage de génération in: Nicolle O, Kaës R et al.. L'institution en héritage*. Paris: Dunod.

Kaës R (2009): *Les alliances inconscientes*. Paris: Dunod.

Kaës R (2015): *L'extension de la psychanalyse*. Paris, Dunod.

Kahn L (2014): *Le psychanalyste apathique et le patient postmoderne*. Penser/rêver. Éditions de l'Olivier.

Kirsner D (2000): *Unfree Associations*. Lanham, MD: Rowman & Littlefield.

Rosanvallon P (2018): *Notre histoire intellectuelle et politique, 1968–2018*. Paris: Éditions du Seuil.

Tuckett D, Amati Mehler J, Collins S et al. (2020): Psychoanalytic training in the Eitingon model and its controversies: A way forward. *Int J Psychoanal* 101(6): 1106–1135.

van der Leeuw P-J (1968): The psycho-analytic society. *Int J Psychoanal* 46: 160–164. Sur la vie des sociétés de psychanalyse. Adresse présidentielle XXV Congrès de l'Association Psychanalytique International de Psychanalyse.

Wallerstein R (1972): The future of analytic education. *J. Amer. Psychoanal. Assn.* 20: 591–606.

Chapter 3

Maintaining and developing a containing institution

A challenge for psychoanalysts?

Gabriele Junkers

I. Introduction

For us as psychoanalysts, psychoanalysis as a theory, a cultural achievement, a method of investigation, and technique of treatment is a precious discovery that needs to be preserved and enhanced. To this end, we need an institution[1] that provides a sound framework for our collective efforts. But many analysts are unhappy with the existing organizations, criticizing above all the quality of communication between themselves and their colleagues. Naturally, we are all fully aware that progress is impossible without debate and dispute and that this frequently creates tension between different groupings. Yet we still find it difficult to uphold a spirit of open-mindedness in coming to terms with the multitude of theoretical and clinical persuasions that our colleagues represent. How, then, can we hope to join forces constructively?

The ideas I want to discuss here are inspired by the desire to cast light on the deeper reasons for the much-maligned communication deficits bedeviling the work of psychoanalytic institutions. The careers of "typical" psychoanalysts have a number of features in common, and I shall first be looking at these from three different perspectives: developmental psychology, professional profiles, and institutional factors. Against this background, I then intend to discuss the personal characteristics conducive to the desire to become a psychoanalyst, the way these characteristics interact with the complexities of theoretical and clinical education and training, and how they relate to the requirements that need to be met if there is to be constructive cooperation within the group as a whole. In view of the effects of unconscious dynamics in analytic groups, clear and transparent structures are indispensable if we hope to regulate such cooperation objectively and with due concern for the tasks in hand. Accordingly, I shall be enlarging both on the necessity of structural cohesion for psychoanalytic organizations and on the aversion to structural concerns that can frequently be observed among their members. In so doing, I hope to enhance our understanding of the anxieties that rear their heads in this constellation and the defense mechanisms marshaled against them in the

DOI: 10.4324/9781003301936-4

context of both structural and social realities. In addition, I shall be indicating some potential consequences, making a number of practical proposals, and suggesting potential new avenues to explore. My aim in this is to encourage debate and constructive dispute within and between different groups.

My perspective on this topic results from a combination of my own experiences as a member of various institutions, observations on those institutions, and an awareness of the different groups existing within my own self.

II. Psychoanalysis as a career

II.1 The desire to become a psychoanalyst

When we decided to become psychoanalysts, we did not yet know that this ambition was very much a consequence of early experiences and the lives we had led *before* embarking on a course of analytic training. But we knew that we needed psychoanalysis, and we can think ourselves fortunate that this was the case (cf. e.g. Ferro, 2003, p. 137). In the families we came from, there may have been something that we felt was "not good" or "not good enough" and that caused us anguish. More or less unconsciously, we set out on an ill-defined quest for something we hoped to find in what we imagined a course of analytic training would be like. The motive force behind this covert desire may have been the (usually unconscious) hope of liberation from anxieties, of achieving greater peace of mind, understanding ourselves better, and deriving greater satisfaction from social relations. All kinds of conceivable causes may have led to an uncertain "sense of being" (Winnicott, 1971, p. 80) and interfered with the development of a stable identity squarely and adequately based in reality. Even after the termination of training analysis, wounds are liable to break open again at a later stage. When we started wanting to become "analysts," we did not know what was lurking behind this unconscious inner blueprint. But we dimly suspected that the projection of anticipated wish-fulfillments might conceal fantasized hopes that we believed could only be realized by "becoming an analyst." Accordingly, the choice of this job and no other appears to be burdened with a powerful, albeit covert promise.

---

(1) One candidate told her training analyst: "I believe that when I become an analyst, it will put an end to all the pain and the unpleasant feelings; everything will turn out fine." At the initial interview, another applicant said: "I'd like to die behind the couch," while a third candidate opined: "The good thing is that you can practice this profession forever, you never have to stop."

Statements like these give us an inkling of the intense longing bound up with the choice of this profession, a longing that can distort a realistic view of the world in order to keep illusions alive.

This "aching" desire means that to practice this profession, we are prepared to accept all kinds of restrictions and sacrifices in terms of time, money, and psychological stress. Analysts are analysts "body and soul." We put all our eggs in one basket. We have opted to embark on the long inward-looking process that the training analysis involves, undertaken in the company of a training analyst we put our trust in. To the extent that the psychic constellation we bring with us "gels" with the training analyst's specific abilities, we can accept, use, digest, and implement what he/she has to offer. Sometimes more, sometimes less.

Like Ferro (2003, p. 137), I am convinced that the psychic problems and injuries that we bring with us in choosing and training for this profession are a *conditio sine qua non*. I also believe that a specific ability to "tolerate pain" can be a sounding board enabling the injuries of the analysand to "resonate harmoniously" in the analyst. At the same time, choosing this profession promises healing both for ourselves and for our primary objects. But not everything can be worked through in the training analysis. Even as experienced practitioners we also have to acknowledge the limitations of the method we use (e.g. Klein, 1975a [1950], p. 45). In our analytic work we must always be attentive to the fact that in conjunction with earlier experiences new injuries can lead to an opening up of old wounds (Ferro, 2003, p. 137).

What can we say so far? Embarking on a career as a psychoanalyst implies an unstinting readiness to place the training, our training analysis, and our future patients in the focus of our lives. If we see the desire to embark on this course of training as a function of our own (hi)story and early afflictions, it is certainly a courageous decision to set out on the long road that leads to personal development. On the other hand, psychoanalysis – both training and the analytic institution – may be unconsciously transformed into a locus of hope that promises the realization of potential ideal images for the self.

II.2 Becoming a psychoanalyst: taming desires and learning an analytic attitude

II.2.1 Combining the inner and outer paths to professional practice

The training analysis as a process of learning, development, and maturation (cf. the Eitingon model) is universally regarded as the core element in the training of psychoanalysts. It is designed not only to enable candidates to achieve *a secure conviction of the existence of the unconscious* but also to experience personally the conflicting claims of the id, the superego, and the ego as well as the defensive forces that are brought to bear against self-scrutiny. As we proceed, we are expected to learn to withstand frustrations, to come to terms with the absence of the object and also the impossibility of possessing it. Early deficits may never be fully and completely remedied, but this idea should not yet be actively entertained.

Only in retrospect do we accept the fact that however ideal the situation of the training analysis may be, we must always expect to be involved in a never-ending clinch with the defensive ego, for the patient (candidate) often fears inter-psychic empathy as much as he/she desires it. *A good analysis is an offer, not a guarantee.* It equips the analysand for forays into the unknown but does not provide a complete map of the regions to be explored (Ferro, 2003, S. 137).

The long years of this grueling apprenticeship are full of twists and turns, new departures, inner turbulence, and instability. Anxiety becomes an important and unavoidable companion.

Like many other authors, Bion (1994 [1975]) stresses the paramount significance of developing a psychoanalytic identity of one's own. Much as we may idealize our teachers and identify with them, in the last resort it is our development in the training analysis that (ideally) instills in us a stable *personal identity* that can function as the foundation for an *analytic* identity worthy of being called a "voice of our own" ("The analyst you become is you and you alone:...that is what you use...", Bion, 1994 [1975], p. 15; cf. also Kaplan, 1993. "To put it in more popular terms, I would say the more 'real' the psycho-analyst is the more he can be at one with the reality of the patient", (Bion, 1984 [1970], p. 28).

At the outset of our careers, we do all we can to adjust to new theories, new teachers, new colleagues, and new institutional structures in the organizations we have little choice but to join. In the various events organized by these institutions, we experience different kinds of work defined in terms of time, place, and interaction of various kinds. The external path of institutional learning is closely bound up with our internal experiences. Henceforth, both will be inextricably associated in a process of complex interaction.

The psychoanalytic theories we learn about provide us with new perspectives that enable us to understand, respond to, and interpret the utterances and behavior of our future patients. Gradually we acquire a notion of what Schafer (1983) introduced into psychoanalytic training as a "positive ideal": *the psychoanalytic attitude.* We begin to intuit the significance of perception and listening, of silence and patience, ingestion and conceptualization as ways of finding access to the unconscious realms of our patients and arriving at interpretations that make those realms conscious in a way that is bearable. We must learn to be abstinent, to keep our own wants and emotional states to ourselves and let nothing penetrate to the outside. In the ideal case, we learn and acquire an attitude derived from psychoanalytic theory and internalized accordingly, as opposed to a cast of mind that stifles genuine thought and operates in terms of right/wrong, allowed/forbidden, analytic/non-analytic. Effortfully, we learn to hold our desires and memories in abeyance, to curb the urge to understand everything completely and utterly, and to blot out the claims of certainty and factual reality. Just as significant as the "analytic attitude" are the analyst's self-perception and the engagement with his/her feelings in countertransference (e.g. Gabbard & Ogden, 2009, p. 311; Brenman Pick, 2018). At this point in the analytic process, the focus shifts to achieving an understanding of one's own fears of potential entanglements and the way they interact with the unconscious dynamics of the analysand (Bion, 1984 [1970]). Only the awareness, the elaboration, and the acceptance of a *genuinely personal contribution* to this process and the responsible handling of that contribution will enable us to learn (and it is a lifelong learning process) to *"speak with our own voice."*

Becoming a psychoanalyst also means learning a new language interwoven with theoretical knowledge one absorbs in the course of training. This psychoanalytic language evolves from a combination of new terminologies with a heightened ability to observe clinical phenomena and see one's own subjective experience from the outside. It extends our linguistic repertoire by providing new words for feelings and integrating aspects we normally leave out of account. It covers things that *cannot* be traced back to sensory impressions alone (Bion, 1984 [1970], p. 89) but can only be experienced as the resonance from one's own emotional sounding-board. Using this language without yet having a full command of it is a major challenge.

Starting out on daily analytic work behind the couch means transcending all our inner uncertainties and at the same time conceding that we are still involved in the open-ended quest for a (n) (professional) identity. It demands the courage to perceive and accept ourselves as learners. Before we present our own work for discussion in seminars and supervision, we have to reflect on it and work it through. Despite all the uncertainty lurking in the background, trainee analysts are called upon to represent an inner standpoint that is clear and understandable for others. Bion (1987, p. 15) warns against the illusory certainty that may be instilled in us by ingenious interpretations and theories that we only use to bolster our self-confidence in the struggle against the fear of not really being an analyst and not knowing how you get to be one. He reminds us that language not only clarifies thoughts but can also be used to conceal them (1984 [1970], p. 3), and we need to be extremely sensitive to this fact when it comes to assessing our analytic progress. Candidates frequently have a desire to appear more self-assured than they actually feel, in other words to regurgitate ill-digested knowledge in the service of a bogus professional self.

---

(2) A European training analyst recalls one candidate who was greatly concerned about adapting and adjusting to his new situation and to that end drew upon the novel "technical vocabulary" of analysis in an effort to emulate his own analytic mentor. He thus ended up in a state of

mimicry because he was unable to connect to a genuine analytic attitude within his inner self. The price for this was that his work remained rigid and inflexible. The training analyst was unhappy to hear (indirectly) that the supervisors were full of praise for this young man, whereas he himself saw almost exclusively the insecure, contorted side of his candidate.

If things go badly, the analytic attitude can turn into a mere replica of a professional model and hence into a suit of armor shielding the analyst throughout his/her professional life. The price paid for this is the loss of flexible adjustment to the inner and outer conditions prevailing in a given situation. The final outcome would be a professional self that is founded on "knowing" and mimicry, rather than on integration of professional knowledge with the personal self.

Doubts about one's own work prompt critical reflection on potential entanglements and are helpful in subjecting one's efforts to an ongoing quality check. Psychologically, however, it is tedious and grueling to constantly cast doubt on oneself in supervisions and case presentations, to be queried by others, and above all to accept the feeling that those queries are justified.

The end of training and the future prospect of working "on one's own" are both liberating and alarming. We know from training analyses how difficult many training analysands find it to tolerate loneliness. But without the capacity to be alone and to withstand loneliness we could not practice our profession. Winnicott (1965) sees the acceptance of certain realities of life and the development of an identity of one's own as prerequisites for "the capacity to be alone." He speaks of the ability to be alone in the presence of others. Ortega y Gasset reminds us grimly that we have no stand-ins, no one to think our thoughts for us, no one to deputize for us in the business of life. Melanie Klein (1975b [1963]) considers "a ubiquitous longing for an unachievable inner state of perfection" to be responsible for the feeling of inner loneliness (p. 300).[2] And we have Monica Bruzzone et al. (1985, p. 411) to thank for their impressive descriptions of the inner turmoil experienced in the course of training.[3]

II.2.2 Everyday psychoanalytic life

To provide our patients with a dependable setting, we adhere to a self-imposed, strict, and inviolable time-plan. We are entirely "our own bosses" in the way we handle the course of the working day and organize our practice as an institution[4] (Bleger, 2013 [1967]; Churcher, 2022). Completing our training and working for a time without supervision/intervision is frequently regarded as a new juncture in which we consolidate what we have learned. Gradually we find our bearings in our own institution(s) and our own society, bringing with us everything we have learned, including all those aspects of attitude and behavior that we have "picked up" from other members (cf. Section III). Frequently we find the group to be a welcome counterpoise to our isolated work in the practice. Here we meet colleagues we find (and who find us) congenial or uncongenial. It is not always easy to acquire an authentic attitude.

What can we say so far? We psychoanalysts are mostly glad to have opted for this profession. Candidates, full members, and the training committee all attach very high, if not excessive, expectations to training analysis. In the best case, this analysis will have been good enough to equip us for self-analysis and enable us to come to terms reasonably well with our own selves. To my mind, regarding the training analysis as a guarantee for sound mental health is unrealistic, erroneous, and based on idealization.

In trying to *find our bearings*, we frequently pin our hopes on an offer misconceived as a promise. It is the prospect of achieving security by learning to assume a professional attitude. Developing an authentic analytic approach is a major challenge. In the framework of training, the superego we bring with us forms an alliance with a professional superego. The professional superego and the "institutional superego system" (Reeder, 2004, p. 153) may be mutually reinforcing.

In the institutional context, the influence of a recourse to *imitative identification* (Gaddini, 1969), i.e. learning from models, as a substitute for reflective assimilation is frequently underestimated. The things we "pick up" from others normally evade conscious, self-critical observation in a social context and function subliminally as a vehicle for unconscious mentalities, "beliefs," and "taboos." We learn how to behave like a psychoanalyst, how to keep our own counsel, establish contact, keep out of each other's way. And sometimes we lose our bearings altogether. In most cases, we resort to the "inner setting" newly acquired for use behind the couch and transpose it uncritically to institutional and social situations (cf. Section III.4).

Membership of the group(s) we belong to – our home institute, our national and international societies – is membership *for life*. We are in there together with three if not four analytic generations: candidates, parents, grandparents, and sometimes great-grandparents. Living cheek by jowl with the analytic family all our lives is a situation that poses special challenges for institutional co-existence, permeated as it is with conscious and unconscious attitudes and transference remnants constantly struggling to rise to the surface (cf. Section III.4).

II.3 Transience and the death of the analyst

We analysts do not have much time to exercise our profession. After qualifying to practice, we can look forward to 20–25 active years before we reach normal retirement age. But in fact we are exempt from this restriction because there is no statutory or institutionally prescribed age-barrier limiting our professional activities. Some psychoanalytic societies do recommend an age-limit (often 70 years) for accepting new training analysands. The absence of "youngsters" is felt to be disquieting, although worldwide trends are part of the explanation. We prefer not to ask ourselves whether it might have something to do with the way we live out our role as psychoanalysts. So how can we come to terms with the challenging situation in which three to four generations have to get on with each other, the older members are in the majority, and psychodynamic factors also play their part?

My observations and investigations suggest that, more than other people, psychoanalysts are inclined to regard transience, aging, and the prospect of their own death as factors that in their case do not count. Many of them live and behave as if they had a boundless future[5] stretching out ahead of them. The following, rather unsettling experience substantiates this impression:

(3) As a member of the executive board preparing an EPF conference, I proposed giving a panel on the subject of aging. I received no verbal response but earned any number of disapproving glances as if I had violated some taboo. Scouring the literature for an explanation, I was dumbfounded to discover that in the years between 1920 and the present, only about 20 articles in the *International Journal* discussed the topic of aging (Junkers, 2006). This, I felt sure, was not just a reaction to Freud's advice to desist from analytic work with people beyond the age of 50. There was obviously a widespread disinclination to come into contact with elderly people and elderly patients. Whenever in subsequent national and international discussions I broached subjects like aging, illness, crises in analytic careers, and taking leave of the analytic profession, the responses were equally disconcerting. Not only did I encounter silence, indifference, and rejection, I also received (I was in my mid-fifties at the time) testy personal letters urging me to stop sticking my knife into older psychoanalysts and advising me to undergo another piece of analysis myself to explore the sinister reasons for the destructive abuse that I was obviously determined to level at the analytic profession.

This confirmed my earlier impression that I was violating a taboo. To find out more, I proposed establishing an EPF work group dedicated to the subject of aging. At the first meeting about 20 years ago, only one participant turned up! Later I was encouraged notably by *women* analysts like Annemarie Sandler, Danielle Quinodoz, and above all Betty Joseph to cast more light on the topic of aging and the problems bound up with it. The collection of papers titled *The Empty Couch* (Junkers, 2013a) documented the efforts of our numerous work-groups, the investigations within the EPF, and the later establishment of the "IPA Committee on Aging – of Patients and Psychoanalysts" (2002). This little vignette tells its own story:

---

(4) One candidate complained that it was impossible to tell from the official list of training analysts whether the analyst in question still offered supervisions or training analyses. Year-long attempts to introduce an "r" for "retired" after the relevant names, as is the custom in Britain, were stymied by opposition from the executive board. When asked why, they said that this was something that analysts could not be expected to tolerate.

What couldn't they tolerate? Being designated as "retired," i.e. someone no longer actively involved in analytic training? Or were we talking about the typical senescent fantasy of being old and hence no longer any use? Much the same happened with a "professional will,"[6] the binding introduction of which was recently rejected by the executive board of a European psychoanalytic society on the grounds that precautionary protection for patients and for psychoanalytic records (including data protection) is exclusively a private matter. It is remarkable that from 1955 to the present day, precautionary measures of this kind have been called for at regular intervals (e.g. Firestein, 1993; Galatzer-Levy, 2005; Gabbard et al., 2001) but have yet to be put into practice.

What is the precise nature of this taboo? Denis (2013, p. 33) points out that the "unconscious notion of psychoanalysis conferring a kind of immortality" is widespread. He addresses the conviction that, in grappling with the unconscious, psychoanalysis is capable of transcending the customary limits of the body. He dismisses it as illusory, citing Dewald (1982), who assumes "that many analysts entertain the fantasy that their personal analysis has immunized them against illnesses that others are subject to" (p. 359). Here we find the conviction of a species of immortality compounded with the conviction of physical invulnerability.

In itself, aging is not a psychoanalytic concept. But we can still attempt to grasp in psychoanalytic terms various aspects of the way in which aging is experienced. Money-Kyrle places the phenomenon of aging and his concept of the *facts of life* (Money-Kyrle, 1978 [1971], p. 443) in a psychoanalytic context and attributes special significance to the acknowledgement of reality in this connection. Fear of death, says Money-Kyrle, is not the same as the recognition of its inevitability. Conscious awareness is forced upon us by repeated experiences of the fact that nothing (good or bad) lasts forever (p. 444).

Linear time and its irreversible progress penetrates all sectors of our lives, including perception and experience of affects and moods. Orientation in time and the development of a sense of temporality are among the neutral ego functions that are (or should be) acquired in the course of individuation.

We know, however, that early traumas can interfere with the development of this feeling, even though the changes this causes may remain unrecognized on the surface. Only when we begin to reflect on our own experiences do we develop an awareness of the past, the present, and the future. Freud linked the subjective experience of time with perceptual consciousness, whereas the Kleinian view connects it with temporal experience from the conflicts of the depressive position, i.e. an *awareness of separateness*.

Personal *identity* can only be constituted by the experience of continuity and of sameness in change. A sense of reality cannot be achieved without a feeling for time and development and hence also for aging. Accepting aging means accepting changes as losses without losing a sense of oneself in the process. Especially harrowing is the loss of fantasies that have turned out to be illusions. I have referred to these developmental tasks facing us as we grow older as "work on the process of aging" (Junkers, 1994). It implies reconciling the inner, limitless world bound up with our wishful thinking – a world without a feeling for time and without a "no" – with external, factual reality as exemplified by our own body, our place in the sequence of generations, and our dealings with the outside world. Accepting my own personal aging as a reality forces me to realize that there are limits to the projection of hopes and wishes onto the future and that in real life the implementation of plans for reparation is increasingly restricted. To square up to "work on the aging process," we must be ready to engage with a process of mourning and be able to place ourselves outside ourselves (Junkers, 2013b) and thus not to allow the soul to recoil from pain, as Freud (1916 [1915], p. 306) explained to his friend Rilke, when he railed against the acceptance of transience. Hanna Segal (1958) concluded from her treatment of an elderly man that at an advanced age it was the unconscious fear of death that could trigger psychic problems in which notably idealization and denial were instrumental.

What can we say so far? Many psychoanalysts appear ill-equipped to deal with the reality of aging and work on the aging process. Fear of helplessness, impotence, illness, need, loneliness, exclusion, and annihilation interfere with an unclouded view of reality.

As a limiting and structuring factor, time is important for our sense of reality. Our analytic activities in the timeless realms of the unconscious may conjoin to detrimental effect with an existing disinclination against time as a limiting experience of reality. The following vignette illustrates one possible repercussion affecting analytic work:

(5) At an informal meeting, one European (female) colleague complained: We have initiated so many important projects and so many voluntary work-groups have set them on their way with any amount of time and energy. But none of those groups have submitted a closing report actually bringing the process to an end.

Completion of lifelong work routines appears to be unconsciously bound up with an intolerable separation, death, or annihilation fantasy: *If I complete my work, I shall no longer feel contained and will have to die.*

If we deny that life is finite, then, as the example of King Lear illustrates, everything has to be rejected that can interfere with that denial. This may extend to the awareness of the significance of *the intact body as the indispensable basis (hardware) for the analyst's "stock-in-trade" (emotional sensitivity and acumen)* if that realization has to be scotomized as something menacingly restrictive. Physical illness can damage our analytic faculties (the ability to analyze). Notably, the progressive diminution of perception and control associated with the onset of dementia can, first insidiously and then drastically, impair the capacity for realistic assessment and self-reflection. Without anyone noticing it, analytic work then loses its substance and becomes ineffective. Denial of these connections is frequently motivated by anxiety: "Who am I without the couch?" Accordingly, the overwhelming but mostly unconscious fear of termination, loneliness, mortality, and exclusion can trigger all kinds of misconduct or aberrant behavior, all the way up to anti-democratic behavior in institutional contexts.

---

(6) This was the fate of a respected elderly colleague from a European institution who was unable to come to terms with the fact that he had decided against a university career and now did everything in his power to "wangle" the election of a young, analytically unsuitable, but academically successful colleague as a training analyst. None of the colleagues witnessing these manipulations dared to criticize his behavior. The situation is given a dramatic twist by the fact that it was only in the aftermath that it became known that at this point in time he was already very seriously ill.

Among psychoanalysts, open discussion and clarification of the somatic/psychic factors determining when they should terminate their professional careers is an absolute taboo. The clinching defensive argument is that we are dealing here with a private matter. But this private matter is significant because (a) we have ethical obligations towards our patients and our training candidates, (b) age-affected behavior can interfere with our analytic powers, (c) age-affected behavior on the part of one member can have repercussions on the dynamics of an entire institution, and (d) there is a taboo preventing (particularly younger) colleagues from confronting older trainers with their real situation.

III. The psychoanalytic institution: from twosomes to public communication

The assumption I proceed on is that we psychoanalysts are responsible for what we feel to be the inadequacy of the containment provided by our psychoanalytic institutions. Only through individual *and* joint reflection and insight can we do anything to change the situation. Undisputed is the fact that we need a group, that we want to be members of a group, and that we need the certainty of remaining a member of that group, even if we turn away disappointed and seek to convey the impression that we do not belong to it.

In the following I intend to

1. outline a framework for the external, formal containment of an organization providing protection for the pursuit of, and engagement with, well-defined aims;
2. report selected critical voices of psychoanalysts with respect to institutional co-existence;
3. describe a number of behaviors displayed by psychoanalysts that can impede collaboration in our organizations;
4. set out my thoughts about the influence of those features on the significance of containment in psychoanalytic institutions;
5. and, in conclusion, discuss impediments to, and potential for, the impact of generativity as a vital factor in psychoanalytic institutions.

III.1 A frame for work in psychoanalytic institutions

A psychoanalytic institute brings together people of different origins and different ages, originally strangers to each other but united by their interest in psychoanalysis, its further development, and the training of young analysts: members, would-be members, candidates, and "trainers." Members with the competence to judge are unanimous that they need a group in order to pursue their declared aims. Newly qualified candidates applying for acceptance as members of the group *implicitly* enter into a quasi-contractual agreement of unlimited duration. By declaring their consent to a training program offered by the group, would-be members and candidates have *explicitly* declared their agreement with the rights, obligations, and commissions formulated by the group.

With his/her individual unconscious, every member of the group contributes to the group dynamic, so that the group is marked by the collective effect of the unconscious psychic activities of all the members. No individual in the group can evade being caught up in the emotional situation obtaining in that group. We know, but in difficult situations too easily forget, that not only the individual but also the group has an unconscious. A group can feel anxiety and can employ defense mechanisms to fend off unpleasant or painful feelings, availing itself of the voices of individuals for that purpose.

To keep the all-pervasive unconscious undercurrents at bay as far as possible, the group needs not only unifying aims but also an appropriate defining structure, a framework providing a container for the organization and its work.[7] Ideally, such a framework will generate in the group a feeling of containment, but members may also experience it as painful due to the limitations and restrictions it imposes. This will prompt those members to look for a way out by engaging in defense maneuvers. Permeable structures characterized by gaps and ambiguities facilitate the incursion of early, archaic anxieties and mobilize corresponding defense processes in the group. My experience has led me to the following conviction: The security of an organization and its success in minimizing gaps conducive to misunderstandings docking on to the unconscious dynamics of the members is proportional to the definition, differentiation, and comprehensiveness displayed by the structure of the organizational framework of that organization.

Designing a structure for a psychoanalytic organization is not something we have learnt. Normally we accept the "inherited architecture" because "it's always been that way." Small groups tend to emulate Freud's example and establish a private circle. But as the group expands, the permanent necessity of work on the organizational structure imposes itself.

The duties accruing to the group require the definition of offices, roles, and periods in office, alongside rights, responsibilities, and (rarely) obligations. Ill-defined contours ("soft" role definitions, etc.) can readily be exploited by individuals whose far-reaching personal ambitions transcend structurally restricted roles that are not designed to sustain them. To keep the inherent conflict potential as low as possible, these roles should be defined with great precision in terms of the tasks associated with them, the powers of decision they confer, and the period their incumbents remain in office. To ensure that all members actively comply with these structures, they should be set down in writing, display sufficient clarity and detail, and be readily accessible to all members at all times. An explicitly defined corporate structure of this kind not only ensures the transparency conducive to cooperation and collective identity but also promotes containment by preventing experiences of shared learning from being relegated to oblivion.

---

(7) The head of a European institution suggested to the executive board and the members that the tasks incumbent on each role should be precisely described and the powers of decision associated with them clearly differentiated from one another. He encountered massive resistance from his colleagues, who insisted that everyone knew how

these things work and that the group should not be over-regulated as that would only provoke opposition. The attempt to go ahead all the same ran into a wall of tacit resistance, and the plan finally fizzled out altogether.

(8) Conflict flared up between the training coordinator and the head of an institution because the latter had communicated to the parent society a decision he had made with regard to a new training regulation. As there was no clear structure defining the various powers of decision, there ensued an acrimonious personal dispute within the executive committee finally culminating in such an impasse that the members called for new elections.

These vignettes show how easily structural ambiguities can lead to personal conflicts. This can be avoided by adapting the "corporate philosophy" to changing external and internal conditions and keeping it up to date at all times. In my experience, the defense against devoting time and energy to the organization is overpowering in its effect. "Institutional self-analysis" (i.e. containment in the guise of ongoing organizational development) is normally rejected as completely superfluous. The apprehensions caused by novelty and change interfere with a triangulating external perspective on the object "group," which in its turn thwarts the opportunity of taking a corrective look at the internal object "my group." This "unpleasure" is reinforced by the lack of institutional knowhow. In addition, the self-centeredness operative here prevents the institution from conceding that recruiting professional analytic assistance from outside might improve cooperation.

(9) A European colleague entrusted with looking after a new analytic group asked me for my advice on the following matter: In its initial stages, the psychoanalytic organization reluctantly elaborated a set of regulations for work within the organization. After lengthy and tedious discussions, an agreement was reached on what the code of ethics should look like. Some years later, the group was confronted with an ethical problem for the first time. On inspection, it transpired that the ethics regulations available differed substantially from the ones originally elaborated. With considerable embarrassment, the group was forced to admit that the person in charge at the time had lost the document in question but was too ashamed to own up to the loss. Instead, she had written a new and much less detailed manual from memory, and in the present case, this sketchier version was causing very substantial problems.

The conclusion is obvious. The call for future-oriented work on the structure of an organization constantly falls foul of reactions designed to evade feelings of unpleasure and displayed by forces intent on adhering to the status quo. While such adherence can go some way to consolidating the collective identity of an organization, it can also encourage and perpetuate stagnation, ossification, and imperviousness to a changing world. To maintain a balance between sensitivity to change and respect for tradition, these factors need to be constantly weighed up against each other.

Given the way analytic institutions have typically been run in the past (and present), it may seem highly unorthodox to envisage such an institution as a complex corporate body similar in many ways to an economic enterprise. But we are too quick to forget the entrepreneurial responsibility[8] implicit in the fact that, alongside the duties involved in training candidates, an analytic enterprise *also* has to deploy and administer large sums of money. There are cases where the high-handedness of their leaders has negotiated organizations into difficult, if not legally precarious, situations. They should be a warning to us all.

Membership of our psychoanalytic organization is for life. This being the case, reluctance to question the things we are accustomed to may also be motivated by a fear of casting doubt on the competence of our parents and grandparents. If so, young analysts have no choice but to believe what their "elders and betters" say and have little chance of participating actively and intelligently in an organizational process and its development (cf. Kirsner, 2001). To my mind, active participation by younger members is a generative prerequisite enabling them at a later stage to shape the future organization in a creative spirit. Nor must we forget that as psychoanalysts we are destined to remain in an incestuous situation in which there is no remedy for all the things we have trouble coming to terms with.

One indispensable precondition for fruitful institutional effort is the ability to establish a "work-group" (Bion, 2003 [1961]) enabling us to fully appreciate the necessity of making decisions. This attitude is of course diametrically opposed to the one we adopt behind the couch.

---

(10) In an analytic institute, an elderly colleague asked the chairman of the training committee not to apply overly strict criteria in the case of candidate F., who was in the grip of a difficult personal situation. The chair of training was a former analysand of the elderly colleague and for this reason ventured neither to refuse his request nor to point out that this personal communication was a violation of boundaries.

The example shows how quickly the boundaries between personal feelings and the institutional task of deciding between pass and fail can be fudged.

Let us pause for a moment and share a brief analytic excursus on *"yes"* and *"no"* to remind ourselves of the way in which boundaries and decisions are essential features of the work institutions are required to do.

In our early development, the first experiences of limits are connected with a "no" (Spitz, 1966 [1957]; 1992 [1957]). In the separation process, the child has to take on various functions of the (love) object itself. At the same time, the objectification of the self goes hand in hand with the objectification of the other (p. 111). The use of the word "no" vis-à-vis adults gives the child self-confidence and hence new autonomy bolstering the perception of the other and at the same time the presence of the self. The "no" thus becomes "the matrix of social relations at the human level" (p. 123). In the subsequent development of the ego, "the supremacy of the reality principle over the pleasure principle becomes more and more marked" (p. 111). Ultimately, the availability of the "no" determines the capacity for assessing reality and action within that reality. The performance of the function of judgment is only made possible by the fact that "the creation of the negation symbol has permitted to thought a first degree of independence from the consequences of repression and thus also from bondage to the pleasure principle" (ibid.).[9]

Affirmative judgments are also closely associated with the verification of reality. Thinking and tentative action as well as the power of judgment are the abilities that enable us to engage actively and effectively with our environment and other members of society.

Yes and No form the basis for democratic action. A disinclination, or indeed refusal, to define boundaries and to make judgments and decisions conducive to development and progress makes realistic and effective leadership of an analytic organization impossible. Instead, it sows massive dissatisfaction among the members and promotes resignation and self-imposed helplessness. At the same time, however, we must always be aware that every decision, every yes and no, is *also* a decision on acceptance and belonging, rejection and exclusion and as such may involve the risk of paranoid processing.

So far, I have been contemplating the largely formal preconditions supporting psychoanalysts in the successful performance of their primary tasks within the organization. With regard to the need for a work-oriented attitude, members should always be clear in their minds that the reason for coming together within the group is to perform tasks. What frequently interferes with this is an expectation implying that the primary purpose of coming together is *to get* something. If members share a secure relation to reality and a clear commitment to the task(s) in hand, then they can achieve something comparable to achievement of tasks by an individual ego. Bion (2003 [1961], p. 75) refers to this as a "work-group," that can realistically *assess* the resources it requires to perform a given task, can *judge* the availability of those resources, and *decide* what it takes to procure them. *All* group members feel equal to the task of making a *contribution* to the fulfillment of the task and are able to tolerate the fact that, despite our powerful desire for certainty, reality to a large extent means precisely the opposite. A work-group is able to put up with such uncertainties because its members can perceive annoyance and disappointment within themselves, deal with those affects within their own psyche, and *only then* devote themselves to the task in hand. Disturbances to the fulfillment of the task invariably crop up when the members of the group tacitly agree to avoid joint anxiety by way of a shared defense process. Bion (2003 [1961], p. 99ff) refers to them as "basic-assumption groups" standing in a close psychodynamic relation to the "personal proclivities" that the group members bring with them (Bion calls them "valencies"). At certain specific points, they can be used to hustle us into certain roles within the group and thus to exploit us as "valves."[10] So even in the group we are by no means masters of all we survey!

The characterization of the framework of an institution would be incomplete if we were to neglect the emotionally charged concepts of authority, leadership, and power. Psychoanalysts in leading positions are frequently reported as having difficulties in relating to power, force, and the exercise of authority.

The members of an organization elect the chair of that organization democratically and thus equip him/her with the requisite authority and power to pursue the aims shared by the group in an efficient manner. They need to be aware that agreement processes in groups are always *painful* and that no leader can satisfy everyone. But what are the criteria by which a leader is elected? Ideally, in the light of what we have discussed so far, he/she should be in a position to withstand pressure, keep projected self-parts to himself/herself, make them explicit in an appropriate way, and decide responsibly on how to enhance the potential for change. As a representative both of the "primary task" and of the "institutional culture," his/her view of himself/herself, the group, and the requirements made of it should at the same time be adequately distanced. He/she must also ensure that boundaries that have been defined as such are respected. So what has happened when, after a democratic election, members start covertly accusing their new chair (whom they have usually known for quite some time) of being enamored of power for its own sake and prone to uncollegial behavior, subsequently resorting to passive withdrawal instead of sticking up for their opinions? Obviously there is something powerful at work in these members that outweighs realistic insight and the decision on whether a candidate is suitable – or at least good enough – for the post or not. Are we perhaps using this person as a vehicle for projective identification in order to make them guilty and sacrifice them? As a symptom of the situation in the group, abuse of power, it seems to me, is always connected with dysfunctional conditions in the organization (basic-assumption groups, Bion, 2003 [1961]). It cannot be regarded separately from the history of individual participation or the history of the group. Lyth (1988) would here assume the presence of a social form of defense marshaled against the anxieties materializing in the course of work.

I have been emphasizing the significance of the institutional framework, but this should not be taken to mean that the solution to the whole problem lies here. However sound a structure may be, it is *no guarantee* that an organization will function well, even under the best of all conceivable circumstances. And we must never forget that in itself everything I am recommending here is a maneuver that both provokes and defends against anxiety.

III.2 What do psychoanalysts criticize about/within their institutions?

We have outlined an ideal institutional framework that can function as a protective setting for the diversity of conscious and unconscious processes taking place in group interaction. Let us now summarize briefly what it is that instills discontent, disappointment, and disaffection in psychoanalysts when they contemplate cooperation in their organizations. This dissatisfaction centers around three things: the way colleagues deal with each other, the response to theoretical and clinical diversity, and denials and secrets that must never come to light.

Freud himself had to deal with "secessionist" strivings (1914) resulting from apparently insuperable *difficulties in coming to terms with people who think differently* (cf. Teising, Chapter 1 in this volume). Over the last 10–20 years, however, complaints about institutional discontent have been increasing (e.g. Eisold, 1994; Weimer, 1999; Kernberg, 1996, 2000, 2004, 2012; Reeder, 2004; Kirsner, 2001; Erlich, 2009; Herrmann, 2014; Utrilla Robles, 2013; Poland, 2009). The grievances voiced and the resultant desire for something to change have either petered out or culminated in radical and frequently garbled recommendations, largely in the form of proposals for training reform. Only rarely has there been any scrutiny of institutional co-existence itself, as if there were some mutual ban on criticizing colleagues. Remarkable is the acrimony with which affects of a sometimes destructive and condemnatory nature have seasoned the criticism voiced by psychoanalysts otherwise notable for their judicious attitudes.

Utrilla Robles (2013), for instance, criticizes the widespread idealization of psychoanalysis as "fanaticism." She links this omnipotent and restrictive wishful thinking (Wunschdenken) with a longing for infallible security on the one hand and a fear of freedom on the other. She pillories the spirit of conformity rampant in training, asserting that candidates are discouraged from expressing doubt, asking questions, or floating hypotheses.

A failure of collegial ethics[11] is the term I would use to characterize the criticisms from Poland (2009) and Beland (2015) of the way in which psychoanalysts deal with *each other*. Beland denounces *aggressive types of behavior* such as *overbearingness and arrogance, loud mockery, attacks and domineering attitudes, contempt, ridicule*, and *crippling lack of interest*. Poland laments an absence of the triadic competence required to behave in a group context without apprehension and with a command of the socially competent behaviors we refer to as "social skills." Tendencies for colleagues to exploit each other are attitudes I have frequently come across and Freud himself criticized (1930 [1929], p. 111) as latently aggressive (e.g. "Could you translate this paper for me [free of charge]?"). Frequently, we meet an absence of authentic gratitude. Psychoanalysts in prominent roles are criticized for being "authoritarian and hierarchical," "highly offensive," and for "not perceiving an interlocutor as a person" (Beland et al., 2002).

Kernberg (2000, 2012) criticizes the psychoanalytic training situation for its "lack of consistent concern for the total educational experience of candidates." This squares with my own observation that psychoanalysts are more likely to defend older colleagues whose analytic powers have been impaired by illness than candidates liable to suffer injuries or re-traumatization at the hands of an unprofessional psychoanalyst (cf. Junkers, 2013a, p. 60; Traesdal, 2013). In 2014, the IPA, then headed by Stefano Bolognini, responded to this criticism by establishing a *Task Force for Institutional Issues*. Surveys in many international IPA societies indicate that a large majority of members are not only generally in favor of clarifying background factors and elaborating concrete recommendations but in fact consider this to be an urgent priority. In its first review of the situation, the Task Force refers to the matters discussed in this chapter as important topics for discussion: fear of death, intergenerational conflicts, difficulties in communicating with other sectors, authority, dependence and idealization, and the family aspect of analytic training. Meanwhile the group has published relevant literature on the IPA homepage.[12]

Finally, I should like to discuss a number of observations gleaned from surveys of psychoanalysts and psychotherapists. Lohmer and Wernz (2005, p. 300) encounter an urgent desire on their part to belong to an organization but note that authorization from within is difficult for them to come to terms with. They show a marked inclination to avoid conflict and prefer not to engage in open disputes. In a similar vein, Kirsner (2001) takes psychoanalysts to task for vagueness in the way they express themselves, which leads to a blurring of intentions and arguments. This encourages faith rather than cogency and militates against an inquiring and exploratory attitude.

The outcome of a survey by Erlich (2004)[13] matches my own observations. He emphasizes analysts' fear of the "outside," notably their reluctance to engage actively with the outside world. Like Lohmer and Wernz (2005), he detects among psychoanalysts "a decidedly receptive/reflective relation to other people and their environment." On the question of *actively* establishing contact with others (professionally, personally, ideologically, cf. also Kernberg, 2000, 2012), he identifies a major *reluctance to seek contact* and a *passive tendency* to leave the initiative to others. In surveys, an outgoing attitude is lauded as a positive and necessary attitude for "psychoanalysis," but those *colleagues actively concerned with interface* have a decidedly *lowly-to-poor status* in all (European) psychoanalytic societies. Especially contact with the political sphere is considered reprehensible, not to say actively dangerous. Psychoanalysts making an appearance in the media are classified as narcissistic because of the damage they can do to psychoanalysis. The public sphere is no place for psychoanalysis. "Psychoanalysis begins [...] at the door to the practice, and it ends there as well" (Erlich, 2004, p. 3). The tendency to self-isolation suggests apprehension about leaving the analytic setting, as this may weaken the feeling of security the analyst harbors in the analytic space. Responders conceded that this was probably due to *not having the skills required for appearing in public.* Erlich (2004) concludes that psychoanalysts consider their identity to be special and different from that of others. We know from descriptions by various authors that different professions attract different kinds of people (e.g. Dartington, 1994; Schmidtbauer, 1977). If we count psychoanalysts among the helping professions, then we can also say of them that they harbor reparatory desires vis-à-vis their primary object coupled with omnipotent expectations of their own ability to heal, all this against the background of a deep-seated fear of losing control and proving ineffectual (Hinshelwood & Skogstad, 2000, p. 14).

III.3 Features and weaknesses that shape the analytic culture in our institutions

Against the background of a "typical" psychoanalyst's career, my own experiences, and the characteristics of "the" analytic personality as set out in the literature, I shall now attempt a synopsis casting light on the particularities of psychoanalysts from a number of unwonted perspectives. These are (a) inner conditions, (b) dealing with boundaries and limitations, and (c) opening to the outside and encouraging social, triangular skills. I intend to focus on things that in our everyday routines frequently escape our attention. Some of these particularities appear to encourage "quagmiring," i.e. getting bogged down in ill-defined work structures. Do we have the courage to take a more realistic look at ourselves *from the outside* and concede that some "weak points" are in fact seriously detrimental? If so, we could check to see whether those points square with features we recognize in our own selves and decide whether to accept the suggestions set out in the following and to use them constructively to explore new avenues.

- *Idealization:* Urgent wishes, passion, and a tendency to idealize are typical features of the path that leads to our chosen profession. We are likely to over-accentuate the significance of psychoanalysis (although we tend to play this down, ironically), ignore the scientific claims of neighboring research sectors, and take a blinkered view of the potential diversity of life. With this attitude, we are particularly susceptible to the influence of charismatic personalities, submitting to their influence while at the same time being tempted to rebel against the boundaries implicit in this constellation. A firmly established, indeed traditional, tendency to idealization serves in an omnipotent way both as a defense against destructive impulses and as a protection against opening out to otherness and alterity.[14] This (self-)idealization accompanies us throughout our professional lives. Hardly any psychoanalytic article considers itself complete without a quotation from the charismatic inventor of psychoanalysis, and these quotations are frequently invested with the status of incontrovertible scientific evidence. On the other hand, it is hard to see how we could bear up under the strain of our (training and) work without a degree of idealization.

- *Reality:* At all junctures in our lives, as we have seen, there are indications of a tendency to phase out parts of reality if they militate against our wishes and convictions. This applies to the way we react and behave in public, in groups, and in the performance of our work, as well as – and above all – to the way we come to terms with limiting realities, notably restrictions from outside. But to engage effectively with our environment and cope successfully with the demands posed by work in the group, we must be realistic in dealing with restrictions and acknowledging the need for decisions.

- Part and parcel of this inadequate orientation to reality is an *unrealistic attitude towards time.* We have talked about the inner conviction that we have unlimited amounts of time, and this erroneous conviction is reflected very drastically in the widespread scotomization of the finite nature of life. A reality oriented accommodation of our actions to the claims of time is indispensable in thinking through and reflecting on decisions and implementing them within a reasonable or defined interval. Procrastination in arriving at institutional decisions and acting on them leads to rigidity, repetition, and a hidebound approach that militates against getting things done and striking while the iron is hot. Thinking through a task or a decision will necessarily need time, but defensively delayed prevarication has to be avoided.

- *Fear of separation and separateness:* Reluctance to recognize the boundaries imposed by reality is widespread and is bound up with a fear of separation. We encounter this fear in the avoidance of a clear-cut "yes" or "no" and in the refusal to make a clear distinction between the professional psychoanalytic attitude behind the couch and an approach that is appropriate to the public sector and to institutional work. This omnipotent tendency is identifiable in the scotomization of the limited nature of our lives, the disregard for rules, obligations, and regulations, and the refusal to recognize democratic voting outcomes. Implicitly we are insisting on the inviolability of our personal freedom. This – usually unconscious – attitude precludes all prospects of a group situation in which a work-group mentality might prevail.

- *Insufficient triangular competence:* We have come across many indications that un-coped-with Oedipal anxieties can impede psychoanalysts in tackling a number of problems that life confronts us with. In terms of Oedipal development, Britton (1998 [1989]) focuses on the denial of the psychic reality of parental intercourse as a defense against the certainty of exclusion. We need to take account of one thing: Training analysis centers around an exclusively dualized situation involving one object, in which work on disillusionment should be prominent. By contrast, stepping into the institutional public sphere involves confrontation with a much more unpredictable, complex, and uncontrollable reality, and with objects experienced as potentially dangerous. If the ability to acknowledge the realities of life is defective, destructive impulses can subsequently attach themselves to everything happening in the group. They reveal themselves in defense impulses vis-à-vis the institutional public, in a fear of "life outside," in a disinclination to accept generativity, and in various degrees of (apodictic) certainty.
- *Passive-receptive orientation and (over-)readiness to adjust:* The anxieties we bring with us promote a striving for sameness and a readiness to adapt, i.e. a willingness to comply with the tacit and incontrovertible codes operative within the group. Having learned to observe minutely the groups we are part of, we have registered precisely what they traditionally hold to be right and wrong but without actively querying those implicit tenets and traditions. Probably based on the unconscious notion that "we all think the same," we encounter a widespread disinclination to be explicit about things featuring in the life of the group, in other words addressing them in an understandable and consistent way. As Reeder (2004) argues, such unspoken laws encourage dependency and, in organizations, a paranoid institutional climate born of unresolved conflicts between love and hate. Here again, the resolution of Oedipal anxieties is part of the equation, i.e. the extent to which our ego can emancipate itself from our superego instead of letting itself be dominated by it (Britton, 2020).
- *Concern to avoid conflict* is a widespread need among psychoanalysts and is closely connected to the complex anxiety and avoidance situation we have been describing. An upshot of the unresolved Oedipal problem constellation is the absence of suitable behavior patterns that in the case of conflict would be helpful in discussing things controversially and yet constructively. This avoidance attitude may also be exacerbated by the unconsciously shared fantasy that any form of spirited encounter between individuals may lead to madness. A very common defensive behavior pattern connected with this is the denying silence that aggressively undermines all efforts to relate and cooperate (verbal exchange is a function of the work-group, cf. Bion 2003 [1961]). These passive-destructive attacks and the lack of appreciation among colleagues frequently lead to

severe injuries, a form of action that is passed on to our candidates as a negative ideal.

- *The quandary between wanting to be loved and not wanting to be recognized:* On the one hand, we psychoanalysts long for the object and for recognition by it, on the other, we appear to be governed by the fear of being seen in a relationship and hence identified, judged, and condemned. In our contacts we are at pains to avoid conflict, but there still "occur" countless instances of indiscretion, injury, insult, dishonesty, and lethal silence. In my experience, this imbalance is reinforced by a widespread lack of *social skills*. By this I mean not merely the ability to correctly assess a social situation, but also the presence of a behavioral repertoire to fall back on for relating to others tactfully and in line with accepted values; in other words, not only making a showing in the outside world but doing so in a firm and upstanding manner.

- *Fear of leaving the protective sphere called "psychoanalysis":* Not only as candidates do we bring many anxieties with us, but also as fully-fledged analysts, for example the fear of not living up to our own standards or what we believe to be the standards of the group and thus being disliked or rejected. Against the background of a triangular deficit, it becomes more readily understandable that many analysts fear leaving the protective sphere of the analytic *solitude à deux* and thus risk misunderstanding their profession as a protective refuge or locus of withdrawal. The remarkable thing is that we transfer this individual anxiety to the institution, tending to consign the organization to a hermetic space that protects it from exchange with the environment and hence from being rejected as a group. For both the individual and the group, a lack of culturally defined *social skills* appears to be partly responsible for this. One such skill, to my mind, is the ability to communicate to others in understandable language what psychoanalysis is capable of achieving. I would indeed go out on a limb and suggest that a repertoire of competent communicative strategies could function as a container and thus reduce social anxieties. If I know how I *could* behave, this will help to allay my anxieties and lower the barrier that prevents me from behaving that way.

- *The temptation and danger of misusing the analytic attitude for institutional communication* – a question of contextuality: The "analytic attitude" we have been at such pains to learn, including not-knowing, not-wanting, not-remembering, and operating in a timeless space, is not suitable for effective work in public institutions (Herrmann, 2014). It encourages procrastination, leaves work unfinished, and gets colleagues' backs up. Vice versa, much the same would be true of an attitude adopted behind the couch that was geared to the realities of time and space. If an analyst were to work in this way, we would not expect any developmental progress for the patient. In this, I contend, we are all agreed. Both attitudes will cause problems if they are used in the wrong place. But why? What we are obviously dealing with here are internal attitudes that we adopt in accordance with our appraisal of the social context and on the basis of perception from our own personal perspective, attitudes we are only implicitly aware of. Our response is based partly on an assessment of what we have learned to be appropriate behavior in various situations and partly on our individual personalities. If it is true that we bring with us a certain deficiency in terms of triangular competence, then we will probably also have less knowledge at our disposal of what would be considered appropriate in various social situations. This may make it easier to understand why we prefer to fall back on something we have learned, i.e. something recognized as valid by psychoanalysts in general. With this acquired attitude we feel sure of ourselves.

What is the difference between these inner attitudes? Behind the couch, our mission is not geared to concrete aims and realities, instead we are called upon in every session anew to create and provide an attitude favorable to psychic development, without restrictions in space and time. It is only the setting that "locates" analysis in external reality. On the other hand, without reality-oriented restrictions in time and space, an effective working attitude geared to achieving aims and performing tasks would be inconceivable in the togetherness of the institution. It would be ideal if we could make a clear and situative distinction between these two very different internal attitudes and deploy them differentially and flexibly. The precondition for this appears to be a complex and anxiety-free form of interplay between perceptiveness, appropriate assessment of a situation, and availability of a corresponding behavioral repertoire. Both excessive permeability and overly rigid demarcation can lead to problems. One special aspect of employing what we have learned in a broader social context is the use of acquired psychoanalytic terminology in public, social communication and institutional cooperation. Here professional analytic parlance can be misunderstood as aggressive, contemptuous, devaluating, and marginalizing and create the impression in recipients that they can expect little or no understanding or acceptance from the people operating behind this impenetrable professional barrier.

- *Fear of judgment/condemnation, the code of ethics and abuse of confidentiality:* Although psychoanalytic ethics is part of the curriculum, there is always a danger of it being neglected when planning seminars. In the organizational context, individual fears of failure or inappropriate conduct may gel into a species of group defense. In institutional terms, this boils down to a defense-determined breach of training responsibility. Also, the urgent and ubiquitous issue of confidentiality, which is something much more far-reaching than mere data protection, poses itself anew (or should do) in every encounter between doors as a question of where to "draw the line" is theoretically treated as a matter of course, but often neglected in practice. Where do we stand in terms of our training responsibility?

Could the overestimation (and under-definition) of personal liberty lead in the institutional context to an avoidance of responsibility despite our awareness of the consequences? How can we deal with this, if we feel that referring to realities as such is tantamount to destroying illusions and is for that reason aggressive and unacceptable?

- *Taboos – switching the mind off:* In all analytic groups we encounter taboos that most of us have not learned to think about. They include topics like aging, transience and death, money, and hourly fees. Another underrated taboo is analysts' omnipotent conviction that they can – and have to – cope with everything alone, coupled with the anxiety prompting them to avoid enlisting outside help for fear of feeling needy. This applies both to individual analysts (e.g. Kavka, 2013, p. 130ff. or Traesdal, 2013, p. 82ff.) and to groups.

III.4 Containment of psychoanalysis via active containment lived by analysts

Containment serves three major purposes: taking in, active digestion, and reintroduction of changed, detoxified content into the communication process. By way of the containment they offer, groups can also serve as a defense against anxiety (Jaques,1955). Organizations have a formal, static containing function defined by the clear-cut, limiting structure for the organization that we have been discussing (a function that requires a work-group mentality). Alongside this, containment lived out and shaped by real people signifies both an *active* and a *passive* process.

The work of the psychoanalyst is distinctive above all for being concerned not primarily with material things but with the unconscious and with affects. Through many hours of the day, we dreamily absorb the raw material proffered by our patients in order to digest and detoxify it. It is eminently understandable that at our evening meetings, undigested remnants from a variety of sources should threaten to spill out into our collective dealings within the group.

By containment in the group I mean a working attitude required not only from the leaders of the group but from all its members. I understand the active concern for containment as a joint effort that all members have implicitly subscribed to in their efforts to create a work-group. If the group feels threatened, either from outside or by individual members, this "infection" can cause confusion, an inability to "think straight," inertia. In severe cases, chronic misunderstanding will lead to escape reactions and coterie formations, or collective inertia will favor unanimous abhorrence for any kind of development. This should not be suppressed but regarded as a symptom and given the scope it needs to reveal itself and grow. Only then can we try to understand, to intervene and clarify, and to restore the necessary "thinkingspace" to the group. Much as in the treatment of our patients, consolation, reassurance, and the satisfaction of needs promise no improvement because thinking can only set in again when sufficient space for thinking is available. Thinking only becomes possible again through the creation of empty spaces. This means that all participants need to recognize frustrations as such and be able to withstand them. Only stoical understanding of this kind can pave the way for progress.

For me, an active containment in groups means the modulation and mediation of relations and tasks. I have already described the significance of group-leaders, the abilities they require, and the tasks they face. What we have not said so far is that they cannot do all this work on their own. The group needs enough members with adequate valencies enabling them to function as a "digestion apparatus" and to act as mediators. They are part of the living structure of the organization and mediate containment for a given situation. If a group-leader falls down on these functions and in addition has hardly any supporting members to stand by him/her, then trouble will ensue, the kind of trouble that undermines trust. Then mistrust will appear to be the only attitude that provides protection. In simplified terms we might ask: How much frustration can a group take? How long-suffering is it? Can it hold up against feelings of mistrust, of not belonging? Can it withstand individual fears of being dropped by the group?

Finally, I should like to look at the concrete external conditions we create as a container for our work in the group. One example is the meetings in our institutions, which normally go on until late at night, a time when for many of us the energy required for work and the capacity for internal processing are exhausted. We will recall that the unconscious of all the members acts in concert. In the event of unpleasurable experiences occasioned by physical fatigue and drained containment capacity, it can fall back on early forms of defense expressed via individuals in the group. This self-created fact has a detrimental effect on constructive cooperation, and the attitude it engenders is passed on unthinkingly to the next generation. It probably stems from the omnipotent conviction of an unflagging and inexhaustible potential for work. But young candidates who have little children to look after and never get enough sleep are the ones who suffer most. Accordingly, communication and the thought capacity of a group, understood as group culture, depends on the extent to which the entire group lives out its containing function. Its capacity for reflective and active digestion is what defines the group's potential for development.

At the last, the definition of aims and work in a well-defined framework can also be understood as containment. Establishing a temporally structured framework will help to create an overview and reduce the risk of overstrain. If, however, groups string their seminars together, one after the other, with no intervals in between, this can be understood as an unconscious expression of unanimity in actively precluding intervals for personal encounters and informal exchange between individual members.

Training psychoanalysts and transmitting psychoanalysis is a task that almost all analysts would see as the primary function of an analytic institution and the most promising way of guarding against decline. But what kind of institute will best preserve generativity? Erikson understands generativity as a link between the life-cycle and the cycle of generations. Creating a future for young analysts via generativity lived out here and now is a challenge.

Merely ensuring that there actually *is* a next generation will not enhance generative capacities at the psychic level. Indispensable in Erikson's view (2013 [1980]) is a mature "adult" capacity for genuine concern with regard to what we want to achieve and what we have achieved. But inevitably the caring attitude of a generation (a group defined by its temporal commonalities) will always be ambivalent given that the oldest members must *at the same time* be prepared to pave the way for their own replacement. To this extent, generative action *also* means creating constructive preconditions for the time after our own future. Erikson (2013 [1980]) contrasts this with a self-regarding, narcissistic attitude (stagnation). If we are really serious about handing down the legacy of psychoanalysis, then the caring element must not be restricted to training analysis but must be adopted by *all* group members as a generative attitude. The upshot of this is a very special appeal addressed to all psychoanalysts, and the elderly in particular. Erikson insists that the final years of our lives confront us with a *developmental* task, the task of achieving the kind of retrospective *wisdom* that is conducive to a capacity to let go, *to look death in the face without flinching*, to accept life as it has been, and, for all the errors we may have committed, to see that life as a boon.

We frequently encounter analysts who find it difficult to acknowledge that life is finite, who are reluctant to step back and leave the field to their younger colleagues. Should we perhaps understand the dissatisfaction marring our institutional cooperation as the expression of a *crisis of transmission*? Should we see the constant urge to generate new proposals for the restructuring of training as a defense against intergenerational tensions? Might it be conceivable that with a view to assuring the transmission of psychoanalysis training analysts agree on a uniformly low fee so as to enable candidates to carry on with their training despite the straitened circumstances many of them have to cope with? Or are we so concerned about the future of psychoanalysis because we project the fears of our own demise onto psychoanalysis itself?

How well are we equipped for co-existence in an institutional framework encompassing up to four generations, in which the instructors themselves fear that by making reference to the realities of life they may deprive their analytic grandparents of life-preserving illusions? In Section II.3, I pointed out that there may come a time in life when physical old age impairs our analytic skills. True, the first thing to aim at in such a case is dialogue and exchange, but positioning, decision-making, and action are equally indispensable. As I have shown elsewhere (Junkers, 2013c), this bid for quality assurance in the transmission process may be overshadowed or even foiled altogether by a thicket of projections, attachments to the past, and denials. Remarkable here again is the experience I referred to earlier: It is the senescent, ailing practitioner who gets covering fire from the community of analytic colleagues, whereas the psychic intactness of a candidate or patient is *always* treated as secondary in importance. Accordingly, we have no choice but to assume that old attachments are very likely to be stronger than devotion to the truth.

Critical voices appealing to the responsibility of the institution and pointing out that the present training system infantilizes the training candidates (e.g. Kernberg, 2000) need to be set off against the desires for dependency that, as we have seen, so many candidates bring with them. The vital task they call on us to fulfill is to not merely acknowledge and work on both the inhibitions and the strivings bound up with individuation and independence in a way that will favor triangular competence, but above all to actively require and encourage that competence. I am convinced that a training analysis without regressive forces will never have any effect. To my mind, opening up access to the unconscious infantile side of an individual (or a collective) is a major asset of the psychoanalytic process. It is essential in ensuring differentiated access to the various *modes of sensing life* which, in conjunction with a capacity for childlike pleasure, produce the maturity and wisdom that can help us not only to *know*, but also to *be* (cf. Mawson, 2019).

IV. Some proposals and recommendations

To preserve psychoanalysis and develop it further, we will need to square up to the reality of our psychoanalytic culture as we are living it at present and to ask ourselves whether what we actually do is an appropriate way of implementing the values we uphold. We are living in an age of turmoil, witnessing far-reaching humanitarian disasters and assaults on the very identity of democratic and open societies. Pessimistic visions of the future impose themselves. How can we carve out a realistic place for psychoanalysis in this changing world? How can we forge a psychoanalytic culture in our institutions that will help us to live and work together fruitfully on the basis of the values we represent?

My assumption is that we psychoanalysts can only do something to allay our institutional discontent if we acknowledge the significance of the particularities we have to offer and what we actually do. Then we might find a way of rousing ourselves from the comfortable inertia of a space where nothing ever happens and replace it with a spirit of research, inquiry, and investigation. Many of the specialities we have looked at are born of an inner need to avoid psychic pain. A broad critical discussion of these findings might prompt us to train our gaze on what we find within our own selves. If we did so, we could surely hope to reduce the risk of damage to individuals, groups, and psychoanalysis itself. To cooperate in the spirit of a work-group, we need to bridge the gap between the social and the psychological with a view to engaging both with structural and instrumental aspects of social life and with the emotional phenomena encountered at the profounder levels of the human personality (Trist & Murray, 1990). We can only change our institutional culture by way of the outer world and *at the same time* via the inner objects of the individual members.

I arrive now at my closing remarks, which I address both to the individual analyst and to institutions. If on various occasions I refer to the necessity for *courage*, it is because I am convinced that courage – in the sense of not flinching in the face of conflict, going out on a limb, and taking up a position – will be necessary to implement changes that – and here I am absolutely certain – cannot be achieved by analytic reflection alone.

- *Courage for introspection:* Could we summon up the courage required for introspection and by training our gaze on our own selves from the outside scrutinize our behavior in the actual social environment? What wounds did *I* bring with me when I embarked on this profession? Can I recall and name them in all humility? Can I accept that my colleagues have their injuries too? For all their differences, can I encounter them in a spirit of forbearance, humility, and tolerance and grant them the benefit of the insight that despite our training analyses we all still have problems and anxieties? What do I *actually do* in my group? If I look at myself from the outside, can I recognize whether in group interaction my behavior can serve candidates as a good analytic model? What is it within myself that stops me from perceiving my share of the responsibility for taking an active part in an institution designed to preserve psychoanalysis? How could I contribute more to encouraging fruitful cooperation and tactful co-existence within the group? Am I ready to honestly inquire whether insight is what motivates my behavior or whether that behavior stems from anxiety and a concern to avoid pain and discomfiture? In a crisis, can I acknowledge together with my colleagues or the institution that the injunction to engage in self-inquiry exceeds my powers and that to gain new insights I need another person? In the mini-sequence of a moment in the group, why do we behave as we do and not differently? Much of this has yet to be investigated. We speak airily of the necessity for self-analysis, at the same time we know how difficult it is in practice.

- How could we achieve *greater courage in perceiving reality for what it is and accepting the limits it imposes on us*? Can we support each other in ensuring that in our seminars the subject of termination of analyses, for example, is not so easily neglected? Here again it would be immensely valuable to attempt more introspection with regard to my relations with colleagues and the group and to actively engage with my own inner discontent with the institution with a view to working it through *within my own self.* Then it might no longer be necessary to evacuate what exceeds the limits of our personal inner containment. But at the same time we must recognize in all humility that this again can only be the reminder of an effort to be undertaken and that, as if driven by compulsion, the diverse currents operative within the dynamics of organizations can repeatedly thwart such constructive attempts.

- Could we summon up the *courage* to achieve greater insight into our own inner resistance(s) against *working consistently on the framework of our group* so as better to understand what is so uncongenial about that work? Might joint discussion of the literature on the subject go some way towards mitigating this disinclination?

- I would welcome more *courage in clearly separating off the private domain of our work from the institutional.* Is the quality of our analytic work, and the described dangers threatening it, an institutional or a private matter? Part of the question of the clear demarcation between private and professional is the frequently evaded issue of positioning: Do we as members only have rights? Or do we have duties as well?

- Can I find the *courage to commit myself to being a member?* For instance, accepting as a member responsibility for the group by asking myself honestly about my motives for electing a director? Do I sidestep my responsibility as a member by telling myself that I am insignificant and that the way I vote makes no difference? Or would I prefer to acquit myself of this "troublesome" chore as quickly and unthinkingly as I can?

- How can we achieve greater *courage* in recognizing discerningly that we can do some things especially well and other things less well or not at all? Must we cling stubbornly to the omnipotent conviction that we can do all this on our own? Can we allow ourselves the *curiosity* of inquiring *what kind of professional assistance might be helpful in supporting the further development of a constructive group*? If we did, we would by the same token accept and confront our apprehensions with regard both to neediness and to things alien. Why should we not commit to offering regular seminars on entrepreneurial leadership at our supra-regional psychoanalytic conferences? Might that be a *structural* way of addressing shame and the excessive demands we make on ourselves?

- Could we be more *courageous* about making theoretical knowledge about groups and organizations an integral part of our curriculum and combining it with theories of Oedipal development? *Practical offerings encouraging joint learning and work in small (project) groups* at conferences could also further the ability to discuss issues (including those of a controversial nature) with strangers, candidates, and analysts with a view to finally elaborating something cooperatively. The supra-regional work-groups of the EPF have taught us not only how much need there is for collegial exchange but also that some work-groups remain in existence for years and come up with important contributions. Exchange along the lines of these groups would also be conceivable between different national institutes. In my view, the supra-regional level has the advantage of side-stepping the familiar dynamics operative in the home institute and making for a more intensive experience in the exchange with unknown others.

- Would it be conceivable for us to *actively relate to the taboo on the aging issue and to do so with greater courage?* Working out a curriculum for psychoanalysis and the ages of the individual[15] might widen our perspectives on work with older analysands (in the face of demographic change) and help us to focus more extensively on generative diversity in our own organizations.
- I would welcome greater courage in *referring our anxiety about the survival of psychoanalysis to its place in our own selves* and devoting greater self-reflection to anxiety about annihilation and our own death.
- Could we summon up the *courage* to establish for all members *seminars on the exercise of leadership functions* in psychoanalytic institutions? Laments about not being able to fill leading posts are becoming more and more frequent. We are only too ready to forget that, strictly speaking, most of us should at least once in a lifetime perform an honorary function in our institutions.
- I would welcome more *courage in accepting the various preferences colleagues may have* about operating more on the internal or the external side (without devaluing the respective other). Some of us are "loners" or soloists, others are good at conveying valuable insights and reflections of our profession to the outside world. One laudable example of the need to showcase the difference psychoanalysis can make is the initiative by some 400 Italian psychoanalysts who offered help for psychologically challenged individuals in the framework of the Covid-19 pandemic, although here of course we are looking at applied psychoanalysis. I see a successful example of the need to show what psychoanalysis has to offer in offering short term Crisis intervention to people in need in the context of the pandemic, to which about 400 Italian psychoanalysts have joined forces, even though it did not imply full psychoanalysis (Niccolò, 2021).
- I think we should have the *courage* to *inquire* probingly and honestly into *generativity* as it stands and the motives behind our training endeavors. (a) Do we perhaps have our own motives in supporting younger members in their hankerings for dependency? Can we offer them assistance of a kind that promotes triangulation competence? (b) Can we make them an offer of good, objective, and transparently elucidatory evaluation instead of condoning unfortunate training outcomes by constantly deferring clear verdicts to a later date? (c) Would it be a good thing to reduce the fees for training analyses across the board so that the training of young colleagues will not fail for lack of financial resources? Or would it be obvious to set the fee for training analyses generally at a reduced amount so that the training of young colleagues does not fail due to financial means?
- The constantly changing *external technological, political, social, and global realities* make both institutions and the individuals working in them vulnerable and invite psychic withdrawal. To tame the resistance to thinking,

I believe that in these troubled times we should accept proposals to enlist the support of psychoanalytically oriented organizational counseling (cf. e.g. Lyth, 1988; Obholzer & Roberts, 1994; Stokoe, 2015) and thus create scope for reflection on matters we have not thought about (adequately) so far.

As a unique theoretical model of the human mind, psychoanalysis will presumably survive for some time to come. But it would be an omnipotent idealization to believe that it is completely invulnerable. If we want to uphold and preserve it as a technique for our analytic approach, then its transmission needs to be implemented carefully and caringly both in thought and action.

I should like to close with Bion's famous remark (1952, p. 238): "The individual is a group animal at war, both with the group and with those aspects of his personality that constitute his 'groupishness'".

Notes

1 In the following I shall be using the sociological terms "organization" and "institution" synonymously. Both refer to public bodies fulfilling a particular purpose and based on a regulatory system designed to predictably shape and stabilize the actions of individuals in a group (as long as they abide by its rules).

2 All psychoanalysts expressing their views on the subject of loneliness were over 60 years old.

3   In the crises we experienced feelings of worthlessness and helplessness mixed with paranoid anxieties of greater or lesser intensity. At these times the training institute seemed to us to be a formless body rather than a group of individuals performing a didactic function. Some of us felt we were joining a dogmatic religious sect which would attack any manifestation of spontaneous thought as if it were a heresy. Then we felt like a group of patients that had given the diagnostic skill of seasoned training analysts the slip, rather than a selected group of students who had been chosen for their potential to undertake analytic training. We believe we were outwardly passive and submissive to the teaching authority, and that this gave rise to an alternation between dependence and competitiveness which impinged on the learning process.

(Bruzzone et al., 1985, p. 411)

4   A relationship that lasts for years with the maintenance of a set of norms and attitudes is precisely the definition of an institution. The setting is therefore an institution within whose framework, or in the midst of which, phenomena occur that we call behavior.

(Bleger, 2013, p. 512)

5 In "Psychoanalysis: A Profession for the Immortal," Paul Denis (2013, p. 32 f) describes this widespread immortality fantasy.

6   A professional will pertaining to a psychoanalytic practice is a formulation of ethical and professional responsibility regulating the questions of who notifies the patients in the case of emergency and what is to be done with the (medical) records kept in the practice. Every psychoanalyst of whatever age should take precautions for such an emergency and deposit the document containing this information in a readily accessible place or in a sealed envelope at the secretariat of the relevant professional institute.

(O'Neil, 2013, p. 150ff)

7   From our experience with patients, we know how important the understanding of early anxieties is and how those anxieties manifest themselves in the way patients deal with boundaries.

(cf. Jaques, 1955; Bleger, 1967, p. 512)

8 Members' dues, candidates' contributions, spending on acquisitions, invitations to guest speakers, etc. In addition, there are the costs for training analyses and supervisions on which all discussion is prohibited (cf. Section IV).

9 Translated by Andrew Jenkins; page references refer to the German Edition.

10 The defense-motivated basic assumption groups described by Bion (2003 [1961]) are secondary formations emanating from an extremely primitive scene taking place at the level of part-objects and bound up with psychotic anxieties as well as splitting mechanisms and the projective identification characteristic of the schizoid-paranoid position postulated by Klein.

11 As far as I know, most codes of ethics in use in psychoanalytic societies fail to go into detail on ethical behavior among colleagues (see the concluding chapter to this volume: Looking ahead).

12 www.ipa.world/IPA/en/en/Unified_Papers/Books_Query.aspx

13 In the course of a study involving European analysts, Erlich questioned the participants on the topic of "interface" and the social reality of analysts.

14 Steiner (2020) has recently reminded us how a paradisiac illusion (of a pre-Oedipal existence) appears to justify mockery, hostility, and ridicule on our part when it comes to engaging with the necessity of protecting ourselves from reality (p. 6).

15 Audrey Kavka (San Francisco) has developed a curriculum for candidates on „Lebensspanne und höheres Lebensalter." Christane Schrader (Frankfurt, Germany) has devised a "Curriculum on Development in Adulthood including Later Life and Old Age, with special reference to treatment technique" that is compulsory for candidates at the Frankfurt Psychoanalytic Institute (FPI) (circular dispatched to all members of the DGPT, 1/2020, pp. 28–32).

References

Beland, H. (2015). Lehranalyse und Institution – Die Progression des Verstehens ist im Rahmen des organisierten Vertrauens möglich. Unveröffentlichtes Manuskript vom Vortrag auf der 23. Konferenz der DPG-Lehranalytiker, Göttingen.

Beland, H., Brodbeck, H., Ruprecht-Schampera, U. & Wildberger, H. (2002). DPV-Transparenzkommission: Berichte über die Untersuchungen des Bewerbungsverfahrens, des Vorkolloquiums und des Kolloquiums. *Teil I. DPV-Informationen, 32*, 17–31.

Bion, W. R. (1952). Group dynamics: a re-view. *Int J Psychoanal, 33*, 235–247.

Bion, W. R. (1987). *Clinical Seminars and Four Papers*. Abingdon: Fleetwood.

Bion, W. R. (1984 [1970]). *Attention and Interpretation*. London: Tavistock Publications. [Reprinted London: Karnac Books 1984].

Bion, W. R. (2003 [1961]). *Experiences in Groups and other papers*. London: Routledge.

Bion, W. R. (1994 [1975]). Brasilia. In: *Clinical Seminars and Other Works*. London: Karnac Books.

Bleger, J. (2013 [1967]). *Symbiosis and Ambiguity: a psychoanalytic study*. [Simbiosis y ambigüedad: estudio psicoanalítico]. S. Rogers, L. Bleger & J. Churcher (translators); J. Churcher & L. Bleger (Eds). New Library of Psychoanalysis. London: Routledge.

Bleger, J. (1967). Psycho-analysis of the psycho-analytic frame. *Int J Psychoanal, 48*(4), 511–519.

Brenman Pick, I. (1985). Working through in the countertransference. *Intern. J. Psychoanal, 66*, 157–166.

Brenman Pick, I. (2018). *Authenticity in the Psychoanalytic Encounter: The Work of Irma Brenman*. Oxon: Routledge.

Britton, R. (1998 [1989]). The missing link: parental sexuality in the Oedipus complex. *Int.J.Psychoanal, 54*, 83–101.

Britton, R. (2020). *Sex, Death and the Superego: Updating Psychoanalytic Experience and Developments in Neuroscience*. London: Routledge.

Bruzzone, M., Csaula, E., Jimenez, J. P. & Jordan, J. F. (1985). Regression and persecution in analytic training. Reflections on experience. *Int Rev Psycho-Anal, 12*(4), 411–415.

Churcher, J. (2022) (forthcoming). The psychoanalytic setting, embodiment, and presence: exploring José Bleger's concept of encuadre, In: C. Moguillansky & H. Levine (Eds), *Psychoanalysis of the Psychoanalytic Frame Revisited: A New Look at Bleger's Classical Work*. (IPA Classics Revisited series). IPA/Routledge.

Dartington, A. (1994). Where angels fear to tread: idealism, despondency and inhibition in thought in hospital nursing. In: A. Obholzer & V. Z. Roberts (Hrsg.) (Eds), *The Unconscious at Work* (S. 101–109). London: Routledge.

Denis, P. (2013). Psychoanalyst: a profession for an immortal? In: G. Junkers (Ed.), *The Empty Couch. The Taboo of Ageing and Retirement in Psychoanalysis* (pp. 32 – 40). London: Routledge.

Dewald, P. A. (1982). Serious illness in the analyst: transference, countertransference, and reality responses. *J Am Psychoanal Ass, 30*(2), 347–363. DOI: 10.1177/000306518203000202

Eisold, K. (1994). The intolerance of diversity in psychoanalytic institutions. *Int J Psychoanal, 75*(4), 785–800.

Erikson, E. H. (2013 [1980]). On the generational cycle – an address. *Int. J. Psychoanal, 61*, 213–223. Reprint in G. Junkers (Ed.) (2013a).

Erlich, S. (2004). *Report on the EPF Working Party on Interface*. Unpublished Ms.

Erlich, S. (2009). Das Unbehagen in der Kultur von heute. Psychoanalyse und gesellschaftliche Anerkennung. In M. Ermann (Hrsg.), *Was Freud noch nicht wusste* (S. 113–125). Frankfurt/M.: Brandes & Apsel.

Ferro, A. (2003). The analyst as individual, his self-analysis and gradients of functioning. *Psychoanalysis in Europe. EPF Bulletin*, 57, 134–142.

Firestein, S. K. (1993). On thinking the unthinkable: making a professional will. *The American Psychoanalyst*, 27, 16.

Freud, S. (1914). *On the History of the Psychoanalytic Movement*. S.E., Vol. 14, pp. 7–66.

Freud, S. (1916 [1915]). *On Transience*. S.E., Vol. 14, pp. 305–307.

Freud, S. (1930 [1929]). Civilization and its Discontents. S.E. Vol. 21, pp. 64–145, 419–506.

Gabbard, G. O. & Ogden, Th. H. (2009). On becoming a psychoanalyst. *Intern. J. Psychoanal.*, 90, 311–327.

Gabbard, G. O., Peltz, M. & The COPE Study Group on Boundary violations (2001). Speaking the unspeakable: institutional reactions to boundary violations by training analysts. *J Am Psychoanal Ass*, 49(2), 659–673. DOI: 10.1177/00030651010490020601

Gaddini, E. (1969). On imitation. *International Journal of Psycho-Analysis*, 50, 475–484.

Galatzer-Levy, R. M. (2005). The death of the analyst: patients whose previous analyst died while they were in treatment. *J Am Psychoanal Ass*, 52(4), 999–1024. DOI: 10.1177/00030651040520040601

Herrmann, A. P. (2014). Warum es so schwierig ist, in psychoanalytischen Institut(ion)en gedeihlich zusammenzuarbeiten. *Psyche – Z Psychoanal*, 68(2), 97–121.

Hinshelwood, R. D. & Skogstad, W. (Hrsg.). (2000). *Observing Organisations. Anxiety, Defence and Culture in Health Care*. London: Routledge.

Jaques, E. (1955). Social systems as a defence against persecutory and depressive anxiety. In M. Klein, P. Heimann & R.E. Money-Kyrle (Hrsg.), *New Directions in Psychoanalysis: The Significance of Infant Conflict in the Pattern of Adult Behavior* (S. 478–498). London: Tavistock.

Junkers, G. (1994). *Psychotherapie mit älteren Menschen. Psychiatrisches Kolloquium* 16.03.1994. Unpublished Ms.

Junkers, G. (Ed.). (2006). *Is It Too Late? Key Papers on Psychoanalysis and Ageing*. London: Karnac.

Junkers, G. (Ed.). (2013a). *The Empty Couch. The Taboo of Ageing and Retirement in Psychoanalysis*. London: Routledge.

Junkers, G. (2013b). Later perhaps ... Transience and its meaning for the psychoanalyst. In: *The Empty Couch. The Taboo of Ageing and Retirement in Psychoanalysis* (pp. 17–31). London: Routledge.

Junkers, G. (2013c). Introduction: when the body speaks and the Psychoanalyst falls ill. In: *The Empty Couch. The Taboo of Ageing and Retirement in Psychoanalysis* (pp. 61–66). London: Routledge.

Kaplan, J. A. (1993). Finding one's own voice: development of the psychoanalytic identity. *Psychoanal Rev*, 80(2), 179–182.

Kavka, A. (2013). The psychoanalysts assistance program. In: G. Junkers (Ed.), *The Empty Couch. The Taboo of Ageing and Retirement in Psychoanalysis* (pp. 130–149). London: Routledge.

Kernberg, O. F. (1996). Thirty methods to destroy the creativity of psychoanalytic candidates. *Int J Psychoanal*, 77(5), 1031–1041.

Kernberg, O. F. (2000). A concerned critique of psychoanalytic education. *Int J Psychoanal*, 81(1), 97–119.

Kernberg, O. F. (2004). Discussion: »Problems of power in psychoanalytic institutions«. *Psychoanal Inq*, 24(1), 106–121. DOI: 10.1080/07351692409349073

Kernberg, O. F. (2012). Suicide prevention for psychoanalytic institutes and societies. *J Am Psychoanal Ass*, 60(4), 707–719. DOI: 10.1177/0003065112449861

Kirsner, D. (2001). The future of psychoanalytic institutions. *Psychoanal Psychol*, 18(2), 195–212. DOI: 10.1037/0736-9735.18.2.195

Klein, M. (1975a [1950]). On the criteria for the termination of a Psycho-analysis. In: *Writings of Melanie Klein*. Vol. III: 1946–1963 (pp. 43–47). London: The Hogarth Press Ltd.

Klein, M. (1975b [1963]). On the sense of loneliness. In: *Writings of Melanie Klein*. Vol. III: 1946–1963 (pp. 300–313). London: The Hogarth Press Ltd.

Lohmer, M. & Wernz, C. (2005). Psychotherapeuten und Macht. In O. F. Kernberg, B. Dulz & J. Eckerl (Hrsg.), *Wir: Psychotherapeuten über sich und über ihren »unmöglichen« Beruf* (S. 292–302). Stuttgart: Schattauer.

Lyth, I. M. (1988). *Containing Anxieties in Institutions. Selected Essays I.* London: Free Association.

Mawson, C. (2019). *Psychoanalysis and Anxiety: From Knowing to Being.* London: Routledge. DOI: 10.4324/9780429055812

Money-Kyrle, R. (1978 [1971]). The aim of psychoanalysis. In ders., *The Collected Papers of Roger Money-Kyrle* (S. 442–449). Hrsg. von D. Meltzer & E. O'Shaughnessy. Strath Tay: Clunie Press.

Niccolò, A. M. (2021). *L'Ascolto Psicoanalitico in Emergenza.* Milano: Franco Angeli.

Obholzer, A. & Roberts, V. Z. (Hrsg.). (1994). *The Unconscious at Work: Individual and Organizational Stress in the Human Services.* London: Routledge.

O'Neil, M. K. (2013). The purpose of a professional will. In: G. Junkers (Ed.), *The Empty Couch. The Taboo of Ageing and Retirement in Psychoanalysis* (pp. 150–160, pp. x–y). London: Routledge.

Poland, W. S. (2009). Problems of collegial learning in psychoanalysis: narcissism and curiosity. *Int J Psychoanal*, 90(2), 249–262. DOI: 10.1111/j.1745-8315.2009.00133.x

Reeder, J. (2004). *Love and Hate in Psychoanalytic Institutions. The Dilemma of a Profession.* New York: Other Press.

Schafer, R. (1983). *The Analytic Attitude.* New York: Basic Books.

Schmidtbauer, W. (1977). *Die hilflosen Helfer. Über die seelische Problematik der helfenden Berufe.* Reinbek bei Hamburg: Rowohlt.

Segal, H. (1958). Fear of death – notes on the analysis of an old man. *Int J Psychoanal*, 39(2–4), 178–181. Reprint in Junkers (2006), (S. 65–74).

Spitz, R. A. (1966 [1957]). *No & Yes: On the Genesis of Human Communication*. London: International Universities Press. (Presently unavailable from Germany.)

Spitz, R. A. (1992 [1957]). *Nein und Ja: die Ursprünge der menschlichen Kommunikation*. Stuttgart: Klett-Cotta.

Steiner, J. (2020). Learning from Don Quixote. *Int J Psychoanal*, *101*(1), 1–12. DOI: 10.1080/00207578.2019.1696657

Stokoe, P. (2015). Ethics and complaints procedures for psychoanalytic organisations: some thoughts about principles. *Couple and Family Psychoanalysis*, *5*(2), 188–204.

Traesdal, T. (2013). The Loss of the Analyst. Wound or groth. In: G. Junkers (Ed.), *The Empty Couch. The Taboo of Ageing and Retirement in Psychoanalysis* (pp. 82–90). London: Routledge.

Trist, E. & Murray, H. (Hrsg.). (1990). *The Social Engagement of Social Science. Bd. 1: The Socio-Psychological Perspective*. London: Free Association.

Utrilla Robles, M. (2013). *Fanaticism in Psychoanalysis: Upheavals in the Institutions*. London: Routledge.

Weimer, M. (1999). Psychoanalyse und/als Organisation. *Psyche – Z Psychoanal*, *53*(1), 8–51.

Winnicott, D. W. (1965). The capacity to be alone. In: *The Maturational Processes and the Facilitating Environment*. London: Hogarth/Institute of Psycho-Analysis. (Reprinted from *International Journal of Psycho-Analysis*, *39* (1958), 416–420.)

Winnicott, D. W. (1971). *Playing and Reality*. London: Tavistock Publications.

Chapter 4

The Sibling Complex and Sibling Attachment

Implications for Conflict and its Resolution in Psychoanalytic Institutions

Harriet L. Wolfe

Introduction

Psychoanalytic groups – small work groups, small and large Societies, national and international organizations – can usefully be conceptualized as versions of families in which the archaic, preoedipal, and oedipal dynamics illuminated by René Kaës interact. To the naive observer, the emergence of destructive rivalries among psychoanalysts represents a shocking, repetitive, and possibly irresolvable family situation. Bitter disputes and a preoccupation with ourselves may discourage patients and young clinicians from pursuing psychoanalysis.

A developmental and psychodynamic understanding of such phenomena informed by the sibling complex offers the psychoanalytic leader a basis for understanding regressive forces and a scaffold for intervention. Sibling links may be disruptive, but they also contain the potential for psychoanalytic organizations to become more collaborative, transparent, and democratic.

In thinking about psychoanalysis today, it is important to place our profession in context. The context is complex. Each level of it involves the psychic development of individuals and groups. First, there is the social surround. This includes the sociopolitical and economic state of the world and our local communities. On this level, we are currently faced with an uncommon level of global crisis. We witness highly variable levels of competence among national leaders. As psychoanalysts, we recognize that needs and fantasies of individuals and groups underlie their transferences to political leaders.

The second level is our complex professional surround. Psychoanalysts are part of an international group, the IPA; of national and regional groups such as the DPV, the EPF, FEPAL, and NAPsaC; and of local groups – our home Societies. The third level is the personal. Each of us has a relationship, real and fantasied, to all of these levels.

How has psychoanalysis prepared us to navigate this complex array of what at all levels can be usefully thought of as forms of sibling and family relationships? I hope to lay the groundwork for our consideration of how we can succeed across languages and across cultures to achieve respect for differences

DOI: 10.4324/9781003301936-5

and support the growth of psychoanalysis as a treatment and as a science. My personal goal is to imagine an International Psychoanalytic Association (IPA) that contains and nurtures difference, similar to good parents raising non-identical siblings – parents who support growth and individuality while insisting on ethical behavior. Given the turbulence of sibling interactions, how do we work effectively with disrupted collegial groups? How can we provide calm, creative leadership?

Expanding our Focus on the Individual to Include the Role of Culture

The clinical practice of psychoanalysis is traditionally based on the high-frequency treatment of individuals. But in the current context of a multilayered global crisis, one that represents a perfect storm of sociocultural, financial, and political stressors, some feel it is irresponsible for psychoanalysts to focus on the relatively small number of individuals who seek treatment with us when large numbers of people suffer alarming levels of distress. This perception of our focus on a select few may contribute to the belief that psychoanalysis is outdated, a thing of the past. How can we, as specialists in unconscious psychic life, respond to the accusation that we have become irrelevant?

Some analysts remain uncertain or concerned about the application of psychoanalytic thinking outside of the consulting room. I believe that our powerful conceptual models of human development and psychic life are not diminished when psychoanalytic concepts are used to clarify societal issues and group processes. I think, rather than being irrelevant, psychoanalysis has never been more needed. In the face of a vortex of uncertainty, psychoanalytic input can disrupt denial of the impact of inhumane policies, like the separation of parents and children at international borders, or the practice of sending refugees back to the impoverished and often violent country from which they came seeking survival.

The central reason I ran for president of the IPA is that the expertise of members of the IPA represents a unique resource for helping our troubled world. For example, we can educate the public about the dangers of nationalist trends and inhumane policies and practices. We can inform citizens about the need for empathy and the dangerous emergence of scapegoating, projection, and emotional decision-making based on past traumas and unconscious processes.

This aspiration regarding the public presence of psychoanalytic thinking has been misunderstood by some as a wish to politicize psychoanalysis. It is suggested that such activity distracts from a focus on psychoanalytic training and treatment. I am well aware that not everyone who practices psychoanalysis wishes to have a public voice. But for those who do, rigorous psychoanalytic training is required in order to have something substantive to offer the public. I do not envision a superficial use of psychoanalytic principles in the public domain, but rather deeply informed efforts to educate those who either unconsciously deny or consciously avoid recognizing the impact of trauma on individuals and groups.

Psychoanalytic treatment and training are proceeding in a changing world. Patients now routinely google their analysts for information. Social media undoes the isolation of treatment from civilian life. Our theories and practices are forced – constructively, in my opinion – to consider the place of culture in individual and group development.

The traditional psychoanalytic focus on the interior of the individual mind has begun to shift to include a recognition of the constitutive impact of culture on individual and group development. Bonnie Litowitz has written about the place of culture in traditional psychoanalytic theory. She observes that culture was viewed by Freud and his followers as external to the individual, an outer layer below which would be found the universal psyche common to all people, with the Oedipus complex at the core (Litowitz, 2003).

But cultures are radically different systems of meaning-making. Karim Dajani, a Lebanese-born American analyst with a special interest in the constitutive impact of culture, writes: "Babies who are structured by different systems (Arab, Japanese, French, Thai, etc.) will learn to be embodied, to differentiate me from not me, and to engage time and space in ways that are particular to their respective systems" (Dajani, 2020, p. 15). In short, there is no way that we cannot differ in significant ways from our neighbors, our patients, and our intimates. *How* we differ is the question, and if or how this difference gets in the way of communication and mutual understanding.

Splitting within Psychoanalytic Organizations: Microcosms of the World

There is a sociopolitical trend in the world today toward nationalist politics and fascist, genocidal, patriarchal leadership. Individual leaders of this type, both past (Stalin, Mussolini, Hitler) and present (Trump, Bolsonaro), project their own humiliation into society. The familial and cultural roots of those leaders' early life experiences of degradation get played out on the larger stage of sociopolitical and economic strain. These leaders seem to recognize disgrace and indignity as social realities. In that sense, they are good observers of the unconscious. They recognize the power of humiliation and the power of the desire for manifest destiny. Their recognition may be conscious or unconscious; in any case, it enables the vengeful motives of such leaders and their followers.

The history of psychoanalysis is riddled with controversy, splitting, unresolved conflict – and also creative compromise. Psychoanalytic historian Pearl King (1991) considers it understandable that controversy exists because theories reflect the deep work that the psychoanalyst does and the way in which the analyst's work is embedded in his/her identity. She writes in regard to the Freud–Klein Controversies of 1941 to 1945:

> Overtly, controversy was mainly couched in terms of scientific differences of opinion about what was considered to be accepted psychoanalytical theory and technique, as formulated by Freud, and what view of it should be taught to students of psychoanalysis or included in public lectures by analysts representing the Society. Inevitably, these issues also masked deeper ones to do with who should decide these questions, and therefore, which individuals and groups held power in the Society.
>
> (King, Steiner, 1991, p. 9)

Thus, King highlights the importance of power dynamics in psychoanalytic groups, a curious phenomenon in that it reflects the murderous rage that can occur among siblings and the envy, jealousy, and irrationality that is potentially operative within a group of enlightened psychoanalytic minds.

There are many similar examples of tension between the fraternal body of psychoanalysts and their predecessors and within the current analytic collective. Both vertical and horizontal dynamics underlie splitting of Societies, specific arguments in administrative meetings, secret alliances between members, and exclusion of those analysts who are for some reason deemed not acceptable. Although a meritocracy allegedly determines advancement and inclusion, those who are excluded often represent the not-me, the other or an outsider who threatens the power balance within the group.

Complex intra- and intergenerational conflicts can arise around aspects of organizational mission – for example, about the nature and value of outreach or empirical research. Splits occur between those who feel psychoanalysis should be devoted solely to practice-related issues and those who think that broader, psychoanalytically informed activities affirm the importance of the profession to the community and the scientific world. In many quarters there is a split between a vision of psychoanalysis as a sort of guild and a vision of it as having sociocultural or empirical value and as benefiting from interdisciplinary collaboration.

Another area of conflict in the profession is expressed related to boundary violations. They occur despite professional training that emphasizes the dangers of incest, real or symbolic. Training analysts shock some – but don't shock others – when they engage in sexual relationships with patients, relationships they describe as "consensual." Idealization of such colleagues can lead to denial or rationalization of unethical behavior and sometimes to the defense of the analyst rather than of the patient.

A tradition of othering within the profession has permitted the presence of systemic racism, childism[1] (Young-Bruehl, 2009), sexism, and homophobia. These societal problems exist within us as individuals and as groups, just as they exist in the broader culture. When we are confronted by social media with shocking and immediate evidence of violence against Blacks, separation of parents from children, large-scale rejection of refugees, and femicide, we are horrified. But when we observe our own collective, we see a dramatic lack of people of color, a historical undervaluing of child analytic work, and an often silent, pernicious homophobia.

These are issues about which psychoanalysts can offer understanding and can predict traumatic outcomes. But many analysts are hesitant to speak out about what they know and instead remain silent. The work necessary for a meaningful engagement with societal prejudices begins with self-analysis. This can be a difficult task for highly trained analysts who have, for example, not thought about their being white and therefore may indeed be racist because their privileged status has never crossed their minds.

How Does a Focus on Sibling Relationships Help Us Understand Our Professional Dilemmas?

I will address this question first in relation to the general problems I just described. Then I will describe two organizational experiences I have had as the leader of a psychoanalytic group and discuss how a focus on siblings – how they can hurt each other and how they can help each other – aided my understanding and management of conflict.

During the Freud–Klein Controversies, the dissolution of fraternal (or, more accurately, sororal) bonds was accompanied by an oedipal dynamic. The Controversies constitute a good example of the intersectional influence of the horizontal and vertical axes of sibling and oedipal dynamics. The rivalry between Anna Freud and Melanie Klein was intense and confrontational. As psychoanalytic siblings, they battled each other along axiomatic competitive, aggressive, and combative lines. Both also acted in relation to Freud as the father, with Anna defending his definition of anxiety and Melanie challenging it.

A group of 28 psychoanalysts participated in the Controversies. Some favored the so-called Viennese theory of anxiety endorsed by Ms. Freud. Others held Ms. Klein's conceptualization of anxiety to be a theoretical advance. The group's reaction divided along several dynamic axes. There were underlying questions about what to teach analysts-in-training and what to accept as the legitimate voice of the society. The power struggle over the nature of the curriculum was a mix of the sibling complex with its aggressive rivalry, and the Electra version of the oedipal striving in which each side may have felt a responsibility to parent or win over the children. It seems the wish for power, the strong identification with the father figure, and the quarrelsome, creative battle between siblings were largely unconscious.

Freud, the father, never made a place for sibling bonds in his burgeoning discipline. The Oedipus complex with its loving and murderous rivalries was emphasized in a generational hierarchy. This may inform the challenge for psychoanalysis still today. Can we contemplate different aspects within ourselves – a "we" and an "I" – coexisting within our same core identity, within our same body ego? The sibling complex means that each of us identifies with the other as "same" as much as we also focus on differences and self-affirmation. This represents not the struggle between siblings for the parent's desire but, rather, the capacity to hold our horizontal connection with the other, to feel the comfort of that connection, even while we might want to be better or best and unique in comparison. When we lose the sibling link intrapsychically, we disown a major part of what constitutes us in the first place. This seems valid on an individual level and equally so when we consider our group alliances since the nature of the group also permeates our identity.

I have the thought that Freud struggled with his own sibling complex – his love/hate relationship with his followers – and that it resulted in a tendency to turn psychoanalysis into a secret guild with him as omnipotent father but without a sibling dimension that could compete or take away from the oedipal structure. This early pattern has left us struggling within each generation to find common cause with our psychoanalytic siblings and find solace and strength in these connections. We may be perilously situated as a vertical profession, equating the other with a parent, rather than someone at our side who can be a companion who shares our fears and concerns (Leonoff, 2020).

Conflicts over the definition of our profession, i.e., what is honorable and useful, reflect the intersection of sibling and oedipal dynamics. For example, a group that must decide whether and how to fund a controversial undertaking may be constituted in part by siblings who become passionate about their version of truth and begin to aggressively oppose colleagues who fail to appreciate their argument for change. Typically, another group of siblings wishes to support continuing the work of an established parental group. The archaic emotions of murderous rage and unbridled envy can enter the boardroom. While colleagues battle it out with allegedly reasonable arguments, the irrational and unconscious level of their disagreements is reflected in their fierce passion, projections, and intensely rivalrous behavior.

The leadership task of working through such a group conflict is aided by an awareness of the archaic dynamics at play. Direct interpretation of unconscious aspects of individuals' alliances or arguments will be experienced as a partisan attack. But when such conflicts are projected onto the leader, she/he is able, thanks to an understanding of the levels of conflict, to remain relatively calm in the face of what feels like unreasonable assault and retain the ability to think.

Crises in Point: Two Local Experiences

I will describe two intersecting organizational crises that occurred about ten years apart while I held different leadership positions in San Francisco. They took place in a stressful societal context between 2001 and 2011. The

U.S. experienced the failure to anticipate and prevent the violent attacks of 9/11/2001, and significant betrayals by the Bush administration and later by Wall Street occurred. A decentering of white America came about with the election of our first Black president in 2008. It spelled hope for the majority of the electorate but also resulted in soaring gun sales (Bump, 2015).

Two professional situations became entangled during that period of time inside my psychoanalytic organization and within me. The experience of conflict – societal, professional, and personal – was intensified because of sibling bonds that had been traumatized and weakened. But resolution of individual and group conflict was possible thanks to intact sibling links. Within those links dwelled the potential for constructive and creative problem-solving.

I will start with the later crisis experienced by the San Francisco Center for Psychoanalysis when I was chair of its Board of Trustees from 2011 to 2013. It involved the loss of the organization's home of about 60 years and a move to a new location. There had been widespread interest in expanding the Center's mission to include psychoanalytically informed service projects, as well as broader educational and scientific programs. Also, a growing proportion of the membership lived and worked outside the city. They lobbied for a setting that was more easily reached by public transportation. However, once a new building that met all these requirements had been selected, resistance to its purchase was both loud and hostile. There were aggressive attacks on the Center's leadership and the emergence of opposing subgroups of analyst members. What became clear in the context of such unexpected and vehement opposition to the move, once it was imminent, was the interpenetration of the past with the organization's present and future ventures.

In the background, there was important, ongoing emotional distress over events that had occurred about ten years prior to the proposed move involving the loss of two respected training analyst leaders, one to cancer and the other to boundary violations. These earlier losses had occurred between 2000–2003 when I was president of the organization.

Change layered on change layered on betrayal of trust contributed to a very difficult and chaotic process which became linked to the current move to a new home. A strident minority of members had complaints regarding ethics, safety, financial security, and culture. Each of these topics was not only serious in itself but also represented an organizational *après coup* (Myerson et al., 2018).

A minor ethical complaint about payment to the spouse of a member for project planning had the sting and echo of a major boundary violation.

The complaints about safety had to do with the location of the new building in a downtown area that was marginal. There were homeless people nearby and drug traffic seemed evident. Some members felt this was an inappropriate setting for psychoanalysts. Other members felt it was time for psychoanalysts to witness the real world.

The complaints about culture were similar to those about safety. The reality of an inner-city culture surrounding the psychoanalytic home struck fear into the hearts of many members. They complained about a mismatch between psychoanalytic and inner-city cultures and unwittingly endorsed the profession as elitist. Although most members agreed intellectually about the need for societal relevance, many did not want to witness the societal realities that concerned them.

This organizational history illustrates in part the intersection of external realities with internal realities. As president of the organization a decade earlier, I had had a personal as well as a leadership stake in the events that unfolded. The Board of Trustees became faced with the sad and very controversial task of acting on an American Psychoanalytic Association (APsaA) ethics committee recommendation to expel a respected training analyst because of boundary violations. There were intense and conflicting reactions from the membership. Although the recommended course of action appeared justified, many of the organization's members were distressed over its severity and felt that their mentor should be rehabilitated rather than expelled.

The Board followed through with the expulsion. But within a year the training analyst who had replaced the expelled member as chair of the Education Committee died suddenly of cancer. I experienced a deep sense of grief and isolation after her death because she and I had become friends while working closely during the investigation of the ethical complaints. My defenses under organizational stress and my incomplete mourning were reflected in the fact I repressed for about ten years the recognition that she and I had been under significant fire while overseeing the ethical process at the same time the next crisis of losing the institutional home was beginning. I did not recognize that a move from our outdated, inaccessible, asbestos-ridden home would be disruptive and another profound loss.

In the case of the analyst expelled for boundary violations, members were divided in their views of the outcome. For some the situation was evidence of an incestuous oedipal betrayal, an unforgivable state of affairs. Other members aligned protectively with the ousted leader and objected strongly to what they considered an unfairly severe disciplinary action. Their denial of the severity of his boundary violations represented a traumatic response on the horizontal level. Their fellow analyst had diminished them as well as himself. It represented an intolerable loss of self-esteem. A middle group recognized both the lost leader's many contributions over the years and the seriousness of his misconduct. Sibling despair was evident in the rage of those who wished to see their fallen colleague killed off. Positive sibling links were evident among the members who struggled creatively to both criticize and appreciate their colleague, to acknowledge wrongdoing at the same time they retained affection.

When addressing the crisis of a move to a new inner-city home ten years later, the Board of Trustees and I acted as if informed by the progressive as well as retrogressive potential of an organizational *après coup*. We responded to aggressive transferences by focusing on realities. We remained committed to addressing members' fears by listening carefully, transparently sharing organizational worries and conflicts, and articulating the rationale for actions intended to address members' concerns. I think this intuitive strategy was the adaptive developmental outcome of the earlier shared trauma. The sibling group had become strengthened in its attachment. It had mourned and assimilated the dreadful loss of an expelled leader, and it was able to work in a constructive, collaborative, transparent manner.

The Future of Psychoanalysis

In thinking with you about the challenges our profession is currently facing and about its future, I would like to emphasize the value in our becoming less isolated, more aware of the influence of culture, and open to the potential advantages of sibling bonds. While those bonds can generate conflict informed by envy, jealousy, and murderous rage, they can also influence the future in a positive way, for they represent the creative, powerful energy of new and youthful perspectives.

I'll start with the benefit of introducing models from allied disciplines into our psychoanalytic conceptual considerations. The complexity of the mind is staggering. Nonlinear mathematical models exist that add to our efforts to understand the mind's complex systems of interlocking levels of co-constructed experience and knowledge (Galatzer-Levy, 2016).

Network neuroscientists use graph theory and describe brain activity in terms of nodes and edges (Bassett & Sporns, 2018). The edges created by nodes of neurons constitute modules, and modules are connected in hubs. These hubs of complex brain connections have been likened to familiar observable hubs, such as those at airports or in power grid systems (Bertolero & Bassett, 2019). Such hubs provide a useful metaphor with which to think about the way that psychoanalytic organizations function and how catastrophic it can be when the hub ceases to function.

A code of ethics is central to psychoanalysis. It is our hub. Boundaries in analytic work are similar to the edges that organize the brain. In my organization, multilayered, potentially destructive group dynamics characterized the aftermath of the boundary violation situation I described. A complicated array of interpersonal communications originating from the couch or in confidential study groups functioned to distort or negate the intolerable reality of the esteemed analyst's misdeeds (Wolfe, 2019). Demoralization at the group level and a moderate degree of splitting resulted, with attendant paranoid reactions to leaders' actions. There was a loss of productive group functioning when the organizing structure of ethical practice was disrupted.

Kaes writes about singular, interpersonal and "ensemble" domains of unconscious functioning (Kaes, 2016). I find these categories of interacting mental forces useful in thinking about organizational reactions to the sort of ethical situation I described. In each domain of unconscious functioning, there are entanglements of unconscious motives, identifications, and conflicting desires similar to the elements of brain structure. A single event is never really an isolated one. There are interlocking levels of co-constructed experience and knowledge.

In my organization, the leadership interventions that preserved basic functioning after the analyst's expulsion involved many levels of contact with the large group. Open meetings occurred in which as much information as possible was shared, and the conflicted feelings of members could be thoroughly aired. Individual help was offered to patients of the expelled analyst. Consultation was offered to subgroups of candidates who had been in classes with him. The Board of Trustees met in an executive session with the organization's lawyer and the Center's most influential senior analyst because he objected strongly to the disciplinary action. Once the details that had been considered were explained, this senior member was satisfied with the outcome, and his paternal support of the collective helped restore a functional group superego.

In the current historical moment, we are witnessing intense conflicts at all levels of organized psychoanalysis. It is incumbent upon us to differentiate the extent to which polarization reflects the current societal surround versus our individual group history and dynamics.

As clinical analysts, we have been catapulted into a humbling circumstance. We suffer the same real crises as our patients, and it is disorienting. We must work harder to maintain an analytic attitude and work differently to establish and maintain an analytic frame. Like our patients, we suffer various levels of death anxiety related to potential infection by Covid-19, and we suffer sociopolitical and economic anxieties that are enhanced by instantaneous social media communication of traumatic events.

The current societal context is one of severe inequity and declining altruism. Economic pressures have required adaptations and have fueled power struggles. Many psychoanalytic Societies around the world are experiencing serious financial difficulties. The requirement of a viable business model in the context of an educational and social mission creates conflicts between those who are unable to contemplate psychoanalytic training from the point of view of a business and those who are responsible for paying the rent.

The imposed condition of remote connection through internet and telephone in both clinical and organizational work requires us to adapt to the conditions of social isolation and anxiety that we share with our patients. At the same time, we must preserve the necessary asymmetry of our ethical responsibility to them. When we practice clinical analysis "on screen," especially when we are new to the medium or awkward with it, we may introduce a strange or alien third rather than a functional third. That is, we are faced with watching ourselves while we work, either subliminally or actually. We risk becoming a character in the action whom we try to control rather than a spontaneous presence open to surprise.

An intervention that many analysts have found helpful is peer group consultation in which clinical work during the pandemic can be safely anonymously shared. Webinars such as those from the IPA have enabled large group sharing of information and support. As artificial as the computer connection can seem, the positive side of internet platforms is their availability for creative connections between individuals and groups. These evolutions in our use of technology are further evidence of the positive impact of the sibling dynamic that represents a bond that includes the other. There is a shared need for survival, growth, and satisfaction – and the potential for collaborative work.

We cannot overlook the fact that, alongside constructive approaches to shared crises, there is a tendency toward discord within and among psychoanalytic organizations. While this has always been true, it has been exaggerated during the pandemic. Conflictual issues must be broached in the absence of informal social contact. When differences of opinion are expressed on screen or online, there is often inadequate opportunity for the sort of exchange that leads to dialogue. Fragmented emotional statements can result in polarization rather than collaboration. In this way, a psychoanalytic organization becomes a microcosm of the world, a world suffering global crises that require but often lack global collaboration to come up with effective solutions. Many groups retreat and seek solace in small familiar groupings. The tendency toward othering may be exaggerated; if so, the solution of retreat into the familiar is a defense against loss of control.

Leaders of organizations are often the target of projections. That process is also heightened in a time of crisis. The helplessness that may be felt by the group is experienced as a parental failure on the part of the group leader to establish order and safety. The murderous rage or deep anxiety that siblings experience can get deflected onto the psychological parents. The depressive position of functional adults can be lost to a paranoid-schizoid position related to the experience of threat to life as we've known it.

On a practical level, the controversies that arise between colleagues must be taken seriously. They must be respectfully and thoroughly heard. Psychoanalysts who have taken active roles in societal conflicts – for example, John Lord Alderdice, who worked to negotiate peace during the Troubles in Ireland – point out that the passionate positions of opponents in a dispute must be completely aired and empathically heard before any possibility of compromise can occur (Strozier, 2019). If a leader can create conditions in which a close listening to the other is achieved, an unexpected sense of common interest may emerge that supports the negotiation of compromise. An American psychoanalyst who consults to organizations, Ed Shapiro, maintains that the most valuable lesson he has learned over his decades of consulting is the importance of listening to how the other person is right – especially the other person with whom one disagrees (Shapiro, 2020). This is not an easy skill to master, but it can go a long way toward opening a dialogue and ultimately to resolving conflicts.

I have found that the opening of my mind as a psychoanalyst and a social being is a direct result of being active in the IPA. It is impressive to hear fellow analysts from other parts of the world, analysts using the same theoretical framework to formulate the psychic life of a patient, say things that are different – mind you: same theory, same patient, but different perception or formulation. It is a fascinating, enriching, mind-expanding experience that helps us become better listeners to our patients and our colleagues. It is a confirmation of the powerful influence of an international psychoanalytic culture, a confirmation of the unique value of intercultural thinking.

Respectful awareness of difference and creative organizational problem-solving flourish when sibling attachment is permitted to thrive. This is a time, as I said before, when psychoanalysis has never been more needed. It is also a time when psychoanalysts have never needed one another more – in order to recognize the purposes that we share, the differences we represent, and the gifts we have to offer one another and the greater world.

There is change on the horizon. How will we, and how will our patients, view remote training and remote treatment after the pandemic? What many of us considered antithetical to our way of working before the pandemic now proves to be possible, although different. If we were previously committed to being in the same room with the analysand and convinced that the embodied presence of the dyad is essential, we are likely to continue to believe that. Nonetheless, there are practical circumstances which may push us to consider an expanded range of options. Will our view of best practices be influenced by the unprecedented experience of the pandemic? How will we consider societal needs as we review professional standards?

While the pandemic may have added to the level of conflict within our psychoanalytic organizations, the baseline of dissension from which we entered this period of crisis was already very high. We were fighting in seemingly intractable ways about issues like frequency, organizational finances, and access to analysands and candidates. What we have failed to do is determine *why* we have been so antagonistic with each other, so mistrustful, so unable to embrace difference rather than consider it a threat. Although the sibling relationship perspective, both positive and negative, illuminates some of the dynamics, the cause of the increased sibling fighting is less clear. I would suggest we focus on loss.

The experience of loss characterizes change. In my story about an agreed upon move to a new institutional home and how it became highly conflictual from an intergenerational and sibling point of view, loss was the central issue. Rational assessments had made the need for a move obvious. Irrational and emotional attachments made acceptance of the move quite difficult and stimulated complaints along the same dimensions that are important in the world today: ethics, safety, financial security, and culture. The move shook some members to the core while it excited others as a positive launch into the future. We needed to take seriously the opinions of all members and to concretely address fears and discomforts.

Working with institutional conflict can yield very gratifying results. The intersection of the parental superego role with the future-oriented sibling pressure to adapt to change results in new phases of organizational growth. Each new cycle of growth brings pressures to act. The leadership challenge is to think psychoanalytically about conflict and loss, which are unavoidable aspects of organizational change. The best rule of thumb may well be to discover how the other – whether internal or external, the not-me who has a different opinion – is *right*, before we move on to the next level of conversation.

Note

1 Childism is defined as a prejudice against children based on a belief that they are property and can or should be used to serve adult needs.

References

Bassett, D.S., Sporns, O. (2018). Graph theory methods: Applications in brain networks. *Dialogues in Clinical Neuroscience*, 20(2): 111–121.

Bertolero, M., Bassett, D.S. (2019). How matter becomes mind. *Scientific American*, July: 26–33.

Bump, P. (2015). In the fix. The Washington Post (online edition). March 11.

Dajani, K.G. (2020). Cultural determinants in Winnicott's developmental theories. *Int J Appl Psychoanal Studies*, 17(1): 6–21.

Galatzer-Levy, R.M. (2016). The edge of chaos: A nonlinear view of psychoanalytic technique. *Int J Psycho-Anal*, 97(2): 409–427.

Kaes, R. (2016). Link and transference within three interfering psychic spaces. *Couple and Family Psychoanalysis*, 6(2): 181–193.

King, P., Steiner, R. (1991). The Freud–Klein Controversies 1941–45. *New Library of Psychoanalysis*, 11: 1–942. London and New York: Tavistock/Routledge.

Leonoff, A. (2020). Personal communication, October 25.

Litowitz, B.E. (2003). The view from inside, the view from outside. *J Amer Psychoanal Assn*, 51(4): 1369–1381.

Myerson, W., Wolfe, H., Hirschhorn, L., Myerson, D., Fruge, E. (2018). Consultation to organizations. In: *Textbook of Applied Psychoanalysis*, eds. S. Akhtar, S.W. Twemlow. London and New York: Routledge, pp. 239–252.

Shapiro, E. (2020). *Finding a Place to Stand: Developing Self-Reflective Institutions, Leaders and Citizens*. Bicester: Phoenix Publishing House.

Strozier, C.B. (2019). The psychology of peacemaking: Northern Ireland, John, Lord Alderdice, and the end of the Troubles. *Int J Appl Psychoanal Studies*, 16(4): 274–284.

Wolfe, H. (2019). The impact of boundary violations by a psychoanalytic leader: Evidence for an "external topos" of the unconscious. *Interazioni/Interactions*, 2: 11–15.

Young-Bruehl, E. (2009). Childism—Prejudice against children. *Contemp Psychoanal*, 45(2): 251–265.

Chapter 5

Reflections on the institutional family of the analyst and proposing a "Fourth Pillar" for education

Opportunities and problems of transferal dynamics in the training pathway

Stefano Bolognini

In the course of several years, I have had the opportunity to discuss in many places – including several foreign societies – this complex, delicate and sometimes even picturesque but far from trivial subject. Because of the shared ubiquitousness of the phenomena described, I have noticed that it has fruitfully intrigued several colleagues, especially in relation to the feelings that are evoked when the deep key of institutional transference is touched.

At every latitude the evolutionary processes of the Candidates within the analytic institution are substantially the same, with more marked differences between small and large societies and with some specific local and theoretical variations. For example, the much greater influence the supervisor has in the French training model, where supervisions usually last longer than in the Eitingon Model and often take place at the end of the Candidate's personal analysis, with the risk perhaps of transferential developments towards the supervisor less "worked through" by an ongoing analysis. Or the different, more colloquial relations between Candidates and Teachers in the little known Uruguayan model, organised in such a way as to establish more cooperative atmospheres outside the analysis, between the two generational groups of colleagues within the theoretical and clinical training seminars.

But for the rest there seems to be a certain "universality" of the processes experienced not only during training, but also in the years immediately following, when certain identity and relational passages of the analyst in the original group to which she/he belongs (somehow comparable to the passages experienced in the family consortium) maintain their own special phantasmatic force: a factual reality that goes well beyond the naive, well-meaning clichés that would somewhat presumptuously describe the analyst as now free for life from relevant transferential influences, given that ideally he would be supposed to recognise and handle them with mastery thanks to his/her self-analysis.

Institutional events belie these fine illusions: neither de-idealisation nor psychological separateness with one's analyst, progressively gained in the final phase of treatment, are sufficient to make the last session (in many cases carried

DOI: 10.4324/9781003301936-6

out vis a vis the first interview) the punctual act of complete re-emergence from the regressive transference experience.

I remember the beautiful note, published in the "Rivista di Psicoanalisi" by Renato Sigurtà (1977), an authoritative Italian training analyst, in honour of the eightieth birthday of his analyst and teacher Cesare Musatti: candidly and with some disconcertment, he reported his residual sense of feeling still partly a child in front of his colleague, in spite of his own (not exactly infantile) age of 70.

As far as I am concerned, after the qualification, it took me ten years to call my analyst by his first name, even if on that institutional occasion he had invited me to do so; yet, it came to me naturally, after ten years, not by a decision at the table nor by solicitation: it simply "happened".

After all, as we all know, these are deep processes, and each one has its own timings and paths, which cannot and must not be planned or forced.

These evolutionary interior steps are certainly complex and not without consequences – sometimes even problematic – on the future social coexistence of the young analyst inside his/her scientific, professional and educational community.

Many of these issues are revisited in retrospect and with interesting subjective sincerity by experienced analysts in the book "Dear Candidate" edited by Fred Busch (2020) devoted to the training experience.

The institutional family: an uneasy area

When in 2014 – during my Presidency of IPA – it was decided to constitute a specific Task Force "On Institutional Issues", we knew we were about to remove a veil that for decades had covered highly conflicting events that spared almost no society.

My colleagues on the IPA Board of Representatives immediately agreed on having the following paragraph included in the official mandate of that Task Force:

Family aspects of training

The familial aspects of psychoanalytic training give rise to powerful emotional factors stemming from the residual effects of transferences, resolved or unresolved. The major difficulty this presents is that life in psychoanalytic societies and institutes is more akin to family life and its related strife (including extended family and tribe) than to organizational life and functioning.

(IPA Mandate of the Institutional Issues Task Force (IITF) as approved by the Board in January 2014)

The regressive (and in some cases even pathological) effects of these underestimated profound analogies between family and institutional events have occurred in many groups and societies since their initial stages. They often started with the famous "Pioneers Syndromes" that were described by Paolo Fonda in 2004 in a Letter to the IPA Members of the Psychoanalytic Institute for East Europe, and that in some respects repeat, with disconcerting predictability, equivalent intra-family paths, as well as the inevitable human tendency to preserve intact the narcissistic illusions of childhood, reproduced in an adult version.

Fonda's description of these phenomena starts with a disarming, delightful personal self-analytical report, which I transcribe here partially but literally, because any paraphrasing would detract from the humour and colour of his precious communication:

The progenitor syndrome:

More than thirty years ago in my region, in the North-East of Italy, there was still no analyst and I was travelling four afternoons a week from Trieste to Venice to reach my training analyst. I was basking in the fantasy of becoming 'the First Analyst' in my city! I imagined a near future, where anything related to psychoanalysis would have to pass through me, where no one would have to talk about psychoanalysis except me and where I would be the natural leader of any analytical group that might be formed there in the future. This fantasy seemed so obvious and natural to me at the time that I did not even mention it to my analyst. In fact I was protecting it from his interpretations. A few years later two other colleagues moved to my city and this abruptly awakened me from my grandiose dream. Interestingly, as we realised a few years later, by moving to a new area, those colleagues had also cultivated similar fantasies. Fortunately for us, and for psychoanalysis in our town, it all ended with a hearty laugh, instead of continuing with endless fights about who would be the real progenitor, and as such the holder of total power over the souls of the region.

But how come one hundred percent of this small sample had been affected by the same syndrome? Is this also common to other professions or is it something specific to analysts? In the following years, however, I could see that this disorder affects analysts very frequently in various parts of the world.

(...)

Is there something in the psychoanalytic tradition itself that stimulates these tendencies? (...) Is this connected with necessary defences, when a still weak professional identity feels threatened by any compromise with others and with a complex reality? Is this the result of a natural selection of narcissistic personalities who may be more willing to bear the heavy sacrifices of psychoanalytic training under such difficult circumstances? (...)

(Letter to the IPA Members of the Psychoanalytic Institute for
East Europe, 2004)

At this point Fonda reflects on the fact that the temptation for pioneers to more or less secretly identify themselves as "little local Freuds" is almost inevitable, but if this fantasy can be acknowledged consciously and made the object of healthy humour and good sublimation, it will do no harm; if, on the other hand, it is not "played" symbolically and is acted out concretely despite the experience of training analysis, it can later create dangerous institutional difficulties within analytic groups.

Fonda also notes that:

> if we consider that in the power struggles in analytic institutions there are generally no significant economic motivations (since managerial functions are more often connected to loss of income than to gain), such a commitment is left with nothing but a narcissistic motivation (...).
>
> (Ibid.)

Testimonies such as Fonda's contribute to give us an idea of the importance and depth and persistence of childhood subjective experiences in the psychoanalyst's evolutionary path when dealing with colleagues and the institution he/she belongs to.

These inner passages are so common that one could perhaps divide analysts into two categories: 1) those who relive their childhood transference in training and institutions ... *and are conscious of that*, and 2) those who relive it in the same way, but ... *aren't conscious of that*! It is clear that the former are much more aware and integrated than the latter.

Furthermore, it is clear that there is an area of partial, analysable, but still ineliminable deep equivalence between the two internal families (the real one and the institutional one) of the analyst at work, as it has also been noted by Lee Jaffe (2001), who in a paper on supervision in training writes: "For the young candidate, parents and teachers can be just as 'present' in the analysis room" (p. 849).

My contribution of years ago on the unconscious equivalences between the two internal families of the analyst, that of childhood and that of analytic training (Bolognini, 2008), had the very specific aim of pointing out the strengths, the potentially constructive and generative aspects of those equivalences, without denying the more problematic or even destructive ones, but without emphasising unilaterally, once in a while, the negative myth of the "family that kills", very common in writings dedicated to the negative aspects of institutions.

With regard to the potential negative effects, it is worth mentioning as a milestone in the analysis of our institutions the famous article "Thirty methods to destroy the creativity of psychoanalytic candidates" by O. Kernberg (1996), dedicated to the risks always present in our training paths, just as in the paths that take place in family environments.

I think that this vision must be integrated.

It is undoubtedly true, in an absolute sense, that many family scenarios have been and are the scene of the worst tragedies, and as such have been celebrated countless times, even in the literary field, starting from the great Greek tragedies such as the Orestea, passing through Hamlet, up to the terrible film "Festen" by Thomas Vinterberg (1998).

But it is also true that, for better or for worse, in the history of mankind life has gone on thanks to families, and that not dissimilarly the analytic community has developed in this way, starting from the scientific "Wednesday evenings" hosted in the living room of Freud's home, the first real psychoanalytic venue.

For this reason, in that work I also wanted to describe the founding and constructive phantasmatic aspects of the "analytic family", not to be taken for granted; those, for example, that Robert Fliess had been able to grasp in "The metapsychology of the analyst" (1942), with his description of the formation of the analyst's "working Ego", and later Roy Schafer in "The analytic attitude" (1983), when he dealt with the analyst's "Second Self" and his "Working Super-Ego".

I will explain this citing a passage from an earlier paper on this topic (Bolognini, 2008, p. 198):

The internal analytical family of the psychoanalyst therefore usually includes the personal analyst (a real complex primary object), the supervisors (often placed in the paternal objectual box, like a 'third party', which denies the uniqueness of the primary object and proposes founding alternatives), the teachers of the training institute (equivalent to uncles, all the more so since they are often the personal analysts of the other candidates) and, precisely, the candidates/brothers, conflicting and often amusing companions of play and adventure in the years of the training seminars.

With regard to the latter, it should be noted that in those years of restoration of schooling one creates with them experiences of indelible, conflicting familiarity, destined to remain as an imprint (…): one has been at school together, and this 'imprinting' characterizes the sense of belonging to a precise litter, and is destined to remain.

As for the 'analytic uncles' (the teachers of the institute, frequently the analysts of the companions/brothers), they often turn out to function as interesting cultural alternatives to the analytic parents. (…). I refer, in this description, to the benign idealizing aspects necessary for growth that valorize the object-self; it is evident that the 'analytic uncles' may also constitute, by splitting and projection, the representative support of persecutory aspects deriving from residual quotas of 'malignant' (in the Kleinian sense) idealization of the object.

Collaterally, an interesting observation that has been communicated to me in various venues, for example, concerns the fact that the most radical and sometimes most damaging idealization processes, because they are carriers of scholastic fundamentalism and exasperated group militancy, are often those related to supervisors: it seems that the risk of becoming absolutist supporters of a supervisor is higher than of one's own analyst.

Candidates therefore evolve 'within their native village' (I intentionally use an image linked to childhood, in order to tune in to a very precise internal experiential level), constituted by their training institute, accomplishing – when things go well enough – a path studded with important introjective moments, which will go on to found and constitute the cultural, theoretical and clinical bases of their 'I of work'.

From time to time, major national and international events (congresses) will bring them into contact with other family tribes (colleagues from other institutes) or even other civilizations, as happens in the IPSO international seminars or in any case in the major intercontinental appointments.

These are invaluable opportunities for growth in which the candidate experiences the possibility of understanding and exchange with analysts who are very distant in terms of style and cultural references; and at the same time he/she can recognise in a deeper way his/her own belonging to a specific analytical family, strengthening the sense of one's own identity.

The transference can condition the theoretical-conceptual openings and closures towards this or that colleague or teacher, sometimes regardless of the actual value or scientific interest of the various contributions proposed (Bolognini, 2019a).

Let me share with you some examples. Rangell described the phenomenon of transference apparently directed towards a theory-object ("transference to theory", Rangell, 1982), behind which there is always a more or less complex involvement towards a figure that inspires areas of high transference significance; and according to Falzeder (1998), who cites in this sense the American "filiations" of Ferenczi and Rank, the inspirational figure behind is predominantly unique.

A special contribution is offered by Laurence Spurling (2003) in "On psychoanalysis figures as transference objects": the author analyses his transference towards the figure of Winnicott, noting the theoretical and affective changes that, over time, have developed in him towards the figure and thought of that master; he argues the usefulness, for each analyst, of a research on his own internal relationship with the author of reference: in his opinion, it is an excellent means of getting to know one's transference more deeply, since the figure in question (the idealised main author) is not a real figure in the subject's mind, but exists only through his writings.

Institutional transference towards analysts actually present in the institution will, if possible, be even more intense and significant because of family-like interior feelings, even if less marked by the idealising omnipotence that is so easily attributed to the spatiotemporally more distant figures.

Given the inevitable high degree of phantasmatic familial equivalence in intra-group relations, as analysts we try to recognise and highlight analytically these transferential "copies", in patients in general and even more in Candidates, just to avoid that the most problematic and disturbing aspects of them are re-proposed in all their childish disruptiveness also at the institutional level; and that they sabotage new, more evolved possibilities of aggregation and collaboration, through such heavy negative unconscious interferences.

At the same time, however, we can also recognise in some cases the physiological generative force of certain fruitful positive transference components that we should neither be ashamed of nor regret, and that we can instead make the most of to foster the growth of our pupils and the livability of our community environments.

We must not forget that in the surprising fluidification of the structures of the internal world induced by analytic regression, the intra-psychic organisation already structured inside the analysand returns to be partially modifiable via the inter-psychic interchange that takes place in analysis; just as the inter- or trans-psychic interchange between the environment and the child may have originally structured the intra-psychic organisation of the subject that was being formed: for the better if "inter", for the worse if "trans-psychic" (Bolognini, 2010).

Reopening of internal channels in the training process

The reopening of the channels between inside and outside (and vice versa) occurs at various levels, both individual and group levels.

It takes place at an individual level, for example, without anyone being surprised or scandalised by it, in the natural phases of the "analytic honeymoon", when this really takes place in analysis: it is a very different condition from the idealising denial that hides the underlying persecution, which is typical of situations in which a disturbed and at least clamorously ambivalent object relationship overturns the superficial appearance of the relationship.

The authentic "honeymoon" consists in a rediscovery – through regression induced by analysis – of a primary phase of good combination with the object, which in my clinical experience is usually accessible only to those subjects who in fact had been able to enjoy it sufficiently in their original experience, having then encountered important subsequent difficulties.

I stress that *rather than a repetition it corresponds to a rediscovery* (Bolognini, 2019b).

In the honeymoon the patient succeeds in being nourished. But the most interesting thing is that his/her desire to be nourished allows the analyst to produce more and better, for a certain period, "analytic milk", in analogy with what happens in the mother–baby couple: in that period, with those patients, we not only experience the subjective sensation of being creative analysts, but we really become one, for a virtuous circle.

As always, of course, it is a matter of seeing if our evaluation of the ongoing process is correct: there can be, tragically, both the error of prejudiced analysts ("suspicion analysis") who mistake this possible, precious temporary phase for a misleading manoeuvre of idealising cover of persecution, and the opposite error of "benevolent" analysts who in an equally neurotic way optimistically misunderstand as a fortunate and authentic analytic honeymoon what is, instead, a defensive idealising split.

And yet, a realistic and unprejudiced evaluation of the founding aspects of these profound equivalences between infantile experience and adult "transferential findings" in the training path of the Candidates allows to give a right value to institutional moments of *status* passage that could be criticised as unnecessarily formal or even infantilising: as for example the ceremony of the concrete delivery of the qualification diplomas and official entry in the Society of belonging, which can in fact be a founding moment that the young analyst will never forget and that will be part of his/her professional history.

Ultimately, there are moments or periods of transferential investment on the analysis, as well as on the analytic institution and on the complex environment of the training, that deserve to be recognized in their real physiological or pathological nature; which, incidentally, comforts me in my personal conviction that it is better to be in analysis for a certain period even during training, given the powerful regressions induced also by the impact with the group of brothers/course mates, cousins/colleagues from other courses, uncles/teachers, and equivalents often inscribed in the paternal series (supervisors).

So it remains to the personal analyst the fundamental role of a complex, multi-functional object, partly maternal and partly paternal according to the intra-analytic events.

The useful effect of the authentic components of the positive transference, which Freud in principle advised not to interpret directly in analysis, could be compared in training to that of the favourable current for a ship going down the course of a great river.

All this, let me be clear, without cultivating the illusion that the analysis of transference in individual treatment solves the question once and for all: by the way, all those who unfortunately have had to experience, to cross (and unavoidably to recognise in their personal analysis) the harshness of a disturbed primary phase, will encounter again the same insidious rapids also in the groupal and institutional transference; and therefore also in their whole personal experience of training, even if hopefully in a somewhat attenuated form, thanks to the reparative reclamation processes preceding the entry into the local analytic community.

Idealisation and de-idealisation in the training process

We must distinguish the healthy regressive recovery of a natural idealisation towards nutritive, really pro-active objects, from the defense that reverses persecution into idealisation.

A certain optimal degree of physiological (= not defensive) idealisation can be useful and even necessary at the beginning and for a certain time, in order to face the duration and the efforts of the training. Nevertheless, from a certain point onward the training itself seems to propose to the young analyst an equally necessary and in any case inevitable path of de-idealisation.

I will not go through the description of these well known passages here, which all have in common the disappointment/disillusionment with respect to the failed acquisition of a secretly coveted omnipotence: a private fantasy that is hard to die for, in spite of years of analysis, as described in the already cited text by Fonda.

I must admit that I find something similar in certain somewhat risky affirmations by colleagues who, in congressional or assembly situations, debating on issues that call into question our competence or understanding, react by proudly affirming that we will not lack the insight and science necessary to handle the most slippery and difficult situations with appropriate confidence; and they exclaim with self-assurance: "Come on, let's go, what's the problem? ... We are analysts!!!".

Unfortunately, the distance between relaxed confidence and illusory arrogance can be dangerously short.

De-idealisation concerns both the student's Self and, correspondingly, the realisation of the limits of the teachers' power. I remember a colleague who said with sincerity:

> When I entered the Institute as a Candidate, I must admit that I thought all colleagues always agreed with my analyst, and I was amazed that this did not happen; even though I rationally knew, of course, that things were not as I imagined!

Regarding the de-idealisation in and of the training, the casuistry of situations reported in the analysis is very varied, sometimes marked by a certain dose of undeniable realism, sometimes instead by an evident negative transference influence, accentuated by the co-presence of brothers/other candidates who provoke confrontations, jealousies and rivalries.

This can raise a certain aggressive tension in the group, of which collateral signs can be perceived: for example, each year class traditionally produces and develops gags and imitations on the various teachers, which constitute the spice and the fun during and after the many hours of lessons in the four canonical years, without this diminishing the real esteem and gratitude for most of the contributions received.

The scholastic atmosphere that characterises the candidates' classes favours, in that period, effects of infantile neoteny (almost all of them during training show an apparent age inferior to the actual one), and fixes an experience of "brood" that will accompany the group of classmates for their whole life.

In my opinion, this is then reproduced also in the life of the local psycho-analytic institutions (Centers, Institutes, Societies), in what I like to call "a school class that never ends".

From the analytic dyad to the group reality

Nevertheless, going back to the theme of de-idealisation, I think that the abandonment of fantasies of uniqueness, of centrality in the mind of others, and of omnipotence, is an almost interminable task in everyday life as in the institution.

It is likely that some of the *desaparecidos* (those who, once they have obtained membership, no longer attend the Society) avoid contact with colleagues because they are deeply disappointed at not having achieved centrality and omnipotence; and that another part of them, on the other hand, avoid con-tact not because they are disappointed, but because they are still secretly convinced – in a split way – of possessing omnipotence, and do not want to risk losing this illusion by frequenting colleagues, and thus becoming aware of the painful recognition that nobody in this world has such centrality and omnipotence: neither colleagues nor they.

Attending the Psychoanalytic Center (or Institute, or Society), that is the common analytic "house", is in short a not insignificant undertaking, espe-cially at the beginning; to some extent it is a narcissistically frustrating situ-ation, after having been for several years at the centre of the welcome and attention of an exclusive parental equivalent, the personal analyst. Even indi-vidual supervision sessions comfort the infantile illusion of being the object of individual and exclusive attention.

But if one overcomes the initial obstacle of the loss of the dyad, and if one begins to distribute the investment also on the peer group, things can gradually change and the interpsychic world can develop in an extended way, according to wider horizontal vectors. One can learn to tolerate the frustrations of loss of uniqueness, and one can enjoy the fun and advantages of team play.

These are only some of the considerations that can arise from an examination of the possible similarities between family and psychoanalytic community.

I wanted to draw attention to this simple equivalence because it is precisely because of its simplicity, elementarity and evidence that it can most often be underestimated and ignored.

I would also add that the entirely legitimate but sometimes somewhat "ideological" desire, present in analysts, to be able to create an institu-tion without family implications simply risks scotomising its ineradicable components, instead of reducing their power by consciously recognising them.

This is what I have tried to present at the institutional level, calling for the expansion of the traditional training model with the introduction of the "Fourth Pillar".

In short, what is the equivalent of this concept in daily life?

It is very simple: from a certain point onward in their development, children and young people should not spend all their time with their parents or at school, but should have a playground where they can organise their own games or activities in a peer group, learning from experience.

Consequences of my reflections: "The Fourth Pillar"

I wish to share here a quadripartite training model I had published, and submitted to the IPA membership. It offers an explanation of the institutional background which generated a new possible vision for a more realistic and productive training process.

Towards a "quadripartite model"?

The IPA training models are officially based on a tripartite model: personal analysis, supervision and seminars. This short note is devoted to a possible further development, which seems to be "in the air". It would consist of adding – conceptually at least – a fourth element that is essential to the future training of analysts: the acquisition of the ability to work together with colleagues and to become an integral part of scientific exchange activities and institutional life, as a permanent constitutive function of the psychoanalytic identity.

As regards the single individual, it is increasingly recognized that psychoanalysts must not be isolated professionals, at the risk of progressive loss of theoretical and clinical knowledge. Psychoanalysis is in constant evolution and there is no reason why the concept of "permanent training", which is accepted in all fields of professional disciplines, should not apply to psychoanalysts as well.

More specifically, though, the exposure – over the years – to the dangers of unconscious contamination from the transference projections of their patients, who so often would like them to be omnipotent, increases the risk of an isolated analyst turning into a local "guru". Institutional exchanges allow for not only scientific updating but also and above all the recognition of our own limitations, through constant comparison with our colleagues.

There are other factors at the root of these considerations.

One positive factor is that a number of contemporary analysts are increasingly interested in sharing their professional experience through working groups. This is demonstrated by the growing success of WPs and WGs at the various Congresses, where groups of 10–15 colleagues work together intensively for one or two days to discuss papers or clinical materials, with specific methodologies and continuity in terms of the composition of the group.

These analysts have shown their appreciation for, and skill in making the most of, the small group dimension, which lifts the individual out of isolation and allows all participants to take an active part in the shared work.

The group dynamic also offers analysts the opportunity to gain insight into the working methods of colleagues from different backgrounds, to emerge from cultural self-referentiality and return to their own familiar work environment, having changed in some way.

One negative factor, which motivates us to consider a possible fourth element of analytic training, is the growing awareness of the historical difficulties experienced by analysts living together in organized and structured institutional settings.

The continual splitting of psychoanalytic societies is the clearest demonstration of this phenomenon, which is almost ubiquitous and shows that, without adequate training and experience in these matters, this situation will continue along its natural course.

The usual oedipal rivalry, both generational and fraternal, and personal narcissistic intolerances find fertile ground in settings that – despite individual analysis – recur with unrelenting and lacerating frequency. The phenomenon seems to affect all areas of the IPA world.

This is why the IPA Board recently approved the constitution of a new Task Force on Institutional Issues, specifically dedicated to the scientific study of this institutional problem and to providing support for societies, if requested.

Naturally, we do not expect to be able to eradicate narcissistic issues and conflicts, working through this area during training, but we can expect that some increased awareness of this phenomenon can considerably improve the internal individual and group attitude of future analysts towards these dangers.

Another negative factor that leads us to hypothesize a fourth training pillar originates from the fact (constant over time and geographical distribution) that many psychoanalysts have a relatively limited participation in scientific and administrative meetings at various levels (Institutes or Centres, national societies, regional federations, IPA).

I remember a meeting of around forty rather despondent Scientific Secretaries / Program Chairs from all over the world at the IPA Congress in Barcelona (1997), in which one finding clearly emerged: in each society, the percentage of average attendance at scientific meetings fluctuated between 25% and 30% of the membership. Over the years since then, I have heard these percentages of participation confirmed by many psychoanalytical institutions.

This finding was matched by the equally ubiquitous phenomenon of colleagues who, once they have obtained the qualification of IPA Member, disappear almost entirely, as if the title of psychoanalyst is seen as a noble title that, acquired "once and for all", does not require a long-term collegial training. This also seems to be a universal and serious phenomenon.

In these many cases, there is a danger that, by consulting the Roster, colleagues who live in different areas direct patients towards psychoanalysts on the sole basis of their IPA member status, even though some of them may not have attended refresher courses or exchanges or shared work with colleagues for years.

Finally, another danger should also be mentioned, one that is less dramatic but insidious nevertheless: that analysts, after qualifying, close themselves off in a devotional and familistic "claustrum" limited to a small reference group (most often, as we know, following a previous supervisor rather than their own personal analyst), to defend themselves against contact with the more complex reality that is psychoanalysis today, so international and so polyphonic.

In this way, the analyst is presented with the possibility/difficulty of emerging from an institutional transference of a strictly familial kind, to open themselves up to the equivalents of secondary school, workplaces outside the family and socio-cultural life in a wider sense.

Ultimately, there are many good reasons to reflect on this often-inadequate aspect of training: the lack of attention – or sufficient attention – to "post-training" and the value of continuous scientific, administrative, institutional and community participation. The opportunities for group collaboration during training are often limited to attending seminars at the Institute with fellow colleagues. There is usually no opportunity for teaching or increasing awareness with regard to the social pathology phenomena that afflict our societies, just as much as they afflict other professional communities.

In the case of psychoanalysts, who are destined to coexist with one another (hopefully in a fertile and fruitful way!) and combine their internal reality with the external reality of their institutions, I believe that the time has come to start thinking in terms of "quadripartite" training, to accustom analysts to cultivating collegiality as a useful and necessary dimension.

(Bolognini, 2014)

This proposal to be integrated in our traditional tripartite training, classically organised with reference to a vertical axis of transmission of psychoanalysis from the competent generation to the generation undergoing training, has aroused genuine interest in many societies.

The importance of the clinical and theoretical interplay shared between trainees has been understood and valued as a gymnasium that helps the constitution of an autonomous and personalised functioning in the clinical work and in the theoretical reflection. Also the libidinal-emotional function of creating stable and active channels of exchange between peers has been well considered, since it could make the future communitarian cohabitation and the collaboration with colleagues pleasant and not narcissistically unacceptable or persecutory.

All this can benefit immensely the future associative life of the analyst, who will not isolate him/herself and will share with colleagues the adventure of such a difficult and demanding profession.

It is evident the deep equivalence of this experiential area with the infantile and juvenile one of the game shared with friends in the backyard: a dimension today rarer in the big cities of much of the world, but infinitely valuable to form human beings not isolated and able instead to recognise the pleasure and usefulness of constructive exchange. We find a well-functioning institutional realisation of this model in the activities of clinical-theoretical interchange organised by IPSO also in their congress which traditionally takes place in the days preceding that of the IPA.

On the other hand, it is also obvious that this emphasis on the horizontal dimension of inter-play between peers cannot be generationally iconoclastic and must not replace the fundamental vertical contribution of competent trainers: it is precisely a matter of responsibly integrating the two dimensions, in order to train analysts who are sufficiently harmonious in their professional functioning and in their perspective of cooperation.

In Italy in particular, several authors have further developed this theme from significant differences in perspective during the following years (Maestro, Bolognini, Foresti, 2021): Bolognini insists more on the experiential formative aspect of the group work of "horizontal peer interview" and intervision of the candidates during the training, as a school of permanent exchange that can be introduced also with regards to the post-Qualification.

Other colleagues are more oriented towards research and training in terms of reconnaissance of group dynamics in institutional settings: Foresti (2019), is more directed towards research and training in terms of recognition of group dynamics in the institutional context, and used the Tavistock tradition as a training tool, which is more focused on learning group skills and institutional analysis. The strand he refers to is the Leicester conferences.

Berlincioni et al., (2016; 2017) have been cultivating for years an experience with Italian and Spanish colleagues, which focuses on the person of the analyst. It is an experiential group conducted with the technique of analytical psychodrama, defined as a laboratory of psychoanalysis in/group for the maintenance of the analytical function of the analyst's mind, and aimed at building a model that can be imported into psychoanalytic training.

Conclusions

All these considerations will require careful elaboration by the psychoanalytic societies, which also have very different histories, training models and internal atmospheres: that is, a cultural richness in itself.

However, in creating the training environment, we must never forget our personal contribution and that of the institution of which we are a part, to the unavoidable constitution of an internal family-like scenario that we have shared with our educators and teachers, we share with our colleagues, and we will share with our students.

The idea of the Fourth Pillar of a quadripartite training model can be useful precisely to integrate the growth factors of the future analyst in an internal and external more socialising professional perspective.

Being aware of all these elements can contribute intensely to the livability and creativity of the analyst's existence, and to those who rely on our imperfect daily work, but willing to heal or to progress.

References

Berlincioni V., Carnevali C., Cusin A., Maestro S., Masoni P., Fiorentino R., Medici T., Vandi G., Zanchi M. (2016): *Gli "oggetti interni gruppali" nel lavoro di manutenzione dell'apparato per pensare*, presentato al *Congresso Internazionale Bion 2016 dal titolo "Emozioni, trasformazioni e vitalità psichica"*, Milano, 30 settembre–1 e 2 ottobre 2016.

Berlincioni V., Carnevali C., Calzolari M.C, Cusin A., Fiorentino R., Maestro S., Masoni P., Medici T., Vandi G., Zanchi M. (2017): Lìmits i intimitat: reflexions sobre una experiencia de treball en grupi de grup per al manteniment de la ment de l'analista. *Edito Revista Catalana de Psicoanàlisi*, vol. XXXIV, no. 1.

Bolognini S. (2008): A família institucional e a fantasmatica do analista. *Jornal de Psicanalise – Instituto de Psicanalise – SBPSP*, vol. 41, no. 74, 197–216.

Bolognini S. (2010): *Secret Passages. The Theory and Technique of the Interpsychic Relations*. IPA New Library. London: Routledge.

Bolognini S. (2014): *Towards a Quadripartite Model?*. IPA NewsLetter, May.

Bolognini S. (2019a): Enchantments and disenchantments in the formation and use of psychoanalytic theories about psychic reality. *The Italian Psychoanalytic Annual*, vol. 13, 11–24.

Bolognini S. (2019b): *Flussi vitali tra Sé e Non-Sé*. Milano: Raffaello Cortina Editore. English version: *Vital Flows between Self and Not-Self*, in publication by London: Routledge.

Busch F. (Ed.) (2020): *Dear Candidate: Analysts from around the World Offer Personal Reflections on Psychoanalytic Training, Education, and the Profession*. London: Routledge.

Falzeder E. (1998): Family tree matters. *Journal of Analytical Psychology*, vol. 43, 127–154.

Fliess R. (1942): The metapsychology of the analyst. *Psychoanal. Q.*, vol. 11, 211–227.

Foresti G. (2019): Il IV Pilastro della formazione psicoanalitica: ipotesi sul training e obiettivi delle attività. *Ricerca Psicoanalitica*, vol. XXX, no. 2.

Jaffe L. (2001): Supervised analysis and training requirements. *JAPA*, vol. 49, no. 3, 831–854.

Kernberg O. (1996): Thirty methods to destroy the creativity of psychoanalytic candidates. *Int. J. Psychoanal.*, vol. 77, 1031–1040.

Maestro S., Foresti G., Bolognini S. (2021): Il quadrupede zoppo. Osservazioni e ipotesi sugli "inciampi" nello sviluppo del IV° Pilastro. Conflitti inconsci nello sviluppo dei sentimenti di appartenenza. Paper presented at the SPI National Congress, February.

Rangell L. (1982): Transference to theory: the relationship of psychoanalytic education to the analyst's relationship to psychoanalysis. *Annual of Psychoanalysis*, vol. 10, 29–56.

Schafer R. (1983): *The Analytic Attitude*. New York: Basic Books.

Sigurtà R. (1977): Il Maestro ed io. *Riv. Psicoanal.*, vol. 23, 341–346.

Spurling L. (2003): On psychoanalysis figures as transference objects. *Int. J. Psychoanal.*, vol. 84, 31–44.

Vinterberg T. (Director). (1998): *Festen* [The Celebration] [Film]. Nimbus Film.

Chapter 6

Curiosity, facing reality, and resistance against structuring psychoanalytic organisations

Philip Stokoe

In this chapter, I shall consider the vital role that the curiosity drive plays in enabling human beings to face reality, and the consequences when groups form around a resistance to this process. I shall describe how this is a characteristic feature of psychoanalytic organisations and consider how an understanding of the unconscious dynamics can help psychoanalysts and psychoanalytic organisations overcome this threat to their development. My analysis of these problems is based in some key concepts that I shall describe first.

Key concepts

I follow Bion, Britton, and Fisher (Bion, 1962a; Britton, 1998, Ch 1; Fisher, 2006) in the view that curiosity, or what Bion called K (the urge to know), is an innate drive at the same level and with the same power as love and hate (L and H). Freud claimed that the human baby, unlike all other animals, masters the pleasure principle by turning to face reality when the temporary comfort derived from a hallucination of the breast, in the context of its actual absence, has failed:

> ...I suggest that the state of psychical rest was originally disturbed by the peremptory demands of internal needs. When this happened, whatever was thought of (wished for) was simply presented in a hallucinatory manner, just as still happens to-day with our dream-thoughts every night. It was only the non-occurrence of the expected satisfaction, the disappointment experienced, that led to the abandonment of this attempt at satisfaction by means of hallucination. Instead of it, the psychical apparatus had to decide to form a conception of the real circumstances in the external world and to endeavour to make a real alteration in them. A new principle of mental functioning was thus introduced; what was presented in the mind was no longer what was agreeable but what was real, even if it happened to be disagreeable. This setting-up of the reality principle proved to be a momentous step.

DOI: 10.4324/9781003301936-7

... Consciousness now learned to comprehend sensory qualities in addition to the qualities of pleasure and unpleasure which hitherto had alone been of interest to it. A special function was instituted which had periodically to search the external world, in order that its data might be familiar already if an urgent internal need should arise — the function of attention. Its activity meets the sense-impressions half way, instead of awaiting their appearance. At the same time, probably, a system of notation was introduced, whose task it was to lay down the results of this periodical activity of consciousness—a part of what we call memory.

(Freud, 1911, p 219)

Fisher argues that there is nothing in the pleasure principle state of mind that can possibly account for this new behaviour:

We are so familiar with this picture that it is difficult to notice the huge gap in it. In fact, it has a delightful 'adultomorphic' quality. We find the mental apparatus in effect saying to itself, it is time to decide to form a conception of the real circumstances in the external world since hallucinating is bringing no satisfaction!

I am suggesting that this is one of the places where Freud's instinct-based theory presupposes something like an impulse to curiosity. There is a conceptual gap here, unless we are prepared to reject an evolutionary view of the psyche and substitute some (perhaps divine) intervention introducing a wanting-to-know into the pleasure-seeking pain-avoiding organism.

(Fisher, 2006, pp 1224–25)

Specifically, Fisher is saying that Freud's theory has to include an impulse towards curiosity for it to make sense of a change that has been unnecessary for all other animals. Only the existence of an innate urge to know can account for this phenomenon. In other words, I take it as axiomatic that the ability and urge to face reality depends entirely on the activation of curiosity (Stokoe, 2020).

The second concept that is essential to this discussion is the continual movement between paranoid schizoid and depressive positions described by Britton (1998 Ch 6). My claim (Stokoe, ibid) is that Klein, describing the paranoid schizoid (P/S) position, is talking about the same state of mind that Freud refers to when he describes the activities of the drives, the pleasure principle, and primary process. Of course, once the baby has started the journey towards consciousness by moving on to the reality principle or, to use Klein's conceptualisation, has worked through the depressive position for the first time, the P/S position is never the same again. Although the unconscious version is the origin of the emotions connected to it, there is an active conscious representation which enables human beings to maintain a form of thinking. By way of a reminder of the characteristics of the P/S position (which I prefer to call the fundamentalist state of mind, because of this conscious version of it), I will list them here:

RULED by the Ideal
GOVERNING PRINCIPLE: Pleasure
ANXIETY is about one's own Survival
LANGUAGE is that of Blame
MENTAL STATE of choice is certainty
SOLUTIONS are all omnipotent
THREAT is difference, e.g.
Help;
Valuing.
RELATIONSHIPS are either mergers or sadomasochistic.

It is necessary for our purposes to focus our attention on some of these characteristics. The first is *anxiety*. There are a number of reasons why we might be pulled from a depressive position to a P/S position, which are explained well by Britton. The one that I shall be referring to is the consequence of feeling suddenly overwhelmed with anxiety. A surge of anxiety will always pull us into that black-and-white state of mind in which we can be certain. My own belief is that this is to do with the more primitive part of the brain reacting to a sense of danger and temporarily disconnecting the higher functions. The fact that the curiosity drive is innate in humans means that we quickly regain some capacity to think, but it is limited by the characteristics of the P/S state of mind in which the need for certainty dominates. I have attempted elsewhere (Stokoe, 2020) to sketch out the way that thinking happens in this state of mind: the salient point here is that while logical thinking is quite possible in this position, the capacity to *think about thinking* is absent and any analysis of the arguments that derive from such thinking make it clear that there is an unconscious (sometimes quite conscious) urge to *prove a belief*. I deliberately say 'prove' a belief, because I'm describing a process that is the antithesis of scientific analysis but can often masquerade as an apparent 'enquiry'. Individuals and organisations caught in this state of mind are always frightened of enquiries. In other words, this is a state of mind in which the central focus is the self. It is a powerfully narcissistic state.

The second characteristic of the P/S position relevant to this enquiry is the way that the universe that somebody in this state of mind believes he or she is living in is *sharply divided between ideal and evil*. The quality of anxiety is life-and-death, but the presence of the ideal provides a rescue. It is an omnipotent rescue, and it activates a particular kind of dependency which is a total identification. Freud talked about this in 'Group Psychology and the Analysis of the Ego' (1921), and you can see this process occur when groups fall into that basic assumption mode that Bion called dependency. It is as if the moment that the individual or the group is overwhelmed by anxiety, there is a rush to establish the direct link to the omnipotent one.

The third characteristic follows from the language of the P/S position, that of *blame*. If you feel that your position of merger with the ideal is threatened, the only thing that you are interested in is who is to blame. What I want to emphasise here is the underlying belief, which is one of entitlement. You believe that you have a right to be with the omnipotent one and therefore, any threat to that right represents an assault to be defended against. This produces behaviour that is on the one hand consistent with a narcissistic state of mind and, on the other, distinct from behaviour that arises in the depressive position, which is often described as concern for the object. In the depressive position, the ideal has been lost but is replaced by what Winnicott would describe as 'good enough'. The attitude of entitlement is now perceived as damaging to the desired object and the consequent (and new) feeling of guilt reveals a new emotional link of concern for that object. This change allows the baby to manage the mixture of feelings with the result that concern can evolve into what might be described as a sense of duty towards others, particularly peers and colleagues. This links to Junkers' chapter in this volume (see Chapter 3).

The next key concept to which I will be referring in what follows is a model which I have described, based upon concepts belonging to the Tavistock approach to understanding organisations. This model has been called the 'healthy organisation model' and it is a way of describing something that, although it does not really happen in practice, or at least doesn't last for very long if it does, nevertheless has the merit of providing a template against which one can understand where any particular organisation might be dysfunctional (Stokoe, 2011).

If we think for a moment about some of the extraordinary developments that take place in the original working-through of the depressive position, one of them might be described as a much more sophisticated version of the infant playing with the hallucination of the breast that I referred to earlier. This more complex version is organised by the creation of what Bion referred to as an apparatus designed to manage thoughts. I don't think that anybody would argue against my assumption that Freud's 'hallucination' is identical to Bion's description of a thought that arises when a preconception meets with an absence. Bion's theory of thinking enables us to understand how a process that develops thoughts also develops conceptions when a preconception meets with its realisation. He shows us that conceptions can develop into concepts, concepts into scientific deductive systems, those systems into algebraic calculus and so on. This is part of a developmental process that began with the raw emotional experience called 'beta elements' by Bion, which are the mind's experience of the activity of the brain. In this way the human being creates a more complex mechanism for managing the original affects. These more complex processes divert us from the requirement to act in order to reduce unpleasure. The un-looked-for consequence of that is the capacity to be creative and to have an impact on the environment that allows us to exert some control over it. Sadly, it has allowed us to destroy it as well.

Simply put, thinking that begins with accepting uncertainty provides a mechanism for helping us to tolerate the urge to reduce uncertainty (which is another form of unpleasure) through immediate action, and might be thought of as *a way to provide space*. Space is required if we are to be able to take up a third position, allowing us to think about our thinking, but massive anxiety tends to result in a collapse of such space. The healthy organisation model is an attempt to describe how an organisation can recreate these processes; the mechanisms that allow us to engage with reality transform what we see into symbols that can be thought about so that, finally, decisions can be made as a result of the thinking process rather than reactively (Stokoe, op. cit.).

There are four governing structures that enable these capacities to be replicated within an organisation:

1. The primary task (or mission statement)
2. Basic shared principles for work
3. A culture of benign enquiry
4. A hierarchy of decision-making.

The primary task is essentially the identity of the organisation, its *raison d'être*, and, as such, it describes the system's relationship to the outside world. All activity within the organisation must be in the service of the primary task. This must also be written down, so that it can remain under review. This is because things change, and a healthy organisation will operate successfully only as long as it remains relevant.

Shared principles for work are also known as the elements of governance; they include financial, ethical, behavioural, and professional standards. These provide the parameters within which work is carried out. As with the primary task, these principles should be carefully created, written down, and monitored for continued relevance. Along with the mission statement, they provide essential reference points for decision-making and activity within the organisation. There is a simple rule of thumb that might be helpful here: whatever principles are applied to the way that clients are to be treated ought to be reflected all the way up the system. We all know of organisations that espouse high standards of respect and consideration towards clients, which nevertheless act in a high-handed, even bullying, way towards their own staff.

The culture of benign enquiry might be thought of as the personality of the organisation. Proper maintenance of the work, of the primary task and shared principles, and of feedback of information will be natural to an organisation that is interested in its own workforce, its own performance, and the attitude of the outside world towards it. Benign enquiry, as a feature of management, provides both a flow of information and a sense of containment. We

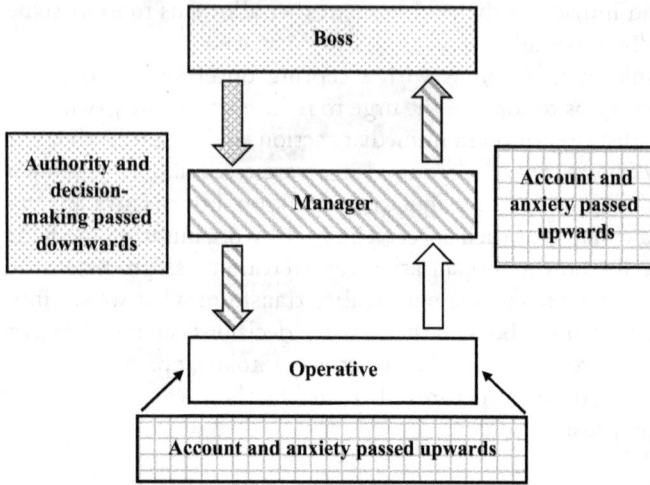

Figure 6.1 Hierarchy of decision-making

might think of it as the essential oil that enables organisational structures to function effectively.

The hierarchy of decision-making (see Figure 6.1) is the organisational equivalent of the circulation of the blood; the structure that enables work to be done, where activities are initiated and monitored. Its purpose is to enable activity on behalf of the mission statement and to absorb information about how it is functioning and about the interface with the external world. In other words, it provides the organisation with an opportunity to link to reality. In its simplest form, it can be described thus: the boss delegates authority to make decisions to the manager, who delegates authority to make decisions to an operative. The important thing is not so much the definitions of delegated decision-making as the fact that this activity is authorised. In exchange for being authorised in this way, there is a requirement to give an account for how each person in role is carrying out their function. The reason for this is that these accounts provide vital information that can be passed up to the right level so that the organisation is kept constantly aware of how it is functioning and how it is being received. Key to the reception of an account is the commitment to a benign enquiry. Specifically, each level anticipates the reception of anxiety. Some anxiety will be consciously transmitted but most will be an unconscious process and management needs to be trained to seek this form of communication. These events of giving account are usually in the form of meetings, and they represent the provision of a three-dimensional space in which the experience, not only of the one giving an account, but of the two of them together in the room, can be thought about from a third position. This represents the organisational process of thinking.

Shared principles

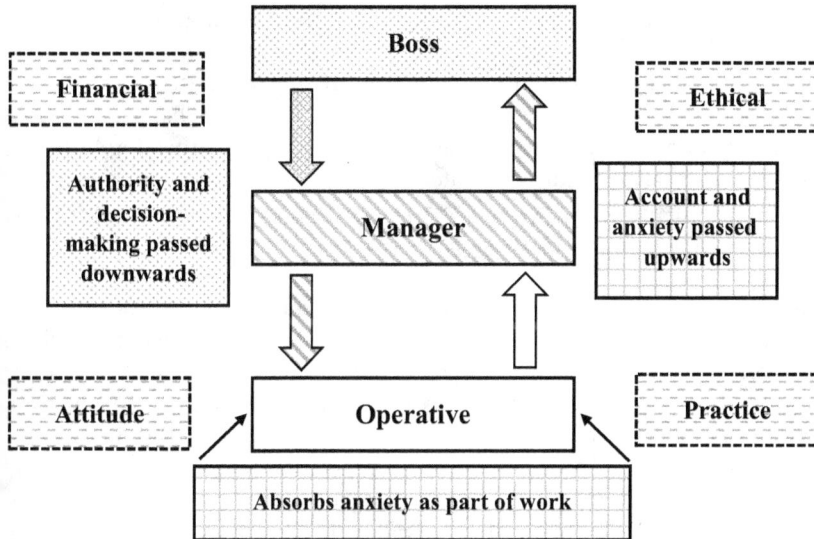

Figure 6.2 Healthy organisation

When this process of thinking occurs within the context of clarity about the primary task and of the shared principles that govern how the work is carried out, then the thinking is contained; an important notion that I describe in further detail later. This is shown in Figure 6.2.

These features have to be created artificially and consciously valued, if not treasured, because you can rely upon it that, when anxiety hits, it is these capacities that will be ejected from the organisation.

Psychoanalytic institutions

There are a number of ways to approach the question of what makes psychoanalytic institutions so difficult to run. I have previously (Stokoe, op. cit.) referred to the importance of the birth of psychoanalytic organisations. I argued that Freud was faced with a very common organisational challenge; basically, the organisation had become too big to be run by one person in a single room (in this case, his waiting room). This is a moment that is faced by most successful entrepreneurial systems. There comes a 'tipping point' at which it is no longer feasible for the entrepreneur to remain directly in touch with the activities of every one of his or her employees. At this point it becomes essential to create a hierarchy of decision-making, which changes the shape of the organisation. I shall come back to this. In my experience as an organisational consultant, such moves are always resisted, even when everybody involved agrees that there has to be this sort of change. It might be correctly inferred that the resistance to the change is, therefore, unconscious. It might also be correctly inferred that a good leader, or an external consultant, will provide time and space to understand the meaning of the resistance. Often this means articulating and making conscious what will be lost in such a move.

Freud encountered exactly this kind of resistance and it took several attempts before it was possible to create the Vienna Psychoanalytic Society and, a bit later, the IPA. One of the characteristics of resistance to change in organisations is that the people instituting or requiring the change will quickly begin to feel that obstacles are created by specific individuals as an expression of their personalities. In this observation we can see something that I think is endemic to all group and organisational dysfunction; that it provokes a tendency to explain what is happening in terms of personalities and specific individuals rather than organisational problems. I thought (and still do) that the struggle against the loss of the entrepreneurial system remains lodged in the organisational psyche of psychoanalytic institutions.

In the same place, I argued that an accident at the point of birth has led to major conflicts within psychoanalytic institutions. The accident was that Freud had hoped that training to be a psychoanalyst would be carried out by universities but, as he was beginning to set up the IPA, he was convinced that anti-Semitism would make it very unlikely that universities would take on such a commitment. He then, somewhat reluctantly, concluded that psychoanalytic institutions would have to take up that task. This has been conflated with the concept called the gold standard and has become an ideal that rules in the organisational minds of psychoanalytic institutions. The application of the idea of primary task enables us to see the importance of a single primary task for enabling good decision-making. Turquet (1985[1974]) describes this very well in his thought experiment in which we are invited to think about whether the primary task of the teaching hospital is to teach or to treat patients. He proposes an incident in an operating room when the consultant is demonstrating a technique to a group of trainee doctors and the patient suddenly haemorrhages. Clearly, if the primary task is teaching, this is an ideal opportunity, and the consultant would stand back and ask the students for their ideas about what to do now. The problem with psychoanalytic organisations is that the imposition from the dead and idealised father of the task of training future psychoanalysts is often mistaken for the primary task of the institution. These are institutions in which, except at their beginning (which is much more like an entrepreneurial system), only a few of the total membership are actually involved in the training, but the misapplication of the primary task fills that group with a tangible sense of omnipotence which has often led to the alienation of the other members of the society. Indeed, some societies have broken up as a consequence.

Taking this analysis further, in this chapter, I would like to consider why this phenomenon goes on repeating across so many psychoanalytic institutions and, indeed, so often within the same institution.

Deeper analysis of organisational defences

Elliott Jaques (1951, 1955) described the way that organisations defend themselves by forming unconscious alliances held together by a single idea. The aim of these alliances is to remove the anxiety that arises as a consequence of being given a task. He called these alliances 'social systems', adding that they were a defence against anxiety. His colleague, Isabel Menzies Lyth, wrote a seminal paper (1960) that makes these processes easy to see and understand.

In 'Group Psychology and the Analysis of the Ego' (1921), Freud, who was interested in thinking about groups with leaders (in contrast to the book by Le Bon called 'Psychologie des Foules', 1895, which had inspired his essay) went on to say that the role of leaders can be substituted by an idea. In this way defensive systems can gather around ideas. For example, many of our current political institutions are developed around ideas generated by individuals who are now long dead. It is significant to notice how often such organisations treat the words representing those ideas as if they are sacrosanct. We are currently living through times in which ideas arising from particular subgroups are treated in exactly this way. 'No-platforming' is a mind-boggling example, particularly when it takes place in those institutions whose whole purpose is to maintain a space for thinking; here I refer to universities and places of higher education.

If you add Freud's description of how an idea can take the place of a leader, to what we know about the impact of anxiety (namely that it pushes individuals and groups into a P/S position) we can see how such an idea will become linked to the ideal in that universe. Thus, the expression 'gold standard' can be seen to represent not only an idea but the accompanying state of mind. We can anticipate that an idea like this, in that fundamentalist position, is not something that can easily be challenged. Indeed, any challenge will be experienced by those protecting the idea as an act of heresy requiring uncompromising retaliation.

Such states have been described by many people studying psychoanalytic organisations. In my view these are extreme expressions of processes that go on continually. What I'd like to do now is to think about the more frequent and, possibly, less noticeable examples of dysfunction. My suggestion is that these all follow a particular pattern, which involves an event that should encourage the organisation to face reality. Instead of doing this, there is an attack on curiosity and a retreat into a narcissistic huddle around a single idea or a single individual.

I should say that the following example is an amalgamation of several, drawn from different institutions, but I believe that it should be recognisable in the sense of being familiar to members of psychoanalytic institutions.

The situation that requires attention has been going on for a long time, sometimes several years. It is the serious reduction in the number of applications to train. Although these figures have been known, nothing has happened until there is evidence of a financial crisis. Whilst the society has been shrinking because new members do not replace those who are retiring or dying, it is only the realisation that the financial base is becoming critical that causes a proper shift of attention. What happens next is significant. The leadership brings the crisis to the attention of the membership and discussions take place. Where voices offer suggestions that the organisation should diversify because that is what happens in the business world when an organisation ceases to be viable, the discussion becomes stuck around an idea that diversification is a threat to the 'gold standard' of the current training. Often those who are suggesting radical change to address the radical uncertainty of the future are the younger members of the society. Only a psychoanalytic Society will be surprised at the discovery that the younger members have a much greater investment in the success of the organisation than those who are more senior. The discussion begins to centre around the personal motivations of those who are suggesting change; some of the least offensive suggestions are based in psychoanalytic ideas like Oedipus or the urge to kill the father. Other, more insulting, commentaries occur, especially interpretations that suggest that the younger members are motivated by envy of status, not having become training analysts.

In this moment of collapse, those who appear to be leading a personal assault on the ones who are pointing out problems demonstrate both the sense of entitlement (in this case, an entitlement to a belief about the 'right way'), and the absence of any sense of concern. What becomes particularly clear in these moments is the unyielding link to the 'right way'. It becomes possible to see the way that this represents the ideal object. For example, there seems to be a view that expressing the need for change is identical with an attack on the gold standard of psychoanalytic training usually linked directly to Freud. It is as if the invitation to face a threat and consider new ways of behaving in order to address that threat has, in itself, become a threat. The response to the threat is to gather in a huddle around the precious object that is perceived as being in danger. Kirsner (2009) describes several examples of this kind of activity. Rangell (1974, p 10), in his Presidential address presented to the 28th International Psycho-Analytical Congress of the International Psycho-Analytical Association, writes:

More insidious, however, I must say from a plethora of experiences and observations, is the too frequent presence in ongoing psychoanalytic life of the same mechanisms I have been describing: the presence of internal conflicts of interest resolved in favour of narcissism at the expense of principles. These occur in small and larger committees, in the large society, in one geographical area as much as another, and at all levels of responsibility. Character assassination by a small number is made possible on a wide scale, if not by the crime of silence, by the sin of omission on the part of many. Impaired morale and ill-will, scientific deterioration and even corruptibility are accompaniments too frequent to be ignored. That unconscious mechanisms are also involved does not absolve responsibility. The whole question of the relation between the unconscious and responsibility needs, in my opinion, a searching re-examination.

This chapter represents an attempt to begin this 'searching re-examination'. There have been other attempts to explore this phenomenon (by Jaques, Lewin, Menzies Lyth, Foulkes, Bion, and Pichon Rivière) but there is already a problem, captured succinctly by Foulkes in 1971:

It seems difficult for many at the present time to accept the idea that what is called 'the mind' consists of interacting processes between a number of closely linked persons, commonly called a group... I believe, however, that there is quite a specific resistance against accepting mental processes as multipersonal phenomena, a resistance based on the very personal as well as general consequences if we accept this truth. These resistances appear to be comparable to those found by Freud against the recognition of unconscious mental processes in the individual.

(2018[1971], Ch 22)

Another way to put this might be: *it is difficult enough to manage the knowledge that we have an individual unconscious that we cannot know directly, but to be confronted with evidence that this part of us can become caught up in unconscious processes generated by the existence of the group feels almost impossible to bear.* I think that Bion's description (1962b) might be the easiest way to approach this. My version is that we become caught up in the swirl of the group dynamic through our valencies, which I think of as the psychic wounds that become the object of our own analysis. These remain acutely vulnerable to unconscious connection and, in the context of a group, draw us into a role on behalf of the group dynamic. Our psychoanalytic training takes this phenomenon for granted in the context of working with an individual; namely that we are going to have more sensitivity in the counter-transference through a sort of harmonic response from our own vulnerabilities to those of the patient. It appears more difficult to accept that this might be the case in the context of a group process beyond the consulting room (see Chapter 3 of this volume, where Junkers addresses this).

Facing reality

I would like to develop the idea that I referred to in the introduction to the healthy organisation model. It might be described like this: the generation of the reality principle is the mechanism by which human beings create consciousness. Our conscious mind develops as a result of the curiosity drive operating as an urge to understand what's happening. Bion called this alpha function. The explanations, which psychoanalytic investigation has shown to be images of ourselves in relation to others or parts of others, accumulate and, following Bion's theory, become more complex as we develop. In step with the increasing complexity, our apparatus for thinking also becomes increasingly complex. It is this apparatus that provides the capacity to tolerate the frustration long enough for us to form a conscious understanding of what is going on so that we can make a decision about what to do about it. This structure (which has to be manufactured artificially in an organisation, and maintained dutifully) is particularly vulnerable to anxiety, as I have suggested previously.

If the organisation has been built around the principles of maintaining structures that imitate the functions that are essential to complex thinking in the individual mind, then challenges to the organisation that provoke anxiety will be manageable because the organisation holds at its centre a commitment to seeking, absorbing, and making sense of anxiety. This represents the institutional version of curiosity. If, on the other hand, the organisation has failed to develop this kind of structure, then it is hardly surprising that it cannot manage the anxiety consequent on a view of reality that appears to threaten it.

If we put together the idea that we, as psychoanalysts, have a predisposition towards a dependent organisation – the group equivalent of a narcissistic personality – with my suggestion that there is an idealisation within psychoanalytic institutions of an arrangement that might be described as entrepreneurial, then we have the beginning of an understanding of the unconscious processes that account for psychoanalytic institutions being so particularly resistant to the developmental process that would lead to a more rationally managed system.

We may further add the observation that psychoanalysts are more comfortable in an environment in which they can analyse personalities, and we can then see an institutional valency that manifests in our organisations. It is a ubiquitous symptom of organisational dysfunction that the individuals within such an organisation become obsessed with an idea that the problems are entirely to do with personalities. All that is necessary is to identify which personalities are the source of all the problems and then come up with a solution about that person. It is obviously unfortunate that our own predilection for looking at the individual leads us into this trap.

Just to pause for a moment to consider an interesting contradiction. Many organisations are happy to reinforce the preoccupation with the search for the individual to blame for the disaster. As a result, they give enormous amounts of money to my organisational consultancy competition (organisations such as PWC, Deloitte, EY, KPMG, and McKinsey & Company) who happily agree that there is an individual or a group of people responsible for the problem, and proceed to apply personality tests like the Myers Briggs to identify the culprits. These people are then offered a training at the end of which, if they are unable to achieve the outcomes they've been given, can be sacked. Of course, the problem re-emerges a year or so later and the whole process gets repeated. It seems likely that organisations are prepared to pay a good deal of money so that systems that might be causing difficulties for staff can be allowed to continue because they are held to be essential to the success of the organisation. This is very much a feature of P/S thinking: that the solution to finding a problematic person in an organisation is to remove them entirely. And here lies the interesting contradiction. Other therapeutic approaches suggest that the aim is to remove or replace parts of the self that are causing difficulty (such as the concept of extinction in behavioural therapy; or, in CBT, the substitution of 'alternative beliefs' for those causing distress). This is an aim that psychoanalytic thinking about treatment normally does not embrace (that parts of ourselves that are problematic should simply be 'removed'); instead, the psychoanalytic approach is to open up the area for further exploration, to help the patient face reality. In other words, we are clinically committed to an idea of encouraging curiosity and a benign enquiry on the grounds that it is our experience that this process leads to the capacity to think about the difficulties instead of acting on them.

This is another example formed by amalgamating stories from more than one psychoanalytic institution:

The board becomes aware that the reduction, over several years, of applications to train is not reflected in other organisations providing training for psychoanalytic psychotherapy in the same City. This raises the question as to why? A small group of analysts are asked to form a working party to think about this problem. The first thing that they discover is that the admissions committee work to a paper providing guidance for their activity. This paper talks about the task and is very specific, it describes the classic psychological definition of the four outcomes of decision-making based on Cartesian parameters in which one axis represents true and false (referring to the result of an

assessment). The other, perpendicular axis represents the range appropriate and inappropriate, although these are expressed as positive
and negative. In other words, there are four possible outcomes of an
assessment (as shown in Figure 6.3).

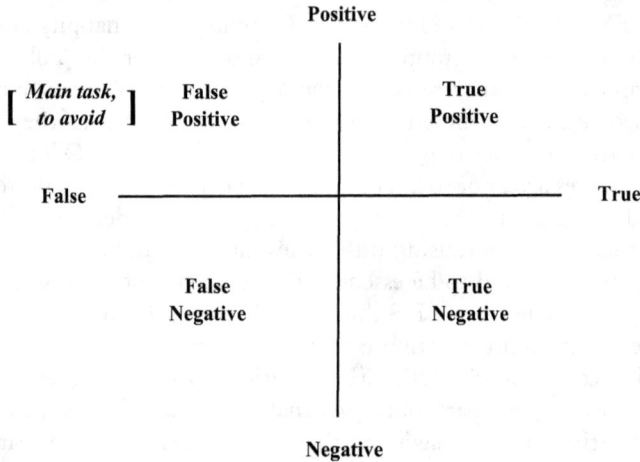

Figure 6.3 Decision-making analysis

The paper concludes that the aim of assessment is primarily to avoid false
positives. In other words, it likens this process to distinguishing the quality
of apples to be put in the same barrel; a rotten apple will damage all the rest
of the fruit.

The working party form the conclusion that this generates an attitude,
in assessors, of suspicion and a level of paranoia. They offer the advice
that this way of thinking is based on an extraordinary assumption that
certain people should not be allowed into the psychoanalytic community.
Two things seem to follow from this. The first is that there is no capacity
for change or development through psychoanalysis. It raises the question
as to whether the institution believes that psychoanalysis has any impact
at all on the individual. The second consequence is that the process makes
assessors so anxious about making a fundamental error that they join in
the creation of incredibly difficult thresholds for prospective candidates to
pass through.

Further investigation derived from interviews with recent candidates and
other interviews with people who were training with psychoanalytic psychotherapy organisations show that the psychoanalytic Institute is perceived

as holding impossibly high expectations of prospective candidates so that nobody wants to take the risk of being rejected.

The working party's report suggested that a different attitude should be assumed by the admissions committee; the attitude ought to be one of positively welcoming interest in the Institute and offering a range of pathways aimed at helping applicants find the right place for them in the psychoanalytic community.

This idea was accepted by the board and passed on to the admissions committee to be put into effect. There was a great deal of resistance to something that was described as, 'opening the doors to all and sundry.' Nevertheless, the committee accepted the instruction and, for a while, things seemed to improve. The salient point for our purposes is that this improvement did not continue. Stories began to emerge from people who had applied for the training to the effect that their initial interviews were felt to be very aggressive. A number of people reported strong challenges about their reasons for applying in the first place. The evidence seemed clear that the openness, the invitation for people to join the community, had relapsed into a very challenging process which, to all intents and purposes, appeared to be aimed at excluding most applicants.

If we think that the entrepreneurial configuration (that is, a group in which each member is connected to the centre, which is occupied by a containing presence) is the group equivalent of a narcissistic state, then it makes perfect sense that such a group would be reluctant to allow more members to join. As Freud pointed out, in the paper that he wrote just after the struggle to move the small group out of his waiting room and create the Viennese Psychoanalytic Society, this sort of group is held together by the phantasy of a direct connection with the beloved leader (Freud, 1921, pp 93–94):

> In a Church (and we may with advantage take the Catholic Church as a type) as well as in an army, however different the two may be in other respects, the same illusion holds good of there being a head — in the Catholic Church Christ, in an army its Commander-in-Chief — who loves all the individuals in the group with an equal love. Everything depends upon this illusion; if it were to be dropped, then both Church and army would dissolve, so far as the external force permitted them to.

I quote this passage from Freud, quite conscious of the irony. Many critics of psychoanalysis claim that psychoanalysis is only another form of religion, in which – while there may be competing interpretations, even heresies – the whole thing is a belief system. We counter this criticism with the claim that psychoanalytic ideas arise out of the scientific approach. Any idea, though it may sound like a belief, is subject to a process of testing. In spite of this, the lived experience of psychoanalytic debate is that, whatever the apparent quality of discussion, there is a background of whispering about whether or not the presentation represents 'real psychoanalysis' or not.

When Bion talks about the defensive arrangements in groups that operate against achieving a working group state, he describes these as 'basic assumptions'. One of them is called dependency. This is the one in which the group unconsciously assumes that the right leader will protect them from all anxiety. Another basic assumption mode is fight/flight; in this state, the group believes that anxiety is created by somebody outside the group. My suggestion is that the urge to create these small groups is an expression of dependency, and any attempt to engage from outside will be felt to be an attack.

One of the first places that Bion talks about alpha function is in the context of the concept of container/contained. Here he describes how a particular state of mind, maternal reverie, allows the mother to use her alpha function to make sense of her child's distress and, by thinking about that, she can come to some judgement as to what she can do about it. This process (not simply the final outcome, but the process) is what gives the child a sense of being contained. In other words, Bion is referring to the mental provision, in this case maternal reverie, of a three-dimensional space in which mother can think about her own experience with her baby. My view is that, whenever a system (whether a single individual or a group) is presented with an anxiety-provoking challenge, the provision of three-dimensional space enables an experience of containment within which a solution can be worked on. It could be argued that every stage of development requires working through the loss of a valued experience in the previous stage. The baby has to manage the loss of the close identification with mother in order to develop the capacity to relate to others. The psychoanalytic institution has to manage the loss of a cosy huddle around an individual, or a specific idea, in order to discover the capacity to bring psychoanalysis into the outside world.

The loss that seems unacceptable to psychoanalytic organisations can be defined in terms of the difference between the process that we would call thinking in an individual and its equivalent in an organisation. I believe that Bion was describing this in his 're-view' at the end of experiences in groups (1989[1961] p 185) where he says simply, "I have been forced to the conclusion that verbal exchange is a function of the work group. The more the group corresponds with the basic assumption group the less it makes any rational use of verbal communication." It is significant that it is only in the pre-view and the re-view that Bion refers clearly to characteristics of what he calls the work group. The entirety of the original experiences in groups contrasts defensive behaviour against an assumed understanding of the work group state. Where he does describe the characteristics of a work group, he prefaces his comments by saying, "It is as hard to define as is the concept of good health in an individual..." (p 25). What I have been doing in this chapter is to try to clarify these differences. To summarise what he calls the qualities that appear to be associated with the work group state of mind, he lists the following (pp 25–26):

a) A common purpose
b) Common recognition by members that there are boundaries to the work
c) The capacity to absorb new members and let others leave
d) The ability to stop subgroups becoming independent units
e) Each member is valued for his contribution to the group and has free movement within it
f) The group must have the capacity to face discontent and the means to cope with it
g) The minimum size of the group is three.

These qualities, along with the claim that verbal exchange is a quality of the work group, fit with my proposal that thinking in an organisation is a process of listening to everybody's contribution, and finding the narrative that connects them all. This is not a narcissistic process. It requires the capacity to respect other people's opinions and *relate* to them. If we take Bion's point (d) and apply that to a system that contains more than one group, it becomes clear that the only way to stop separate groups from becoming independent units is to apply the principle of boundaries and structures. All of this would require the membership of the organisation to give up making individual thinking the primary aim, and, instead, giving collegiate thinking priority. It seems to me that, unlike in other organisations, this is a step too far for psychoanalytic organisations. At the risk of offering an interpretation, one might suppose that we psychoanalysts are less confident of our integrated individual identity than we would admit. One of the joys of plunging into an engagement with the group is not knowing where it will take you. The journey is often more important than the arrival, but it seems to me to be a sign of true maturity. I am reminded of the Chan Buddhist story of Confucius and some of his disciples walking beside a fast-flowing river. They arrive at the point where an enormous waterfall cascades into the rocky basin. It looks terrifying. Suddenly, an old man appears, takes off his clothes and jumps into the water. Confucius and his companions are very concerned about this, and are enormously relieved when the old man reappears further down the river, jumps out and comes back to collect his clothes. They surround him and they ask him, "Old man, how is it that you can survive in such a dangerous environment?" The old man replies, "Go with the flow."

Conclusion

I have suggested that psychoanalytic institutions present unique resistances against evolving into managed systems. This leaves them fundamentally fragile, because they will not be able to evolve in the face of a changing external world. I have tried to understand something of the reasons for this resistance against change, and conclude that it arises from a combination of unconscious beliefs and an organisational fear of thinking. The acceptance of the organisational equivalent of thinking requires giving up the idealisation of individual thinking. There are two main unconscious beliefs at stake here: one is that the best shape for any thinking space is one in which everybody has direct connection with the leader (or with a treasured idea). The second is that the dying founder required each psychoanalytic institution to protect and idealise the training. These two beliefs operate to make change exceptionally difficult because it threatens the 'gold standard', and because clustering around a narcissistic centre does not allow anything new in. Compounding this, the idealisation of individual thinking at the expense of the creative potential of organisational thinking means that all structures suggested to provide a more efficient decision-making are felt to be an attack on each and every individual.

It is, in fact, possible to design an efficient structure for allowing all functions of a psychoanalytic institution to take place. This will follow from recognising that the most sensible primary task is something like *the provision of a safe and developing home for psychoanalysts and psychoanalysis*. Sub-tasks arising from this will include training in psychoanalysis, but will probably also include training in psychoanalytic applications. Another sub-task would include looking after members and supporting them in their psychoanalytic endeavours. A further sub-task will include taking psychoanalysis, as a collection of ideas, into the community and into society in the form of consultation to other professionals, and engaging with public debates about all aspects of the culture in which the individual institution finds itself. These activities will only be possible if there is a single decision-maker in charge of operations and answerable to a board which is responsible for strategic direction and governance. Governance in psychoanalytic institutions is very important because it is here that the psychoanalytic approach and the psychoanalytic mind can be expressed and demonstrated. In saying that, of course, I am already suggesting that the actual psychoanalytic mind doesn't belong to any particular individual, but is a concept represented in the thinking of the institution. This simple template can be modified to fit all sizes of institution and all kinds of complexity.

My motivation in writing this chapter is the same as my motivation when consulting to psychoanalytic institutions; I believe that the psychoanalytic approach to thinking about human beings and the human condition is more powerful than any other that I have encountered, precisely because it takes account of the unconscious. One of the things that we learn from our own analysis is that our unconscious remains unconscious. It is, therefore, important that our institutions as well as our individual members model in our interactions with each other and the outside world our equanimity in the face of the knowledge that other people will see things about us that we don't notice. It seems to me to be an expression of maturity as a psychoanalyst always to be interested and accepting of feedback about our own unconscious.

Let us stop making the mistake of creating narcissistic institutions that act against the opportunity for a real intercourse.

References

Bion, W.R. (1989 [1961]) *Experiences in Groups and Other Papers*. London: Routledge

Bion, W.R. (1962a) *Learning from Experience* (Maresfield Library) (pp. 42–3 & 52). London: Karnac Books.

Bion, W.R. (1962b) The Psycho-Analytic Study of Thinking, *International Journal of Psycho-Analysis* 43: 306–310.

Britton, R. (1998) *Belief & Imagination; Explorations in Psychoanalysis*. London: Routledge.

Fisher, J.V. (2006) The emotional experience of K. *International Journal of Psychoanalysis* 87: 1221–1237.

Foulkes, S.H. (2018 [1971]) *Selected Papers of S.H. Foulkes: Psychoanalysis and Group Analysis*. London: Routledge.

Freud, S. (1911) Formulations on the two principles of mental functioning. *SE* 12: 218–226.

Freud, S. (1921) Group Psychology and the Analysis of the Ego. *SE* XVIII (1920–1922): 65–144.

Jaques, E. (1951) *The Changing Culture of a Factory; A Study of Authority and Participation in an Industrial Setting*. London: Routledge & Kegan Paul Ltd.

Jaques, E. (1955) Social systems as a defence against persecutory and depressive anxiety. In *New Directions in Psycho-Analysis*. London: Tavistock Publications; New York: Basic Books.

Kirsner, D. (2009) *Unfree Associations*. Northvale, NJ: Jason Aronson.

Menzies-Lyth, I. (1960) A case-study in the Function of Social Systems as a Defence against Anxiety. *Human Relations* 13(2): 95–121.

Rangell, L. (1974) A psychoanalytic perspective leading currently to the syndrome of the compromise of integrity. *International Journal of Psycho-Analysis* 55: 3–12.

Stokoe, P. (2011) The healthy and the unhealthy organization: How can we help teams to remain effective? In Rubitel, A. & Reiss, D. (Eds.) *Containment in the Community: Supportive Frameworks for Thinking About Antisocial Behaviour and Mental Health* (pp 237–259). The Portman Papers, London: Karnac.

Stokoe, P. (2020) *The Curiosity Drive*. London: Phoenix.

Turquet, Pierre (1985 [1974]) Leadership, the individual and the group. In Gibbard, G.S., Hartmann, J.J. & Mann, R.D. (Eds.) *Analysis of Groups* (pp 337–371). San Francisco, CA: Jossey-Bass; reprinted in Colman, D & Geller, M.H. (Eds.) 1985; "Group Relations Reader 2"; A.K. Rice Institute, Florida USA, pp 71–87

Chapter 7

Some dark sides of institutional life and of institutional intimacy[1]

B. Miguel Leivi

I'll begin my presentation recalling a small anecdote, funny in some way. More than 20 years ago we received in my institution here in Buenos Aires the visit of Elliott Jaques, by then a seasoned and very renowned analyst who had devoted himself predominantly to institutional analysis. He gave a lecture of which I can hardly recall the content, but I remember instead very well his enormous sympathy, the charming person he was, and that he established a very close and warm contact with his audience. At the end of the lecture, when question time arrived, somebody began by making a reference to what Jaques had written years before (1955) about the relationship between an institution and any of its individual members, who defensively use the institution to deposit their own psychotic anxieties in it. Jaques kindly interrupted him with a smile and pointed out: "that's true, I wrote that a long time ago, but nowadays I think it is the other way round: it's the institution that actually drives its members mad". The colleague tried to resume his question and repeated Jaques' former ideas, but he was interrupted again by the lecturer, who insisted that his points of view had meanwhile undergone a 180 degree turn.

In this curious discussion between Elliott Jaques and Elliott Jaques 20 or 30 years later, as if they were contemporaries, as if the time span didn't exist, who was right? Personally, I'd rather think that both of them were in some way right, probably emphasizing each one's different perspectives of the issue. However, if the problem is considered from the point of view of the proposal that brings us together in this panel, any possible relationship between institution and madness, no matter the order of the causal chain, constitutes, in my opinion, a central aspect of the dark side of institutional life and of institutional intimacy.

I'm of course speaking about madness and not about psychosis, as I believe also Jaques did, even when he had spoken about psychotic anxieties in institutional functioning. Madness is a far less specific term; I find it for that reason, very useful here, because it allows me to encompass a great variety of situations and conflicts that seem, in a similar way, to defy the rational purposes

DOI: 10.4324/9781003301936-8

and expectations placed on any behavior, on any relationship, on any task. And also on any institutional objective and on any regulated and organized functioning.

What is this madness made of? Our clinical experience is full of such phenomena, and they don't certainly lack in any human relationship, nor in any institutional experience, of which I'll only be able to consider a few.

As Freud points out, the appearance of a transference-resistance manifestation in the course of an analysis has very frequently some sort of mad presentation: the patient "is flung out of his real relation to the doctor [...] he forgets the intentions with which he started the treatment [...] (and) feels at liberty to disregard the fundamental rule of psychoanalysis" (1912[1958], p. 107); the whole situation "exceeds, both in amount and nature, anything that could be justified on sensible or rational grounds" (Ibid., p. 100). The therapeutic scene has by then completely changed.

Things are very similar when it comes to the functioning of human groups, be they therapeutic or not, and Bion's theories on groups point in that sense. There is the rational side of any more or less permanent and organized grouping that "meets for a specific task" (Bion, 1961, p. 98), has some aim towards which the individuals cooperate voluntarily, and performs with rational methods "a task that is related to reality" (p. 143). As we know, Bion calls this aspect of group mental activity "work group" (Ibid.). This rational activity of the group is, however, very frequently obstructed, diverted, disturbed, "by certain other mental activities which have in common the attribute of powerful emotional drives" (p. 146). These other group configurations he called "basic assumptions" (Ibid.).

Workgroups, on the one side, and *basic assumptions*, on the other, are in some way the bright and the dark sides of any group functioning, both inextricably linked together like the two sides of the same coin. Since the human being is not a wholly rational creature, since the light of reason doesn't rule thoroughly his/her reality, there's nowhere, at no level of human behavior, complete luminosity, except when a strong idealization is operating; in such cases, the shady zones, so easily disregarded and denied, or perhaps projected onto some external enemy, must always be taken into account lest they produce a growing malaise or they finish by bursting into the open beyond control.

I think that these ideas fully apply to institutional life as well, and that is perhaps Jaques' main contribution to this issue. They certainly apply to any institution, no matter its character. After all, an institution is but a more organized human group with defined aims, roles and positions, rules and mechanisms of functioning.

In many aspects, a psychoanalytic institution is an organization like any other, subject to the same contrasting double sidedness of lights and shadows. But, beyond this general condition, a question could and should be raised: is there, or should there be, anything specific in that respect when it comes to a psychoanalytic institution, or is it totally like any other one?

There's at least one absolutely obvious answer to this question, some-what tautological: a psychoanalytic institution is specifically composed of psychoanalysts. But psychoanalysts are people who devote themselves to studying and exploring the dark sides of human behavior, beginning pre-cisely with the analysis of their own personal shady sides. One could therefore expect from such people and from such an institution not of course thorough rationality, something deemed impossible, but at least some higher degree of acknowledgement of these aspects and some increased preparation and ability to recognize them and to deal with them. This is, in my opinion and in my experience, more a yearning, a sort of John Lennon's dream, than a real fact.

There's another aspect of our psychoanalytic institutions which is quite spe-cific to them: they aren't like most professional institutions, created to gather colleagues who share the same discipline, its knowledge and its practices, who have been trained elsewhere, mainly in some university, and come together to exchange their wisdoms, their difficulties, and their experiences. The main function of our institutions is, on the contrary, the training of the analysts-to-be before they become members. The training is, therefore, the very heart of our institutions, the only entrance route into them: there's no member of the institution that hasn't been previously trained by the institution itself or, at least, by some equivalent institution. In this way, the very survival of any of our institutions depends absolutely on the functioning of its training.

But these rational purposes of the psychoanalytic institutions produce their shady counterparts, which stem to a large extent from the complicated and entangled transferential networks thus created. To be clear on this: every institution, as well as every human group, is permeated by transferences of every kind, even if, as a rule, they are ignored or not taken into account. But the training demands of our institutions add to those general and unspe-cific transferences another set of increased density: candidates and training analysts, supervisors and supervisees, teachers and pupils, all cohabit in a sort of complex endogamy that produces an intricate entanglement of cross-linked transferences of any kind. The institutional intimacy is thus interlaced by lasting lineage relationships, brotherhoods, personal and group sympathies and enmities, rivalries, different sorts of family ties and of family rifts, etc.

Unlike transferences within analysis, where they are dealt with, analyzed, interpreted but hopefully not acted out, things are different in the jungle of institutional transferential ties. Powerful emotional and passionate drives flow there, and many times these latent bonds make themselves noisily heard. In my experience, narcissistic passions are those that create more problems and are the most difficult to manage; as Lacan (1948[1966]) says, the most universal and most typical of all human passions. They never lack. But I'm not going to expand on this, it's no more than a hint.

This complicated structure is not exhausted when the formal training period of a candidate finishes, but remains well beyond it, tingeing thus permanently the internal relationships of the group. The institution has in this way a sort of twofold structure: on the one side, the formal, daylight structure, established in its Constitution and bylaws, made up of different regulatory positions, functions and responsibilities, working rules, terms of office, and so on; on the other side, a shady, nocturnal structure, made up mainly of that network of transferential ties, that have no regulations and, especially, no terms of office; for these reasons, it is far more lasting and enduring. The formal structure is subject to changes, as stipulated by the institutional documents: the authorities change in due time, and even the rules can be modified following certain well defined procedures; the transferential structure has, on the contrary, no regulation at all or, better said, it's possible movements and changes depend on other kinds of factors, just mentioned. These different levels of institutional relations do not coincide, nor do they overlap; they coexist very frequently in a quite conflicting way that is a source of malaise and, sometimes, of open confrontations.

Going back to training, the core of our institutions with its lasting consequences on the dark side of institutional life, it must be said that conflicting dilemmas appear frequently, and sometimes call into question ethical issues. I mean here not problems of conventional morality but, specifically, of psychoanalytic ethics. For instance: formal regulations have been established that try to guarantee the quality of the training; but they have been bitterly criticized by many outstanding authors for the undesirable effects they frequently produce. So, among many others, Michael Balint (1948, p. 167) questioned long ago their tendency to dogmatism and authoritarianism, which make candidates submissive and "far too respectful to their training analysts"; Siegfried Bernfeld (1952[1962], p. 458), on his part, considered that the formalized training "distorts some of the most valuable features of psychoanalysis and hinders its development as a science and as a tool by means of which to change behavior", and Martin Grotjahn (1954, p. 254) wrote that "the rules inhibit spontaneity and enforce regularity and even rigidity in analytic training". Nearer in time, Otto Kernberg (1986, p. 799) deplored the "atmosphere of indoctrination rather than of open scientific exploration" they create, the "distortion of the psychoanalytic process in the training analysis itself" (p. 802), and the "diminished creative thinking and scientific productivity" (p. 806) they frequently produce. In summary: Bernfeld (p. 468) affirmed that "in psychoanalysis, as elsewhere, institutionalization does not encourage thinking", and Adam Limentani (1974, p. 75) added that "institutional training is probably antithetical to analysis; under ideal circumstances it produces a degree of infantilization which could hinder the process of individuation and maturation fostered by the analysis".

Since we cannot do without any of them, because there's no institution without training and there's no training without institution, we find here another case of light and darkness closely bound together, a structural contradiction we have to live with, a source of malaise that pervades the institutional life and requires trying to find solutions which we know will never be final. Here's a small example of those kinds of conflicts: when a colleague applies for training and is in analysis with some analyst who either does not belong to the institution or isn't a training analyst, he/she's regularly demanded in most institutions to quit his/her analyst and begin another analysis with a training analyst. In such cases, not at all infrequent, we are surely following the rules, but are we acting according to analytical principles? If we all agree that the analysis is the cornerstone of an analytical training and that there's no analysis without transference, do we really consider that transference is freely transferable on demand, as if it were a cash check? Don't we have here a specifically psychoanalytic ethical conflict? These kinds of situations lack no consequences; sometimes, unfortunately, the potential candidate can choose going on with his/her analysis and relinquishing the training; ironically, an analytic success at the expense of an institutional loss.

Both levels of the institutional structure, the formal and the transferential ones, are power structures as well. But power is allocated and operates differently at each level, in every institution, including psychoanalytic ones. Power distribution, power circulation, power regulations, power ambitions and struggles are usually very important aspects of the functioning of an organization, the political side, one could say, of institutional life. Could any difference be expected thereon in psychoanalytic institutions?

One of the main functions of the formal rules of an institution is precisely this one: regulating and, especially, limiting power, in order to preserve for a long time Bion's work group functioning, its rational aims and operation, its luminous side, as it were. No institution lacks such tools, the effectiveness of which cannot however be taken for granted, precisely due to the existence of the dark side we are dealing with, that overflows the prescribed regulations. Formal limits are thus not enough; ethical limits to power must likewise be considered.

Psychoanalysis should have here some specific contribution to make, because our method is, from a certain point of view, a device constructed to limit the power that transference confers on the analyst, imposing on him/her ethical boundaries to his/her actions within the analytical setting. The foundations of our practice and of our fundamental technical rules are mainly ethical; they only secondarily aim at efficiency. Abstinence rule is, in particular, a completely ethical rule, perhaps the basis of ethics specific to psychoanalytic practice, "for which there is no model in real life", as Freud (1915[1958], p. 166) says: he formulates mostly negative prescriptions for the analyst, what he has to abstain from doing, instead of positive ones, what he has to do. Lacan, on his part (1969–1970[1991]), also conceives the analytical position – the discourse of the analyst, as he calls it – as opposed to the position of a master, to the discourse of power, and opposed also to the power granted by knowledge – called by him the discourse of the university – which is no more than a variant of the discourse of the master. Being an analyst supposes relinquishing to be a master, to be a sage, to exercise the power granted by transference, in order to keep transference working analytically. Even considering the undeniable differences there are between conducting an analysis and participating in institutional life, why should such an ethical principle not be applied in some way to deal as well with many of the issues created in our institutions by the dark side of power? Could this be another case of no more than a John Lennon's dream?

These questions are experienced in different ways at different stages of the development of an institution, but they never lack. At the beginning, formal and transferential powers, the light and the shady ones, are more likely to coincide with almost no conflict at all. There's no darkness. In its first steps, a new and small group usually needs a strong transferential leadership to direct it and guide it; one or only a few transferential figures are thus naturally invested with the formal power, and there's barely any need for specified rules. The resulting structure is mainly a vertical one. But things change as the group grows and becomes larger and more diversified; it tends then to evolve gradually to the situation described earlier. Transferences become more complex, the leadership is no longer concentrated in one or very few recognized colleagues, and even theoretical and clinical references frequently begin to multiply. The vertical structure ceases to be functional to the group's operation, and the authority of the transferential leaders begins to be felt as authoritarianism. In order to cope with the new state of affairs it becomes necessary to turn the primary group into an institution, with its formal rules and regulations, division of tasks, posts and power boundaries, and also with a new kind of leadership, more democratic and negotiating; in short, a more horizontal structure that allows all its members to actively participate in the activities and decisions, and a way of functioning subject to the agreed rules. As we have seen, the transferential leaderships and powers do not for that reason disappear, but they persist as the dark counterpart of the formal organization that is being constructed.

The transition that a new institution has to go through from one stage to the other is usually not easy, neither for the initial leaders, now questioned, nor for the confronters, whose demands may not be at the beginning well definite. A climate of upheaval and jeopardy makes itself sometimes felt, and political differences between diverse ways of conceiving the institution and its future projection begin to appear. The ensuing struggle between the defenders of the old order and the paladins of the new one, that is only gradually taking shape, can be emotionally overloaded with personal rivalries, enmities, feelings of disloyalty, of ingratitude, even of treason and of long lasting resentments that sometimes complicate the process, until the new institutional order hopefully becomes more consolidated. However, as we have seen, its maturation doesn't imply the disappearance of these differences, but their submersion beneath the rational surface of the institutional functioning into the depth, where they continue to beat, feeding the groundswell that agitates in the shadows that dark side of the life and of the intimacy of any institution, no matter how mature that institution is.

As a way of illustration of these processes and the issues that appear on the road, we can take the beginnings of our institutional organization as Freud describes it in his well known "On the History of the Psychoanalytic Movement", written in 1914[1957] mainly as a reaction to the first serious institutional crises that occurred shortly after the creation of the International Psychoanalytical Association, in 1910. After the first ten years of his "splendid isolation" (p. 22), when he was the only practicing psychoanalyst, "a number of young doctors gathered round me with the express intention of learning, practicing and spreading the knowledge of psycho-analysis [...] Regular meetings took place on certain evenings at my house, discussions were held according to certain rules..." (p. 25). This small group, which kept on growing as more people gradually became interested in Freud's creation and was quite informally organized around the master, was far from being an institution, even when Freud mentions it once as a "private Vienna Psycho-Analytical Society" (p. 26). That's why Freud speaks, from the very title of the article, about the *psychoanalytic movement* and not about the *psychoanalytic institution*.

But even then, when the movement was composed by no more than a small group of interested people with an undisputed leadership, things were far from paradisiacal and there was no lack of conflicts. Freud stresses thereon that "there were only two inauspicious circumstances which at last estranged me inwardly from the group". The first one was that "I could not succeed in establishing among its members the friendly relations that ought to be obtained between men who are all engaged upon the same difficult work"; we could say, in Bion's terms, the *work group* condition to be expected when a common task brings individuals to cooperate voluntarily. The second inauspicious circumstance was that "nor was I able to stifle the disputes about priority for which there were so many opportunities under these conditions of work in common" (p. 25). Even at this initial stage, working in common frequently fell under the sway of some *basic assumption* climate or, perhaps, became the victim of narcissistic ambitions of the members and of the ensuing fierce competition between them, thus disturbing the common task.

The need of creating an institution out of that small initial movement was only considered by Freud when a new group, closely related for some time to Freud's one, appeared in Zürich: "what I had in mind was to organize the psycho-analytic movement, to transfer its centre to Zürich and to give it a chief who would look after its future career" (p. 42). Why an institution?

I considered it necessary to form an official association because I feared the abuses to which psycho-analysis would be subjected as soon as it became popular [...] instructions should be given as to how psycho-analysis was to be conducted and doctors should be trained, whose activities would then receive a kind of guarantee.

(p. 43)

As can be seen, strategic considerations led him to transform the movement into an institution, the International Psychoanalytical Association, and to yield its location from its birthplace, Vienna, to Zürich, and its leadership from himself, the creator and founder, to Jung: "I wished to withdraw into the background both myself and the city where psycho-analysis first saw the light" (p. 43). Needless to say that not every initial leader yields voluntarily the power he is invested with for the sake of the future of the institution or its mission:

> there must be someone at the head [...] an authority [...] who would be prepared to instruct and admonish. This position had at first been occupied by myself, owing to my fifteen years' start in experience which nothing could counterbalance. I felt the need of transferring this authority to a younger man.
>
> (Ibid.)

As we well know, Freud soon regretted having chosen Jung as his follower in the leadership of the new institution, not only due to the theoretical differences that quickly burst out between them: "I had lighted upon a person who was incapable of tolerating the authority of another, but who was still less capable of wielding it himself, and whose energies were relentlessly devoted to the furtherance of his own interests" (Ibid.). As can be seen, also their personal interests and their leadership aptitudes very soon separated them.

The new institution was also meant by Freud as a place where "the adherents of psycho-analysis should come together for friendly communication with one another and mutual support". But these expectations of his didn't realize; the secessions of Adler and Jung followed shortly, and they weren't the only ones. "I was to find that it would not proceed in the direction I wished to mark out for it" (p. 44). The rest is a well known history that extends to these very days, full of conflicts of every kind. Even so, we still have a living institution.

As I said before, however necessary, the formal rules of any institution do not suffice to deal with all this. The ethical restrictions that our method imposes on us to make our clinical work possible can also be useful resources to address these unavoidable transferential and power conflicts, these dark and mad sides of institutional life, that aren't bound to disappear, neither by themselves nor by any effort of will. As I also already said, I think that one might expect that an institution composed of psychoanalysts, people who are trained to deal with such forces, should be in that respect in a better position than other kinds of institutions. But, unfortunately, such a dream only very seldom comes true.

Note

1   Expanded version of a presentation during the IPA Buenos Aires Congress, 2017, in the panel *"The Dark Side of Institutional Intimacy"*.

Bibliography

Balint, M. (1948) On the Psycho-Analytic Training System. *I.J.P.A.*,29: 163–173.
Bernfeld, S. (1952[1962]) On Psychoanalytic Training. The Psychoanalytic *Quarterly*, 31: 453–482.
Bion, W. R. (1961) *Experiences in Groups and other Papers*. New York: Routledge.
Freud, S. (1912[1958]) The Dynamics of Transference. In: *S.E.* vol. XII. London: Hogarth.
Freud, S. (1914[1957]) On the History of the Psychoanalytic Movement. In: S.E. vol. XIV. London: Hogarth.
Freud, S. (1915[1958]) Observations on Transference-Love (Further Recommendations on the Technique of Psycho-Analysis III). In: S.E. vol. XII. London: Hogarth.
Grotjahn, M. (1954) About the Relation Between Psycho-Analytic Training and Psycho-Analytic Therapy. *I.J.P.A.*, 35: 254–262.
Jaques, E. (1955) Social Systems as a Defense against Persecutory and Depressive Anxiety. In: M. Klein, P. Heimann, R. E. Money-Kyrle (eds.) *New Directions in Psychoanalysis*. London: Tavistock.
Kernberg, O. (1986) Institutional Problems of Psychoanalytic Education. *J.A.P.A.*, 34: 799–834.
Lacan, J. (1948 [1966]) L'agressivitéenpsychanalyse. In: Écrits. Paris: Seuil.
Lacan, J. (1969–1970[1991]) *Le Séminaire, Livre XVII: L'envers de la psychanalyse*. Paris: Seuil.
Limentani, A. (1974) The Training Analyst and the Difficulties in the Training Psychoanalytic Situation. *I.J.P.A.*, 55: 71–77.

Chapter 8

Psychoanalytic institutions and how they will help psychoanalysis – if we let them

David Tuckett

Our Editor, Gabriele Junkers, has suggested that there is a significant disjunction between the anticipatory excitement and conviction many psychoanalysts experienced when they first encountered psychoanalysis and wanted to train to become psychoanalysts, and the dissatisfaction with "institutionalised" psychoanalysis many increasingly feel, once they have succeeded.

In this short contribution I will draw on my participant–observer experience living and working inside psychanalytic institutions for approaching fifty years – that is as a member of the Publications Committee of the British Society[1] for nearly twenty years, Editor of the *International Journal* for 12 years, President of the European Psychoanalytic Federation for four years, director on the IPA Board for four years, CEO of Psychoanalytic Electronic Publishing for nearly thirty years and as someone living, researching and writing about psychoanalysis on my own and in small teams of colleagues for nearly fifty years.

My experience of most psychoanalytic institutions is, indeed, as Gabriele suggests, that they tend, although not inevitably, to be particularly dysfunctional – even to the extent that psychoanalysts as a group often become the enemies of psychoanalysis, with disastrous consequences for training, clinical work and relations with other clinicians, scientists and the interested public.

Most human organizations are more or less filled with personal rivalries and defensive behaviours that misalign incentives and common purpose to an extent they interfere with outcomes. This will be particularly the case insofar as feedback mechanisms are fuzzy and failure takes a long time to be recognised. The most effective institutions are well-lead by trusted leaders able to take decisions and to inspire cooperation for common purpose. They create agile and responsive frameworks sensitive to feedback and results. The crucial commodity in an effective organisation is timely knowledge of what is going on and the institutionalisation of enquiring adaptive capacity to respond. The essentials of all of this are well described at a high level by psychoanalytic authors such as Wilfred Bion with his ideas about work versus basic assumption groups and attitudes to curiosity and emotionally grounded knowledge (K and -K). A work group is focused on the tasks the group has

DOI: 10.4324/9781003301936-9

set itself not the personal peccadillos and fragilities of group members. My reading of Freud's crucial insight in *Civilisation and its Discontents* (1930) is that there is a constant tension between pro- and anti-social tendencies, and we know that in the resolution of this tension societies can be creative and innovative or descend into stupor.

The central challenge in a psychoanalytic institution, as in any other, is whether it can be organised as a work group. This means clarifying its purposes and working to achieve them. The three central purposes I see are (1) training, (2) "scientific" research and exploration of clinical methods and (3) relations to outside institutions, particularly those necessary to communicate to a wider public that psychoanalysis is a desirable form of treatment. The three purposes have variable requirements. Fair and meaningful evaluation and feedback systems are necessary to ensure high standards are actually achieved in training. Definable clinical paradigms whose outcomes can be shared and debated as effective are essential to advancing clinical work. And respectful specification of psychoanalytic treatment approaches and theories that make clear their utility and allow differentiation from other approaches are a prerequisite for relations with other fields. Above all, a core feature of a confident institution would be that it has open and transparent procedures and welcomes feedback and the opportunity to learn and to adapt as it goes forward.

On the whole this is not what we find in psychoanalytic institutions. Rather more common place than confidence and transparency, are:

1. Paranoid relationships to outsiders and oversight.
2. Significant degrees of despair and alienation from the institution.
3. Low participation rates in working psychoanalytically within the frequency parameters of training.
4. Ambivalent attitudes to colleagues who apply psychoanalysis outside the conventional clinical frame.
5. Severe problems developing transparent and felt fair systems of progression or appointment.
6. Problematic attitudes to peer review judgement.
7. Failures clearly and respectfully to differentiate different ways of doing psychoanalysis from each other or other forms of psychological therapy.
8. Secrets and cliques and hidden transgressions.
9. Arrogant and high-handed relationships with neighbouring professions.
10. Difficulties treating psychoanalysis as a rigorous subjective discipline focused on consensually implementing an evidence base rather than a system of authority to resolve contentious issues.
11. A marked tendency to confuse constructive critical relationships with institute or other procedures with whole scale efforts to abandon rules, procedures and particularly hierarchies (such as teacher-taught, training analyst) altogether.[2]

To elucidate this argument and to suggest that it is well within our capacity to do much better, I will argue that the central problem to recognise about psychoanalytic institutions is that they have to cope not only with the everyday problems of all institutions, but also with the problems potentially liberated by idealisation of psychoanalysis and incomplete training analyses – in which neither training analyst nor candidate-patient have been sufficiently enabled to undertake the emotional work necessary to give up idealisation to achieve a "third position" in relation to each other and the Institute. For this reason, problematic generational relationships of hidden envy, hatred and rivalry persist and are acted out tending to make many psychoanalysts the enemy of psychoanalysis. Psychoanalytic institutions, and so psychoanalysis as an institutional form, are then hard to *live* as *work groups*, able to be sensitive to and deeply aware and protective of the core findings of psychoanalysis.

In my view, organisations such as the International Psychoanalytic Association and American Psychoanalytic Association[3], who relate to and at some stages have had the role to endorse local institutes, have a crucial potential role as a benevolent third party. The evidence, however, is that they too have been captured by the same idealisation of psychoanalysis and suppressed hatred towards it. They have, therefore, been falling down on what I see as their principal task. While they could and should be focused on the work task of helping local organisations to face the incestuous tendencies inevitably liberated in psychoanalytic training, by offering to act as benign thirds, they have avoided it. They have not then been able to bring issues to light for thinking so that societies can solve them and function effectively as work groups focused on their core tasks: training, advancing the standard of clinical work, outreach.

I will suggest in the following sections that there is evidence and even enthusiasm for the idea that, if supralocal organisations would focus on this work task, or if local organisations would band together to request it, they would both bring relief and be successful.

The challenge: the Oedipus constellation

What we now think of as the Oedipus situation constitutes a kernel of conflicts, identified by Freud as crucial to any science of human psychology and caused by the need to avoid feelings which result from one or more of the following:

1. The recognition of difference from the parent of the opposite sex and sameness with the parent of the same sex.
2. Rivalry with the parent of the same sex and possibly envy of or feeling of lack towards the parent of the opposite sex.
3. The recognition of the existence of time or bigness and smallness, or in other words generational difference and capacity.

4.   The recognition of exclusion from the parent's relationship or in other word's the primal scene.

The feelings of jealousy, rivalry, envy, shame, guilt and hatred that go with these situations are hard to tolerate. They are also exactly the feelings that run through and create havoc in psychoanalytic institutions even more so than in others.

In their extreme form, wishes provoked by these feelings may lead to murderous destructiveness in fantasy or in fact. But Freud bravely recognised them in himself (1897) and was willing to admit them and argue they are inevitable in every human being[4] – setting out his most up-to-date views in his last works (Freud, 1938, 1939). They can, therefore, be expected to emerge in every psychoanalysis; and so also by both patient and analyst in every psychoanalytic training – whether in the experience of the personal analysis, learning to provide psychoanalysis to a patient, in supervising and being supervised or in all the various forms of evaluation and appointment that institutional life necessitates.

Freud wrote that the "creation of a superior agency within the ego is most intimately linked with the destiny of the Oedipus complex, so that the super-ego appears as the heir of that emotional attachment" (Freud, 1933: 64). He added that:

A child feels inferior if he notices that he is not loved, and so does an adult....[and] the major part of the sense of inferiority derives from the ego's relation to its super-ego; like the sense of guilt it is an expression of the tension between them. Altogether, it is hard to separate the sense of inferiority and the sense of guilt. It would perhaps be right to regard the former as the erotic complement to the moral sense of inferiority.

(Freud, 1933: 65–6)

In what follows I will take it as given that the nature of the Super-Ego we form within ourselves as a result of *working through the Oedipal situation* or not, in childhood, in our personal psychoanalysis and in our subsequent experience, is fundamental to the way we manage our life and anticipate our end. It was our executive function, conceived as "the" Ego, that Freud (1923: 55) put at the heart of our capacity for judging the reality of our perceptions or, as we would now say, beliefs. Therefore, it is how far our Ego is emancipated from our Super-Ego rather than being dominated by it (Britton, 2021) that makes for reliable self-observation and self-judgement. It determines our capacity for taking a third position – that is for sound critical judgement in making the necessary and realistic decisions we must make if we are to have effective training, advance the standard of clinical work or undertake outreach. Dominated by our Super-Ego and so frightened of judgement, we will be likely to be attracted to rebellious omnipotence and omniscience, wishing to free ourselves of rules and procedures or becoming enslaved by them in the absence of real judgement.

What's been going on?

Two vital areas for institutional psychoanalysis are the ways scientific life and training are organised. Both, in fact, are survival issues.

Training

Psychoanalysis is unusual among medical and other helping professions in that it was the invention of one person, not hard to identify as "the" father. The key founders around him thought that, to protect its specificity, its training should have international rather than national or more local systems of accreditation.

However, there was a tension over this from the start and over the past thirty years the system of International Psychoanalytic Association (IPA) "oversight", as it was called, had been increasingly unstable due to locally applied variations from the original "Eitingon model" originally used in Berlin but then generalised by the International Training Committee, chaired by Max Eitingon, to all other Institutes in the next few years (Bulletin, 1935).

The main characteristic of the Eitingon model was fully to institutionalise training by laying down three pillars to structure it: personal analysis, supervision and theoretical learning, all organised for the duration of training and conceived as a holistic package. In IPA regulations (its procedural code) prior to 2017, the Eitingon model implicitly retained the "traditional" load on candidates of a frequency of four or five sessions a week for both personal analysis and the analysis candidates conducted. It also referred to systems to appoint designated individuals (training analysts) to conduct candidates' personal analysis as well as their supervision. Formally, it was adopted at first by all and still by 80% of IPA accredited societies, with modifications introduced for complex reasons[5] in French-language orientated areas and in Uruguay.

In 2005, in an effort to contain what had become ever growing differences at the local level, the IPA tried both to accept that variation had been implemented (institutes were training psychoanalysts in significantly different ways) while trying to retain some degree of quality control or oversight. Three distinct "models" of training were proposed, any one of which would be acceptable, and an Education and Oversight Committee of the IPA was formed. Its purpose was to develop transparent descriptions of the core features of each model and to be available for consultation to local institutes struggling with implementation that risked divergence from IPA standards (Letter, 2006).

In practice, a large group of training institutes, especially in Latin America and the US, but not exclusively, were suffering internal conflicts over who had the authority to pronounce a candidate's training complete (e.g., Pyles, 2016) and were also having difficulty recruiting candidates and/or patients for candidates to treat. In this situation some argued that changes to the status of "training analyst" and control by what Kernberg (2000) calls "training analyst cliques", as well as reductions in the load on patients and trainees required, would help adjust to what were seen as real-world pressures. Squiteri (2011) has reviewed the debates. He noted how it was often not well specified whether a reduction in the load on candidates by reducing the frequency of attendance was to apply to a candidate's personal analysis or to the analysis he or she would give a patient under supervision, or both. At this time, except in Francophone countries, psychoanalysis was loosely differentiated from psychotherapy by frequency (minimum five or four times a week versus three or fewer) – see Wallerstein (1998) for an informative account of these issues.

In 2015, a president of the IPA was elected who believed along with others that, in fact, many societies conducting IPA approved training had not been following the rules. The IPA Board soon voted to change them – the representatives from two regions, North and Latin America unanimously, but with only two out of seven voting in favour from Europe. A meeting of about one hundred IPA Institute Training Directors at the IPA Congress in 2017 illustrated the complex arguments that had been debated over the years (for example, Aisenstein, 2010; Conrotto, 2011; Erlich, 2010; Erlich and Erlich-Ginor, 2018; François-Poncet, 2009; Kernberg, 2000; Kuchuck, 2008; Larmo, 2018; Reed and Levine, 2004; Sahlberg, 2018; Wallerstein, 2010; and Zachrisson, 2018). To summarise the five key talks in this debate, four speakers took the view that the Eitingon training regulations had become more or less unrealistic (making economically unrealistic demands on candidates and patients in what were construed to be inauspicious times), prevented survival adaptations to 21st century reality and were unnecessary inflexible. They added that they did not allow candidates to be supported to deal with the realities of modern patients who won't lie on the couch or free associate, needed to meet by phone or other means and in general were the imposition of hierarchical authoritarianism, imposing an inflexible setting which rested more on dogma than learning from experience. At the meeting one of the speakers recognised the challenges but pushed back at the proposed solution of reducing the load by stressing that only an in-depth high frequency analytic immersion in personal experience could prepare a candidate to manage doing psychoanalysis. Throughout this whole debate, as published accounts by Larmo (2018) and Sahlberg (2018) testify, although formally the countervailing positions in the IPA Board concerned "frequency", a great deal of dissatisfaction was expressed. One aspect of what was at stake seemed to be existential anxiety and pessimism about the future of psychoanalytic institutes and even the value of psychoanalysis itself. At the meetings several colleagues stated that traditional frequencies didn't necessarily "work" better and Sahlberg noted a great deal of ambivalence about the training analyst system. In Sweden, apparently, psychoanalysts no longer wished to apply to be training analysts.

The doubts at the meeting summed up the debate. After it, the IPA Board confirmed they would change the rules. First, they altered the minimum frequency requirement to be used in training downwards and then gave IPA component societies the authority to vary training models in regard to frequency requirements, "without reference to anyone else" (Ungar, 2018). They also changed the name of their Education and Oversight Committee to Education Committee, dropping the term "Oversight".

For my purposes in this chapter, what was interesting about this debate and this outcome was that for over thirty years, while the arguments raged and became quite angry and accusing, no systematic evidence for any of the positions of any sort was put forward in writing, peer reviewed or published. Data that did exist, as evident from public ethical violations, pointed to rule-breaking due to corrupt practices and obvious abuse of candidates.

However, following the IPA decision, the training organisations of nine European psychoanalytic societies, concerned that the new training requirements potentially lowered standards and might increase difficulties distinguishing IPA psychoanalytic training from broader psychotherapeutic training, started a research project. A paper summarising the results and arguments has been published, following peer review (Tuckett et al., 2020).

The research was conducted through a series of visits to the different trainings in which four visiting training analysts interviewed a variety of people and participated in a variety of events – most particularly in presentations of candidates' work and progress and discussion about them. Their findings were then discussed in a wider group and eventually with the training analysts in the place visited and by a much wider group. They have been presented at major conferences. The striking point about the findings was the enormous amount of good will and freely given effort put into training in all Institutes and the significant problems posed by conflicts and tensions in the training group, which it had been hard to face prior to the space provided by the visit.

To summarise the main points exemplified in the research report:

1. Variations had taken place in the formal rules set out by the Eitingon architecture in most places and were having problematic consequences. For example, because candidates had given up their personal analysis (which is not meant to happen) but were still very inexperienced with patients and their effects on them, they found it very hard to do psychoanalysis with difficult patients, such as those who contested the frame.
2. Psychoanalytic learning typically created challenging emotional atmospheres for "teachers" and "learners". Vignettes illustrated various challenging experiences.

3. Emotional challenges were regularly and ordinarily suffered by candidates and supervisors which potentially interfered with transparent and simple feedback and evaluation.

4. Conflicts, that may have started around apparently practical obstacles or tasks like evaluation, had frequently turned into painful psychological conflict (anger, humiliation, anxiety, guilt, envy), potential generational conflict, and potential institutional and personal discomfort in managing it.

Additionally, and linked to these main findings, the researchers noted several linked phenomena: emotional role confusion and reversal; interference from peer pressures (such as a norm that if you hadn't finished personal analysis after three years you were odd); and candidates sometimes unintentionally left in limbo as systems became paralysed in the face of unbearable anxiety, disappointment, resentment, etc., in the training group.

The different issues identified were to recur in one form or another in every visit. The researchers thought that perhaps because the structure of the visit programme meant participants were first playing one role (e.g., "visitor") and then the other ("visited"), it allowed difficulties to be explored without too much sense of shame or "us" and "them". In other words, as it came to be discussed, the visits were structured to provide a containing "third position". They provided, so to speak, a theatre and an audience who could collaborate reflexively. Able to observe and discuss the tensions and difficulties, silences and eruptions in someone else's institute made it easier to explore one's own. What was then clear was that the central issue for training institutes was how to be alert, to recognise, to think about and routinely to deal with the conflicts candidates experience and present. Institutes unaware of difficulties and able to avert their attention to them would be likely to be institutes with hidden problems (including ethical problems) with "atmospheres" waiting to erupt.

A particularly striking observation was about how the emotional pressure in evaluation becomes even more pronounced linked to the function of Training analyst – which has caused so much rancour in the IPA debates. As noted earlier, the psychoanalytic theory of the Oedipus conflict and how it evolves has come to be understood as in part resolved via the creation of a benign rather than harsh Super-Ego, sometimes referred to as the ability to take and tolerate the "third" position – a position outside the "primal scene". One way of looking at the struggles the researchers observed about evaluation in training institutes is that they are inevitable; part of an ongoing and never complete struggle to help candidates internalise "third" positions in relation to themselves and others, including their patients. Incomplete success spills over into conflicts in institutions and all kinds of dysfunction and acrimony and also leads to a failure of training.

Researchers also reported on feedback meetings with the trainings after they had been visited. They write that it was clear that the visits had been experienced as creative and helpful, allowing recognition and insight into some of the destructive mechanisms and structures within the training analysts' groups. In some places it became possible to work out specific changes to some elements in the training that had been controversial both in the group of training analysts and amongst the candidates. However, other conflicts turned out to have deeper roots in the history of societies and complex relationships between people, which gave rise to disturbance that needed more time to be worked on. In these instances, the outcome was to look at and discuss the organisational structure of the society related to training and to examine how this was influencing the cooperation of members. The researchers stress in their report that they did not want to make the visit process sound either too easy or too difficult. In fact, they describe it as like everyday psychoanalysis. Just as neutrality (observation from a third position) is at the heart of psychoanalytic clinical methodology, so attempted neutrality was at the heart of the visit protocol – enabled by the frame mentioned earlier in which everyone played the part of "visitor" and "visited" and no one was above examination. The same neutrality was also at the centre of what proved a productive approach to providing feedback to societies –framed as "this is what we see", "this is why we think that", "this is what you might want to think about", "up to you what to do next", "we have done our job". What I would describe as empathetic neutrality is never easy. Turning a "blind eye" between "visitors" and "visited" is as easy to happen as between patient and analyst or supervisor and candidate.

The point that becomes evident is that psychoanalytic training inevitably produces challenges – all manner of parallel processes and the unearthing of unwelcome facts that necessarily evoke more or less unbearable thoughts and feelings. There are no guarantees. Some personal analyses will end in fragile idealisation or unconscious hate. Patients will produce effects that are partly unconscious to supervisors and candidates and evoke responses. Candidates and supervisors (to an extent) are provoked to act out in the countertransference. Unconscious rivalries are stimulated and described. Above all, learning clearly takes time and for some longer than others. The question becomes: Is all this recognised, surfaced and discussed, or are "sleeping dogs" left to lie?

Crucially, the visits sensitised everyone to unrecognised or evaded unconscious residues of how all such conflicts had been managed and worked through, or not, in the past.

It was interesting, as reported earlier, that during the "visits" there were early signs of difficult atmospheres everywhere. But equally important, inhibitions would quite quickly evaporate when the group got to work.

When the teams met together at a review meeting, by which time most present had experienced both "visitor" and "visited" roles, everyone was quite quickly able to realise with relief, first, that everyone else also felt they had "dirty washing" they were frightened to have to hang out. Second, everyone learned that all the difficulties that they had worried were unspeakable, at least to a degree, were to be expected.

Put simply, when we could collectively observe, we could see in every institute the omnipresent consequences of more or less well managed transference and countertransference evoked unconscious relationships from personal analysis – themselves unconsciously stimulated by the unconscious conflicts and associated anxieties and rivalries, etc. The conflicts might emerge directly from the analyses candidates were having or attempting to undertake or via the way supervisors and the system handled them.

At the visits, practices and outcomes emerged they were touched by senses of shame, guilt, threat, helplessness or malaise. Unresolved difficulties between training analysts were often at the heart of these problems – something discussed nearly forty years ago in the psychoanalytic literature (Zimmermann, 1983) but not in the controversies about oversight by IPA. At the same time, it was striking how easily and quickly "visited" and "visitors" were able to use the structure they had framed to get to work. A collegial and respectful rapport quickly developed as they quite easily and quickly got over their inhibitions, shared experience, raised the difficult questions and managed to "converse" about the hard issues. The widespread problems people feared to share were shown to be normal and manageable.

Being challenged can be tolerated or even enjoyed if it unearths problems. It leads to growth!

It seems, therefore, that societies who have resisted oversight and successfully campaigned to end it at IPA level may be making a mistake. In the light of the visits described, the deeply felt existential anxieties and grievances held by the advocates of changing requirements in those debates could be understood differently. In effect, defining training through rules and requirements imposed from outside has led to perverse systems dominated by the underlying and unresolved conflicts necessarily evoked in psychoanalytic training. And they have often gone unaddressed and uncontained.

Malaise, lack of interest in being a training analyst, declining numbers of candidates, perceived absence of available and suitable patients, declining participation in the training, problematic relationships between the training group and the host society and pessimism about the efficacy of psychoanalysis at traditional frequency using a traditional setting, are all very likely to be the outcome of a breakdown in idealisation – ending in varying degrees of alienation spawned by institutional retreats from facing the everyday psychic conflicts of training. It is this situation an outside "third" can assist.

Scientific life

In 1988 I was appointed joint editor in chief of the *International Journal of Psychoanalysis*. I was lucky to be able to have a five-year period of apprenticeship under Tom Hayley so that when I took over the sole editorship, I was well-informed and determined to do what I could to make it a genuinely international vehicle allowing real debate between all traditions.

I wanted to address what I saw then and now as one of the greatest problems of our discipline – a tendency to replace reasoned evidentially based argument with a great deal of opinion often expressed or supported in an authoritarian way[6]. The situation was such that many people had the impression publication in the journal depended not on any kind of judgement standards but on agreement or not with the opinions in an article, who was expressing them and where they came from. To me this belief in a form of mafia like system, which was mostly not in any case accurate, was no way to select papers and to build a discipline which would be well founded in sound argument and be strong, optimistic and confident and so able to retain and maintain a robust psychoanalytic contribution. Unchanged, however, it was leading to all kinds of narcissistic and ideological problems in which "authority" in psychoanalysis was perceived as based on idealisation, opinion and charisma and so both hated and despised. The challenge was transparently to base judgement on reason and evidence and to help the psychoanalytic community accept it.

With the help of many international colleagues (notably Jorge Ahumada, Arnold Cooper, Jean-Michel Quinodoz) in the succeeding years we made progress. For example, we tried to get everyone thinking about clinical facts from their different points of view in rigorous ways. We made the submission and review of papers to the journal anonymous. We made peer review double blind. We held a series of discussions and practical exercises to test how we reviewed papers and out of this we developed and made public our method, which is to attempt to leave people free to argue for their opinions but to conduct assessment on the basis of the quality of their arguments (Tuckett, 1998). I would not exaggerate the progress made – particularly as hostile ideas about conspiracy and personal hostility would occasionally surface, but it was a good experience for those involved and to me demonstrated the tremendous value of cross-national and cross-cultural teamwork and communication. We had a work group.

In 1999, actually at Gabriele's prompting, I successfully stood for election to the European Psychoanalytic Federation. At the point I agreed to stand, I had to prepare a manifesto and so was forced to consider both what the point of such an international organisation was and what I should try to do.

I noted I had enjoyed EPF meetings due to their diversity and success at allowing participation. I suggested the aim should be to further develop it by encouraging our most creative and articulate colleagues to attend and to contribute. I also thought the core task should be to identify and encourage ways of grounding more rigorous thinking in detailed sharing of clinical psychoanalytical work, so that psychoanalysts tried to clarify and explain their thinking to each other and particularly to those who might not share their assumptions (Tuckett, 2017).

These ideas, building on what had happened under Alain Gibeault's leadership and in collaboration with contributions from the executive team of that time (Gabriele Junkers, Emma Piccioli, Imre Szecsody, Henk-Jan Dalewijk and Eike Wolff), led to what was called the New Scientific Policy. It involved a new approach to conferences and the creation of working parties designed to "work at" problems to make incremental progress over time.

By 2003 the success of and enthusiasm for the working parties, begun in 2001, had grown. They came to involve an inner core of some one hundred people working hard for 12 months each year and also three or four times that number attending the workshops then organized about the work at the conference.

Signs of appreciation and success then led the Executive to propose to the EPF Council (the presidents of the European societies) what was called a *Ten-Year Scientific Initiative*. (One of the reforms initiated to create a work group was for the Executive voluntarily to give up voting in meetings so that the presidents had first to be convinced about a project and then after discussion to vote for it.)

The initiative was aimed at what was being widely discussed at IPA level at the time and termed the crisis in psychoanalysis: fewer patients apparently willing to undertake full psychoanalysis, fewer candidates (especially those in their twenties and thirties) apparently wanting to train as psychoanalysts, and widespread lack of understanding among psychoanalysts as to what were the essential characteristics of a specifically psychoanalytic session. The initiative was to be enabled from a €500,000 fund we had built up due to the success of the new conferences which would be used to pay for people attached to the working parties to meet in between conferences and to bring their work to them. To try to leverage this effort we also asked the IPA to contribute and perhaps to consider encouraging similar efforts in other regions but they would not[7].

The EPF Council (with only one abstention) accepted the initiative with enthusiasm. The idea was that over the following ten years it should concentrate activity on aspiring to achieve 12 reasonably ambitious objectives such as (1) transparently describing the various types of working psychoanalytically so that which one someone was using could be recognised; (2) assessing the effectiveness of each way of working psychoanalytically and its advantages and disadvantages; (3) creating a European patient referral and diagnostic programme in which what worked could be shared; (4) creating transparent means to assess training outcomes; (5) publishing studies of the effectiveness of different educational systems; (6) creating an established body of outreach programme expertise; (7) establishing a peer-review-culture tradition for the selection of papers at the EPF conference; (8) creating ongoing interacting peer groups – 100 or so committed research workers, 100 committed outreach workers, 100 committed research clinicians and 100 committed training analysts scattered across Europe and able to understand and trust each other;

(9) creating university links; (10) establishing peer-reviewed publication as the norm; (11) creating some university-based psychoanalytic training; and (12) creating the means to improve referral to full psychoanalysis and regularly monitoring the demand for practice and for training.

At the time, apart from proposal 11, there was not only agreement and enthusiasm but also a strong commitment to the programme. My successor, Evelyne Sechaud, was elected unanimously as President-Elect at the same meeting and set out her vision for implementation a few months later. In practice the initiative and its ambition was gradually subverted.

Looking back, I think all those who attended workshops arranged by the different working parties knew that despite their ambitions, achieving their objectives was hard. For those who chaired them (all originally selected by the Council) it was tough work and always a struggle. Nonetheless, participation was rewarding and fecund. Many of the working parties were copied across the world. The concerns that drove them were always centrally preoccupied with deep issues of psychoanalysis and how to capture and understand unconscious functioning. Four of the original five working parties went on functioning, published in the *International Journal* and in three cases produced books. Some are still "working".

Why was the initiative subverted despite the enthusiasm and why was it that its aims become controversial in the EPF, particularly among those who had not attended them in person?

I do not have a definitive answer. But some of the issues raised – such as questions as to whether some of the ways of working were truly psychoanalytic or whether the EPF should fund some but not all people to meet – appeared to have clear insider–outsider origins. Very little attention was given to results – to the outcome of the work. So, despite the original intention, working party chairs were not asked to come to the Council and give an account of their work – this despite the fact that, on those occasions when they had, everyone had been delighted to escape the administrative agenda to focus on interesting work. Gradually, with the rapid rotation of presidents[8], those who had experienced the need for and voted for the initiative were replaced by others who had not had that experience. Significant objections began to be raised about the working parties being led by the same people and pursuing the same topics – with a limit eventually being placed on the period chairs could work and the length a working party could exist. In this way, rather than seen as best efforts to engage with a common problem, they became perceived as individual vanity projects. Today working parties can be formed on any interesting topic and the objectives of the initiative and the obligations the Council had set itself in 2003 to review progress on the key topics has been forgotten. On top of that, who was and was not in a working party became fraught with rivalry, raised emotions and personal politics. Outside of Europe being a chair of such a working group became a status symbol. But with the exception of Marie Rudden and Abbot Bronstein

(2015), I know of no published work that followed. Indeed, a colleague once joked to me that working parties were now seen as "parties".

Perhaps the initiative was, from the start, too ambitious and too provocative – based as it was on the hypothesis that the prevailing status quo of "anything goes" rather than "disciplined pluralism" was problematic. But the problems the initiative sought to tackle remain with us. They are just as, if not more, urgent as they were in 2001. Alternative ways of addressing them have not evolved.

Work groups and the psychoanalytic attitude

I have described what was going on in some areas of training and scientific exchange in psychoanalytic institutions over the last twenty years. From my vantage point it is a history of potential for work in institutions, but not enough actual work.

The future of psychoanalysis as a discipline – its scientific life and development and its education and training – requires the collaboration of psychoanalysts in institutions and, therefore, in institutional roles. Authors and candidates, for example, require judgements to be made and supported in a transparent manner. At the same time honest feedback has the potential to disappoint or even exclude, destroying idealisations and creating feelings of shame, guilt, rivalry, triumph, envy and so on. As I suggested, these are precisely the feelings Freud believed to be associated with the unconscious dynamics of the Oedipal constellation. They are bound to be difficult. They will be unleashed in the transference-countertransference situations at the heart of training. In this way psychoanalytic institutions have all the problems of ordinary institutions but also suffer the consequences that follow from the fact that the personal and the professional take an enormous amount of emotional work to separate.

From this viewpoint there is a clear conclusion: institutional psychoanalytic capacity is the ability within the institution to take itself as the object.

Consequentially, I think training or scientific or other boards and committees that seek to claim they are progressing psychoanalysis need to be much clearer and more transparent about the problems. Working with Central Banks and other financial institutions I use my psychoanalytic background to suggest that anxiety is a signal that requires attention, not a signal to run away from and bury. Given uncertainty, if anxiety is buried, we can be sure risk-taking will become excessive and there will eventually be a crash (Nyman, Kapadia and Tuckett, 2021).

Surely similar advice should be applied to our own institutions. Oedipal dynamics and incestuous desires will be evoked in every analysis and every training. We should expect it and expect it to take time to work through. We should be highly suspicious if its signs are absent. Therefore, psychoanalytic institutions intent on quality and survival need to instantiate routine procedures to show to themselves, transparently, how they attend to the dynamics just mentioned and how they take a neutral or "third" inquisitive stance towards them.

The feature of psychoanalytic training and scientific production which is apparently most alarming is a fear of evaluation, which often takes the form of naïve opposition to empirical research based on arguments that are usually de-bunked in the first year of university. Other defences against knowledge of reality, such as the argument that creating criteria for measurement is somehow un-psychoanalytic (Junkers, Tuckett and Zachrisson, 2008), or that psychoanalysis is somehow a special subject closed to the usual scientific methodology, have been prominent too often. What is overlooked is that if judgements are not made on transparent shared criteria, then they will either not be made (anything goes) or alternatively be made by fiat authority.

How to make knowledge generalisations about the subjective processes we deal with in psychoanalysis is certainly a challenge. Criticism of naïve empiricism is also pertinent. But to take such arguments seriously we need to ask what better alternatives are being put forward. Are they advanced to support a better way to substantiate clinical approaches and theories, or ways of doing evaluation, or rather designed to remove the requirement to try?

I hope the various experiences and findings I have described usefully elaborate my argument, made at the beginning of this chapter, that psychoanalytic institutions are at particular risk for becoming dysfunctional as basic assumptions groups – groups of individuals banded together to evade their perception of reality. In this way psychoanalysts as a group in institutions can become the enemies of psychoanalysis, with disastrous consequences for training, clinical work and relations with other clinicians, scientists and the interested public.

But this outcome is not inevitable. We have the tools to form and structure work groups and knowledge as to where to look to see signs of trouble. We can then reflect on the more negative developments I have described as symptoms of deeper oedipally situated anxieties about our capacity and ways of dealing with them. We can both surface these anxieties and, as in the structure of the way Gabriele and I tried to organise the EPF Council, or the ways my colleagues managed the European Exchange Visit Programme (EVP), we can create simple procedures and institutional rules; ones to manage anxieties, shame, guilt and other feelings so that they can be surfaced, contained and learned from. This was done in the EVP by creating the right framework for the visit programme to Institutes. It can also always be done by creating teamwork based on work group principles – defining the task and then working together on it. Well organised peer review is another example.

Personally, I have had many occasions to hate peer review and the judgement of colleagues. There was, for example, the blue pencil applied by my professor to just about every sentence of what became my first book. There were the rejections or "revise and re-submits" from the *International Journal* and other journals in Economics, Sociology, Brain Science, Management Science. There were the grant applications turned down by numerous foundations and research councils even when some of them were recommended by Nobel laureates. Did I agree with these judgements? Immediately? Never! I had tried very hard to get things right. In time? Sometimes. Were those eventually accepted after revision better? Yes, always! Have I given up? Sometimes you have to. "Life is not fair"[9].

As I have argued, the psychoanalytic attitude requires a third position – the willingness to experience the situation and then to try to reflect on it with curiosity and interest from outside it and then to re-engage. Institutions need to be work groups focused specifically on limited and agreed tasks, expecting trouble and sticking to the task. They are not playgrounds. In the EPF, Gabriele set the example to me for four years. Always interested in potential dissent, always trying to understand it, always coming back to the original point. We cannot expect ourselves as psychoanalysts not to get caught up in rivalry, shame, guilt and hatred any more than is possible in other disciplines. But knowing it, we can prepare for it and create institutional mechanisms to manage it rather than to turn a blind eye. And we can speak out when we have doubts. Our doubts may be the only feedback that is available other than extinction.

Notes

1   This is the committee which reviews the policies of the external publications of the British Society, such as the *International Journal*, the International Psychoanalytical Library, the Publications of Freuds' work in English and the new Library of Psychoanalysis.

2   Readers may think of Moses and Monotheism (Freud, 1939).

3   The European Psychoanalytic Federation (EPF), the Federación Psicoanalítica de América Latina (FEPAL) and some other supralocal organisations may be able to exercise the same function but hitherto have not had the responsibility to do so.

4   To be completely honest with oneself is good practice. One single thought of general value has been revealed to me. I have found, in my own case too, falling in love with the mother and jealousy of the father, and I now regard it as a universal event of early childhood, even if not so early as in children who have been made hysterical. (Similarly with the romance of parentage in paranoia-heroes, founders of religions.) If that is so, we can understand the riveting power of Oedipus Rex, in spite of all the objections raised by reason against its presupposition of destiny; and we can understand why the later 'dramas of destiny' were bound to fail so miserably. Our feelings rise against any arbitrary, individual compulsion [of fate], such as is presupposed in [Grillparzer's] Die Ahnfrau, etc. But the Greek legend seizes on a compulsion which everyone recognizes because he feels its existence within himself. Each member of the audience was once, in germ and in phantasy, just such

> an Oedipus, and each one recoils in horror from the dream-fulfilment here transplanted into reality, with the whole quota of repression which separates his infantile state from his present one.
>
> (Freud, 1897)

5 An initial reason for divergence can in fact be traced in some accounts to a secession led by a son (Lacan) away from his (parental) institute and the fear that the lower minimum frequency he advocated would prove highly competitive. In time the minimum became the standard. Today far more than just frequency is involved.

6 As Martin Bergmann (2004) has shown, this began with Freud. When he disagreed with Adler in the Vienna Society, he did not hold a discussion and set out the arguments in the Society; he used his authority. It has tended to go on like that. This confusion was later added to by excluding the discussion of work (e.g., Adler, Jung, Klein depending on the Institute) rather than discussing it and what the problems perceived with it were.

7 Neither was I successful later when although twice elected to the Board with overwhelming support from European members, I failed miserably to persuade it either to reduce its bureaucracy in favour of such expenditure or to focus rigorously on educational and clinical standards. In fact, they are never discussed in any substance.

8 Most EPF Society presidents had two-year terms.

9 To me this phrase belongs to Betty Joseph. She used to tell this to my children on our holidays in such a serious and lively way they could usually accept the deprivation at stake!

Bibliography

Aisenstein, M. (2010). Letter from Paris. *Int. J. Psycho-Anal.*, 91(3):463–468.

Bergmann, M.S. (ed.) (2004). *Understanding Dissidence and Controversy in the History of Psychoanalysis*. New York, Other Press.

Britton, R. (2021). *Sex, Death and the Superego: Updating psychoanalytic experience and developments in neuroscience*. London, Routledge.

Bulletin (1935). II. Conclusion of Report of the Thirteenth International Psycho-Analytical Congress—General Meeting of the International Training Commission. *Bul. Int. Psychoanal. Assn.*, 16:242–245.

Conrotto, F. (2011). On the Frequency of Psychoanalytic Sessions: History and Problems. *Ital. Psychoanal. Annu.*, 5:123–134.

Erlich, H.S. (2010). Letter from Jerusalem. *Int. J. Psycho-Anal.*, 91(6):1329–1335.

Erlich, S. & Erlich-Ginor, M. (2018). Psychoanalytic Training—Who is Afraid of Evaluation? *Int. J. Psycho-Anal.*, 99(5):1129–1143.

François-Poncet, C. (2009). The French Model of Psychoanalytic Training: Ethical Conflicts. *Int. J. Psycho-Anal.*, 90(6):1419–1433.

Freud, S. (1897). Letter 71 Extracts from the Fliess Papers. The Standard Edition of the Complete. *Psychological Works of Sigmund Freud*, 1:263–266.

——(1923). The Ego and the Id. *The Standard Edition of the Complete Psychological Works of Sigmund Freud*, 19:1–66.

——(1930). Civilization and its Discontents. *The Standard Edition of the Complete Psychological Works of Sigmund Freud*, 21: 57–146.

——(1933). New Introductory Lectures on Psycho-Analysis. The Standard Edition of the Complete. *Psychological Works of Sigmund Freud*, 22:1–182.

——(1938). An Outline of Psycho-Analysis. The Standard Edition of the Complete. *Psychological Works of Sigmund Freud*, 23:139–208.

——(1939). Moses and Monotheism: Three Essays. The Standard Edition of the Complete. *Psychological Works of Sigmund Freud*, 23:1–138.

Junkers, G., Tuckett, D. & Zachrisson, A. (2008) To Be or Not to Be a Psychoanalyst—How Do We Know a Candidate is Ready to Qualify? Difficulties and Controversies in Evaluating Psychoanalytic Competence. *Psychoanalytic Inquiry*, 28:288–308.

Kernberg, O.F. (2000). A Concerned Critique of Psychoanalytic Education. *Int. J. Psycho-Anal.*, 81(1):97–120.

——(2002). Presidential Address. *Int. J. Psycho-Anal.*, 83(1):197–203.

——(2004). Discussion: "Problems of Power in Psychoanalytic Institutions". *Psychoanal. Inq.*, 24(1):106–121.

Kuchuck, S. (2008). In the Shadow of the Towers: The Role of Retraumatization and Political Action in the Evolution of a Psychoanalyst. *Psychoanal. Rev.*, 95(3):417–436.

Larmo, A. (2018). Reflections on Björn Sahlberg's article: training analysis and training models. *Scand. Psychoanal. Rev.*, 41(2):137–139.

Letter (2006). Final Education Motion. *Int. J. Psycho-Anal.*, 87(3):8.

Lewin, B.D. & Ross, H. (1960). *Psychoanalytic Education in the United States*. New York, Norton.

Nyman, R., Kapadia, S. & Tuckett, D. (2021). News and Narratives in Financial Systems: Exploiting Big Data for Systemic Risk Assessment. *Journal of Economic Dynamics and Control*, 127.

Pyles, R.L. (2016). The Good Fight Continues. *J. Amer. Psychoanal. Assn.*, 64(1):161–175.

Reed, G.S. & Levine, H.B. (2004). The Politics of Exclusion. *Psychoanal. Inq.*, 24(1):122–138.

Rudden, M.G. & Bronstein, A. (2015). Transference, Relationship and the Analyst as Object: Findings from the North American Comparative Clinical Methods Working Party. *International Journal of Psychoanalysis*, 96:681–703.

Sahlberg, B. (2018). Training Analysis and Training Models: There's More to it Than Yes or No. *Scand. Psychoanal. Rev.*, 41(2):119–125.

Squitieri, G. (2011). Il modello Eitingon. *Rivista Psicoanal.*, 57(4):925–939. (See www.pep-web.org/ for full text translation.)

Tuckett, D. (1998). Evaluating Psychoanalytic Papers: Towards the Development of Common Editorial Standards. *International Journal of Psychoanalysis*, 79(3):431–448.

——(2017). *The EPF from 1999 to 2004: On the History of the EPF*, www.epf-fep.eu/eng/article/the-epf-from-1999-to-2004

Tuckett, D., Amati Mehler, J., Collins, S., Diercks, M., Flynn, D., Frank, C., Millar, D., Skale, E. & Wagtmann, M. (2020). Psychoanalytic Training in the Eitingon Model and its Controversies: A Way Forward. *International Journal of Psychoanalysis*, 101:1106–1135.

Ungar, V. (2018). *Further Communications on the Development of the Eitingon Model*. Published at www.ipa.world/IPA/en/en/Training/VU_development_Eitingon.aspx

Wallerstein, R.S. (1998). The IPA and the American Psychoanalytic Association: A Perspective on the Regional Association Agreement. *International Journal of Psychoanalysis*, 79:553–564.

——(2010). The Training Analysis: Psychoanalysis' Perennial Problem. *Psychoanal. Rev.*, 97(6):903–936.

Zachrisson, A. (2018). The Question of the Training Analysis System. Notes from the debate in Oslo. *Scand. Psychoanal. Rev.*, 41(2):126–128.

Zimmermann, D. (1983). Relationships among Training Analysts. *Ann. Psychoanal.*, 11:99–122.

Chapter 9

Developing, holding and containing new psychoanalytic groups

Cláudio Laks Eizirik

In this chapter I will describe and discuss some aspects of the development of new psychoanalytic groups within the International Psychoanalytical Association (IPA), a work carried out by the International New Groups Committee (ING).

The IPA is an association including 12517 psychoanalysts as members, 5333 analysts in training and works with 83 constituent organizations. It was founded by Sigmund Freud in 1910. The Board of the IPA delegates the responsibility for the development of new IPA groups to its International New Groups Committee, whose members ordinarily consist of the Chair of ING and the three ING Co-Chairs for each IPA region. The ING purpose is to stimulate the development of psychoanalysis by facilitating the development and progression of new groups, ensuring the proper development of a group's capacity to work as a scientific society and to produce high quality training programs.

This is a complex and delicate process, to which many IPA members have dedicated and continue to dedicate their honorary tireless efforts and skills. Among these skills are their capacity to hold and to contain all sorts of anxieties, side by side with huge amounts of work and trust in the development of psychoanalysis.

Despite having previous opportunities of dealing with and even taking decisions concerning this extremely important activity, during my four year term as IPA President, and my ongoing interest in psychoanalytic institutions and psychoanalytic training (Eizirik and Foresti, 2019, 2018, 2019a, 2019b), it was only during the last four years, as ING Chair, that I was able to engage directly and intensely on the development, holding and containing of new psychoanalytic groups.

The ING process and the role of sponsors

The ING currently works with 14 Sponsoring Committees, monitoring Study Groups; nine Liaison Committees, working with Provisional Societies, the

DOI: 10.4324/9781003301936-10

European Psychoanalytic Institute – EPI (formed jointly by the IPA and the EPF), the Latin American Psychoanalytic Institute – ILAP (formed jointly by the IPA and FEPAL) and the China Committee – working in China to train IPA candidates.

Jointly, these bodies train over 400 candidates. The ING also includes Allied Centers, composed of people interested in psychoanalysis, such as mental health workers, in places where there are no IPA societies.

The ING Committee works through a continuous communication among its Chair, Co-Chairs, Sponsors[1], Liaisons and the London Head of the ING office and her assistant, with whom the ING Chair holds weekly online meetings. There are also meetings with Sponsors or Liaisons when a specific situation requires. From now on, when I say 'we', I mean this central team described.

Broadly speaking, a future new group represents a new initiative in places where there may exist, or not, an IPA Society or is the result of a split in an existing society.

When a group first contacts the ING to apply for Study Group status we assess the readiness of the group. An IPA Study Group must be composed of at least four IPA members. These members must maintain membership in their IPA Constituent Organization or be Direct Members of the IPA. They must live close enough to each other to enable the group to function as a cohesive unit, meet regularly and develop a strong training program. All four members must be actively involved in the group and its development. We also take into consideration potential ethical issues. From the documents that are sent to the ING by the group, and the exchange of letters with the applicants, we try to assess how the group was formed, what amount of experience and what kind of identification with psychoanalysis they have and what achievements are already in place. It is important to study the history of each group, their previous engagements, if and why all IPA members are or are not included and so on. This initial assessment includes both procedural aspects and offers a preliminary prognosis of what can happen in the future development.

Basseches (2019) considers that there are organizational issues that emerge when new groups begin to form and develop, presenting challenges to their successful and creative development. Each new group has its own challenges, based on the unique characteristics of its local circumstances. Initial issues such as having sufficient number of IPA members – some of whom must function as Training and Supervising Analysts – being able to convene together easily in an accessible location, having basic financial resources to operate, and a pool of potential candidates to train, are all hurdles to be faced.

Moreover, according to Basseches (2019) there are cultural, historical and political aspects of such groups that may or may not be helpful to forming a psychoanalytic entity. Included in this latter perspective are historical and legal traditions within the local mental health establishment which support or discourage participation by one or another professional specialty. These traditions often run counter to IPA expectations of who could or could not be trained to become a psychoanalyst, and force potential new groups to struggle with whether to join the IPA's psychoanalytic approach or to remain nestled in their previously held boundaries.

If we are satisfied with the information provided, a small committee is appointed to visit the group and assess its application in person. In this first visit, the site visiting committee is asked to observe the group dynamics, the quality of relationships among the members, in group and individual interviews, trying to evaluate the ethical values and foresee any possible problems. This process is extremely important and challenging at the same time. Sometimes it is compared with the initial assessment of patients for analysis or potential candidates for training, but in my view this is an unfortunate comparison. Group dynamics, history, motivation, limitations and possibilities present a very complex situation, and one of the challenges we face is to select colleagues who are able to perform these functions well.

A sponsor or a liaison has to be a training analyst in his/her Society, with a lot of analytic and institutional experience, and a particular ability to connect with colleagues and to work with groups. Usually there are two sponsors working with a study group, but sometimes three, according to the size of the study group or its specific needs. In my experience, these couples of sponsors mostly develop a positive working relationship and very often a personal friendship. They work together for many years, and they face several challenges, connected with their role, both objective and symbolic. Mostly, the sponsors are felt as inspirational objects, and even protective ones; they mainly visit the groups twice a year, for an intensive immersion in the group's life, achievements and problems, dedicate long hours of voluntary work to reading documents, reports, theoretical and clinical papers.

Sometimes, however, sponsors are unconsciously seen as agents of an external power, the IPA, trying to impose rules, procedures and requirements that the new group or part of its members feel as unacceptable. Then, at some point of their meetings with the sponsors, one or more members of a study group may recall the experience they previously had in their countries with dictators, tyrants and other dangerous people, associations that may show how the sponsors are being perceived at that moment. Sometimes, there is a splitting in the group's mind, leading to viewing the sponsors as the benevolent parents and the ING Chair and Co-Chairs as the persecutory ones.

All these situations are better dealt with when the sponsors have a strong connection between them and are able to discuss and deal with these challenges taking into account their institutional and psychoanalytic experience. In general, the understanding of unconscious fantasies producing group conflicts or the presence of the basic assumptions described by Bion (1961) provide knowledge/background for the sponsors to deal with the group; in others, it is necessary to discuss them openly with the group in order to have a joint understanding and move forward with the group activities.

According to Flechner (2019), at the beginning, we can see a period of adaptation between the group and the sponsors; paranoid anxieties inside the groups are sometimes handled as feelings of strangeness that come from a sensation of surveillance from the IPA representatives, but over time the sponsors end up being accepted and considered as true collaborators. Sponsors accomplish their task with admirable dedication. Their commitment and interventions in each visit or virtual contact with the new groups allow them to carry forward their growth, maintaining the ethical parameters required by the IPA.

When a Study Group is approved by the Board, a Sponsoring Committee is appointed with the task to guide and set the basis for a future psychoanalytical society: the organizational structure, training, scientific life, ethical code and outreach activities. Sponsors play a crucial role in the development of a group at all stages, but perhaps more so during the initial one, when there is a strong need to obtain and develop a feeling of belonging to the IPA, the group's own identity as separate from previous analytic or other groups, and a growing trust on the ability to work analytically.

Basseches (2019) stressed the impact on groups of IPA Sponsoring Committees. She believes that their role can be pivotal in the way that group foundation can be enhanced or undermined by their interventions and emphasizes that the ING needs to pay close attention to the chemistry of those who function in these outside group supportive roles to be sure that it is actually a collaborative and supportive role and not an authoritarian one.

ING maintains a close relationship with all sponsors, through their reports, sent twice a year after each visit, and also through a meeting in person each year. At each regional and IPA congress, we hold a general meeting with all sponsors and liaisons from the relevant region, where we discuss some theoretical or practical issues related to their activity. In recent years, these joint meetings discussed relevant issues such as: "First generation officers (founders) of new analytic organizations and their relationships with the Sponsors", "Splits in psychoanalytic societies and new groups", "The first steps of a Study Group after a traumatic split", "The history of a Study group that developed successfully and the role of its Sponsors". In each of these meetings, both sponsors and liaisons and ING Chair and Co-Chairs present initial papers, to introduce the discussion.

In addition, we hold a private meeting with each Sponsoring and Liaison Committee, where they can speak more openly and discuss complex issues or concerns, including ethical ones. For example: how to deal with an aging training analyst, with early signs of dementia, to whom some of his colleagues continue to refer patients and supervisees; how to face rivalries between two leading members that threaten to impair the development of the group; how to face strong demands from study group members to become a provisional society before the time established in our procedures and the maturational work is completed; how to deal with fights for power that may involve ethical breaches at a study group, splits and conflicts among the generation of pioneers which can continue in the following generations (Aisenstein, 2019a; Eizirik, 2019a).

These private meetings are a continuous source of learning for all participants, because the chair and co-chairs do not have prepared answers to each of these and many other questions, so what often happens is a candid exchange of previous experiences, to establish reasonable ways of facing difficult situations. It is a conversation among colleagues with institutional and psychoanalytic experience that helps to find new ways of understanding and thinking about individual and group dynamics.

When a group has accomplished all the tasks required and the sponsors and the ING feel they are ready to be accepted for Provisional Society status, and this decision is approved by the IPA Board, a Liaison Committee is appointed to visit the group once a year to guide them through the final stages of development until they are ready for Component Society status and complete autonomy. This last stage towards becoming a Component Society is also not without conflicts and struggles involving autonomy versus dependency, the wish to have freedom to develop its analytic life versus the fear of not being able to do so, requiring to be carefully worked through with the liaisons.

Since the beginning of the coronavirus pandemic, ING activities have been undertaken online. From the reports and the meetings we have had with sponsors and liaisons, following our usual procedure of monitoring, holding and containing, we can assess that the work continues, with the unavoidable losses of in person communication and meetings, but at the same time with the effectiveness that the circumstances allow. This new situation will have to be studied and evaluated as time goes by.

Splits in psychoanalytic societies and the beginning of study groups

In order to introduce some remarks about splits in psychoanalytic societies, I will describe the history of a fictional society (inspired by observations about several ones). This fictional society was founded in the fifties, developed well until being recognized by the IPA in the early sixties, became one of the main societies of the country and in the early nineties went through a split: some of its members joined other analysts who had arrived from another country to begin a new IPA study group in the same city.

This split was a traumatic event that went beyond the walls of the existing Society and the new group, and produced several wounds that took many years to heal, or did not heal at all. Friendships ended, analyses were interrupted, confrontations were publicly exposed and a strong competition was established, both into the psychoanalytic movement and in the external community. Apart from the fact that the newcomers from the foreign country brought some theoretical new emphases, analysts from both groups, the old and the new one, remained connected to the main authors and theories that prevailed since the beginning of the old society, and both groups followed the natural theoretical developments of our field. In short, there was no theoretical reason for the split.

As time went by, new generations of analysts were trained in both societies, relatives of members of one society went into analysis with members of the other, members of one society married members of the other and then even the main characters of the drama of the split resumed their former relationship, of course somewhat cautiously. In this new scenario both societies organized joint activities, received hosts from other places and shared national boards of analytic institutions.

So, the first question is: why did this split happen?

In my view, the basic reasons can be found in Freud's Totem and Taboo (1913), Group Psychology and the Analysis of the Ego (1921), and in papers by Bion (1961), Jaques (1976), Kernberg (1998), among others. So I will suggest one possible way of understanding the origins of that split.

It seemed that the relationship of the founding members was very good, under the leadership of the founding father, with strong ties and a feeling of joint work, with concrete results and a real pride in the group's achievements. However, one of the brothers apparently was or at least did his best to look or to act as if he was the favorite son. Maybe this was the view of his colleagues, many of them unhappy with his analytic development. The original pact was broken and in a complex network of crossed transference and countertransference, involving the third generation (candidates in analysis with members of the second one), this supposed preferred son was slowly undermined in his ambitions and eventually decided to leave the society with all his candidates, and to join with the newcomers.

Looking from a psychoanalytical perspective, he was symbolically killed, and then there was no other possibility except to leave. One could also consider that this fight was also a way of attacking the founding father, who was still alive but too old and unable to manage this crisis, as he had done with past ones. What could be the origin of this crisis? The brother's narcissistic needs? The envy of the other brothers of his national and international prestige? The feeling that the founding father loved him more than the others? The long repressed rivalry, competition, jealousy, envy among the brotherhood and all those bad feelings that apparently did not exist under the disguise of a happy family? All of those?

Elliott Jaques (1976) distinguished two types of social organizations: requisite and paranoiagenic. Requisite organizations are structurally sound – that is, authority and accountability are matched, and it is possible to get the right number of people for the right task at the right time; they are organizations with a functional administrative structure. Such organizations, according to Jaques, enable people to relate to one another with confidence and to rule out suspicion and mistrust. Paranoiagenic organizations, notes Jaques, make it impossible for individuals to have normal relationships of confidence and trust. They force social interactions into a mould calling for forms of behavior which arouse suspicion, envy, hostile rivalry and anxiety, and put brakes on social relationships, regardless of how much individual good will there might be.

In my view, we can observe, in our psychoanalytic organizations, the alternation or predominance of one of these two structures, and when the second one prevails, splits or endless crisis will occur, but we can also observe these two kinds of functioning in the same institution, simultaneously or one after the other. In Kleinian language, we can describe these ways of functioning as schizo-paranoid and depressive, obviously.

In the aforementioned fictional example, it seems to me that the requisite organization of the first years was substituted by a paranoiagenic one and that this type of functioning remained between the two societies for a long period, until more recent developments.

The second question is whether this split could or should be prevented. On this point, I strongly agree with Aisenstein (2019b), when she states that our first attempt should be to reconcile, but sometimes it is better to let each one, be it a couple or two groups, follow his or her or their way. In this case, it would be impossible to reconcile, and the split stimulated each group to follow its own way. The paranoid atmosphere naturally led the old group to call the new one irresponsible, untrustworthy, psychopathic and so on, while the new one called the old one conservative, reactionary, rigid, old fashioned and so on. But both groups devoted their effort to study, train candidates, publish, research and develop psychoanalysis. When they were able to meet and to talk, eventually, they could share mutual experiences, difficulties and achievements.

According to Aisenstein (2019a) the reasons mentioned to explain splits are often theoretical and technical divergences, but she recalls the fine example of the British Society and the passionate Controversies between Anna Freud and Melanie Klein in London during the war.

She recalls that London was being bombarded while the psychoanalysts were fighting with words over psychoanalytic concepts…and today, the Kleinians, Anna Freudians, Independents and Middle Group coexist, not without tensions, but without being separated, within the British Society.

In other words, it seems to her that divergences, even profound ones, can be fruitful if dialogue is not severed.

Aisenstein is convinced that the deep and implicit causes of certain splits are linked to the confrontation of characters and narcissisms that cannot tolerate each other.

She is, of course, in favor of attempts to bring about a conciliation between the parties in conflict, and the IPA often takes on this third party role, sometimes very fruitfully.

On the other hand, she thinks that just as there are bad marriages in which two personalities of quality would benefit from separating, there are toxic confrontations.

Taking into account her long experience with new groups, she prefers to have two good groups that are in rivalry but work well, rather than just one group that is paralyzed by conflicts and hatreds that impede creativity.

The role of leaders in the development of new groups

We are well aware of Freud's insights on the role of leaders and their relationship with the group or the masses (Freud, 1921). Previously I mentioned several analytic thinkers who discussed this issue more recently.

What I will present here are recent reflections from two ING co-chairs, Harriet Basseches and Marilia Aisenstein, based on their past and current experience and then I will describe my own views on this relevant issue.

According to Basseches (2019) the first issue that deserves attention is rivalry. Rivalry may occur between two leaders of an organization, a rivalry that disrupts and sometimes defeats group formation with both parties leaving; or such a rivalry may end up with one leader successfully defeating the other and thus emerging as the dominant leader. If both leave, the wounded group may still emerge with a lesser leader stepping in. Then it becomes a matter of whether the surviving group members can be generative enough to pass on to new generations their psychoanalytic organizational seed. While at first it may be a weaker entity, with time it can emerge as a stronger union in the absence of the powerful, charismatic leader. Here Basseches is referring to the concept of generativity, proposed by Erikson (1963), to denote a concern for establishing and guiding the next generation.

The question that gets worked through, especially by the later generations, is whether the original traumatic rivalry stays buried in the fabric of relationships emerging later as transgenerational trauma, or whether the later group can use awareness of that danger to stay alert to it and avoid temptations and thus to unite.

Basseches (2019) describes that one of the most successful new groups she monitored has been led primarily (although not exclusively) by women. In this particular case, it happened that men provided guidance (as Sponsoring Committee) and a situation where a man was the original leader, but, like Moses, did not go on to the promised land of becoming part of the study group.

Basseches reflects then on the charismatic leader. She thinks that when the founder is such a leader, he or she brings enthusiasm and intensity to their role that draws a strong organizational group around them. It is then a meaningful challenge for such a person to not only provide the strong foundation for the group, but then, in the spirit of generativity, to help the next generations, to be able to continue the development of the organization. To let go of his or her centrality and transfer their leadership to others does not diminish but rather enhances their stature and respect. It seems to Basseches that the Moses metaphor mentioned earlier, though a lot to ask of someone who has achieved so much, creates an organizational triumph by letting go, to build the greater legacy of a cohesive and forward-looking institution that can survive.

The issue of leadership was also explored by Aisenstein (2019b).

According to her, as the groups are totally disparate, their organizations different, their sizes variable and their stories not comparable, we have to look for what she calls the 'common denominators'.

In her view, we underestimate the immense efforts made by 'charismatic leaders'. We underestimate this because we arrive as IPA members when the group is ready to be evaluated. We do not know about the years of prior work on the ground led by the 'founding leaders'. Often these people have sacrificed significant years of their working lives and their family lives to see a Study Group recognized by the IPA. They are by definition strong, charismatic and passionate personalities, as described by Basseches (2019).

Aisenstein (2019b) mentions the book *"Fanaticism in psychoanalysis, upheavals in Psychoanalytic institutions"*, by Manuela Utrilla, that offers a close study of the psychic construction of 'leaders'.

According to Utrilla (2013), 'charismatic leaders' always create their 'followers'.

Passion for their ideals, conviction and positive narcissism (as described by André Green, 2001) are indispensable traits in becoming a charismatic leader. In order to surround oneself with a group, to carry it onward, to fight to have it recognized, one needs a passion for ideals with which the subject risks ending up identifying him/herself totally.

So, in such men or women these characteristics probably exist in an embryonic state but are barely discernible. What are the conditions that lead them to their climax? And how could we best manage them?

Aisenstein (2019a) mentions that several scenarios may exist. There are 'leaders' whom the exercise of power tranquilizes and improves.

Others, on the other hand, seem incapable of living without what they consider their *mission*: that is, to educate, to convince, to transform according to *their own image*. But when they feel they are losing their power, it often happens that they become destructive both for the group and for themselves.

This is where she thinks we could see ING playing a role. Those kinds of initial fights between two or three historic leaders will be transmitted to their analysands and supervisees and create tensions and hate within the group.

Aisenstein (2019a) thinks that often we believe in continuity, but continuity is sometimes a trap. According to her experience, Sponsoring and Liaison Committees are themselves vulnerable and may remain too close to leaders. Or, on the other hand, they may unwittingly push groups into conflict with their 'founders'.

Now I will get back to the fictional example of a split into a society and the formation of a new study group in that city. While reading and summarizing the ideas put forward by Aisenstein and Basseches, another possible way of understanding that split came to my mind. The first idea is that it was an example that a split may be a positive outcome for a conflict, as it happened in that situation. The other idea is connected with the charismatic leader, so well described by them and by Manuela Utrilla. It is possible that the so-called preferred brother was a charismatic leader, both on the positive and negative versions of this kind of character. In any case, we must take into account the huge effort of the founding psychoanalysts and be more careful and compassionate when they reach the final steps of their productive careers. We had situations in which the ING was able to help some of these colleagues and their groups, but this is where confidentiality draws a line.

Concerning the issue of leadership, my own experience includes the opportunity of working with several different leaders, as well as observing different leaders of new groups and Sponsoring Committees, and, last but not least, occupying the role of leader in many different circumstances. I agree with the important points raised by Basseches and Aisenstein, and I would like to add some others.

There is something in a leader that stimulates his or her colleagues to search into themselves for the best way of taking part in the joint enterprise they are all included in. This is the capacity to lead, to not be afraid of taking risks and to convey to the group the feeling of complete devotion and commitment to his or her mission. It is impossible to be a leader without some amount of narcissism, but what I am stressing here is the fact that a leader needs to be identified with his/her mission and to have a view on what is to be achieved. This ability to inspire and to stimulate can be connected to what Freud (1921) described as the group members projecting their ego ideal into the leader.

Another important trait of the leader is that his/her choices should not be motivated by his/her own interests and that he/she does not appoint or invite people to occupy group functions only among his/her friends. The true leader chooses people according to their expertise and competence. The true leader is able to endure challenges and even heavy criticism or attacks without being destroyed or having the need to retaliate. Another important aspect of the true or charismatic leader is the ability to listen to the colleagues or followers, to try to understand their needs, complaints or criticisms and to change the course of action when new facts and evidences so require. A certain amount of compassion is also required, the empathy that allows someone to put him/herself in the other's shoes and to feel what they are feeling.

I was able to witness and work with groups that were suffering the situation described by Basseches and Aisenstein: leaders who were unable to withdraw from their position, because they felt this loss would mean their own death. Guilt, hatred, feelings of betrayal and of lack of gratitude were identified in group members, producing a dark atmosphere and the risk of splits, or even their reality. That's why I consider it so important for the work of sponsors and liaisons to help all leaders to work through their motivations and the need to stimulate and prepare younger colleagues to take over when the time comes. The democratic structure of all groups, new or old, is of paramount importance, and it needs to be clearly stated on the procedures and into the mind of all members.

I was also able to witness and work with groups whose leaders had a clear notion of their importance and the centrality of their work, but at the same time were able to accept that new leaders were emerging and would help them in the first stages of their work. More than once, I witnessed new leaders expressing their gratitude to old ones, and promising they would remain as eternal consultants and even a kind of guru.

Some of these old leaders felt deeply disappointed when this did not happen; others were able to understand that new leaders need to have their own plans and ways of leading. In short, to be a charismatic leader includes some degree of vulnerability, due to narcissistic needs, as if the power would be for life, thus helping to cope with primitive fears and anxieties. What I mostly witnessed is this kind of leader in our new study groups, colleagues who fully devoted their energy and skills to their task and who, afterwards, were admired and even loved by their colleagues. At a certain point in their careers, they did not need any formal position, because their colleagues, old and new, knew they were there to help, to give advice, to support, to hold and to contain for the rest of their lives.

Ethical issues and the development of a culture of confidentiality

The ethical dimension encompasses the field of our relations with others, mediated, explicitly or implicitly, by codes of prescriptions, for the legitimization of behavioral patterns. However, this ethical dimension involves human beings in reflexive relations, relations to us and to others. The metaphorical figure of the ethical dimension is the home, the place where we live. Etymologically, ethos is the root of habit, practice and home. Home is a place of shelter, hosting the conditions for the possibility of protection, food and pleasure. To take ownership of our work is to gain some kind of serenity to experience life outside the shelter, to experience challenges and possibilities of the double condition of existence, being thrown into a world that is not chosen, and to recognize the need to build an inside and an outside world to be in. Relations with others are built in this mediation, where there is reliability and risk, differentiation and protection, responsibility and challenges (Figueiredo, 1995).

Ethical issues play a central role in the development of new groups, despite the fact that many times a group of analysts who begin to develop a new group feel so committed to the task and so united around a joint purpose that they cannot even imagine that ethical breaches may happen at some point of their future development. That's why Sponsoring Committees always include work on an ethical code, and the discussion on ethical principles and problems in their joint meetings with all group members. In this chapter, I am stressing the importance of the position of sponsors as collaborators, inspiring objects and providers of guidance and the need to follow and behave according to the IPA procedures and ethical requirements. Seminars, case discussion and open discussion on ethical issues may contribute to a better understanding and even the prevention of future problems.

When ethical breaches really happen, sponsors will smooth the way for the study group to seek the help of the IPA Ethics Committee.

Among so many dimensions of ethics and ethical problems, I will focus mainly on the challenge of fostering a culture of confidentiality, and describe some issues and concerns that were discussed within the ING community. In order to do so I will review some relevant points of the report of the IPA Confidentiality Committee and then I will describe and discuss the current state of our work concerning confidentiality in reports and communications among us.

About confidentiality

The Report from the IPA Confidentiality Committee from November, 2018, is an extremely important resource to help us when facing problems and dilemmas concerning confidentiality. I will highlight some of the main points they express and their main recommendations, since this is a relatively new document. I suppose not many colleagues have had the opportunity of getting in touch with their relevant contributions as is the case with the ING Committee.

In their general conclusions, the Committee mentions that the principle of confidentiality is one of the foundations of psychoanalysis, which is stated by the IPA in its Ethics Code, and this has consequences both for the IPA as a professional organization and for its individual members. Confidentiality is a matter both of ethics and of technique. It is essential for the well-being and future development of psychoanalysis, as well as for the well-being and benefit of patients. Ensuring the maintenance of confidentiality can be a complex, difficult and challenging task. The Committee considers that in our current professional culture there are gaps between the theory and practice of confidentiality, as we know, even if only anecdotally, that in actual psychoanalytic practice the thoroughness with which confidentiality is maintained is highly variable.

In this report they have identified major risks to confidentiality across three broad areas: 1) sharing of clinical material with colleagues, which is for the benefit of individual patients and of patients generally, but which can come into unavoidable and ultimately unsolvable conflict with the need to preserve confidentiality; 2) telecommunications and use of technology, especially but not exclusively in 'remote analysis', which is creating new risks for which only partial protection is possible; 3) requests from patients and from third parties for access to process notes, where ethical and technical considerations are at risk of being subordinated to legal or political ones.

Furthermore, across all three of these areas, problems arise concerning the possibility of obtaining 'informed consent', given the complications due to the transference in any psychoanalytic situation and the inherent unpredictability of unconscious psychic content at all stages of an analysis. Despite the fact that the IPA has a responsibility to provide guidelines for its members concerning all of these risks, psychoanalysts cannot escape the obligation of making difficult ethical and technical decisions on a case-by-case basis, often with insufficient information. For this they may need not only guidelines but also institutional support. Psychoanalysts generally need to become better informed about the risks to confidentiality. This implies a need for continuing professional development by individual analysts and a corresponding need for the IPA, its committees and its component organizations to develop ways of meeting this need.

The overall recommendation of the Confidentiality Committee is that the IPA should foster and strengthen a culture of confidentiality in every aspect of its operations.

This is something that the ING has already begun trying to do, as I will describe now.

The issue of confidentiality in relation to reports from the ING Committees

The ING Committee has discussed the issue of confidentiality at its regional meetings with Sponsoring and Liaison Committees, including how reports of visits should be written, reports from Supervisors, the circulation and storage of such reports (including the deletion of them when they are no longer needed). It was stressed that a report should be written with the view that those mentioned in the report will read it. It is important to manage the content of Supervisor reports and recommendations for Direct Membership, ensuring that only the competency of the analyst is addressed – there is no need for information about the case or the patient, biographic data or any information that potentially identifies the patient. The ING is striving to ensure that all of our new groups are mindful of the importance of protecting their patients, candidates and themselves and that groups hold regular ethical seminars.

The ING has received supervisor reports from key people in Component Societies that contain details concerning the case and the patient. This information is unnecessary and puts the candidate, supervisor and anyone who circulates the information at risk – not to mention the potential emotional damage to the patient should they discover that information about their case has been circulated by email. The ING highlights the problem when it presents itself, by redacting sensitive information and requesting original copies are deleted from computers. However, the issue also needs addressing from the source, i.e. the Institutes themselves.

The written case reports from candidates are the most problematic as it is sometimes necessary to include detail in these papers. These papers should be handled with extreme caution, stored on a secure server, protected by a password, not circulated by email and deleted when no longer needed. All Institutes must have a clear procedure for handling these papers. During one of our meetings with our sponsors and liaisons it was suggested that one way of handling this problem could be meeting personally with candidates to carry out most of the assessment in order to negate the need for detailed clinical information to be written down and circulated.

Another final issue is ensuring that supervision, carried out over any form of telecommunications, including fixed and mobile telephones, VoIP applications, email, and any other application which uses the internet, is secure. The problem with any such security issues is that they vary from country to country and therefore it is important that those concerned research what is possible in their own environment.

Several important points were raised during our discussions

Some sponsors feel that there is a danger that Committees will submit reports that don't give any information rather than include something that may be problematic, in the sense that we will lose what is essential from a psychoanalytic perspective, and some even considered that the reports may become void of the very soul of analytic essence. It was considered by other colleagues that it is a difficult balance, even if most of them understand the current need to develop a culture of confidentiality.

It was stressed that there is a chain of confidence which negates the need for detailed information. The ING Committee was appointed by the Board and it is not therefore necessary to include detailed information to back up recommendations. We appoint Sponsors because we trust their judgment and the same should be said for supervisors – they make a recommendation based on their knowledge and experience – it is not necessary for them to include details of the case or the candidate to back up their views.

It was suggested that a candidate could give his or her consent to have information about the supervised case shared. It was pointed out that it would not be appropriate to do this when there was information about the patient included in a report as the patient's confidentiality must also be protected.

There were general concerns about how to keep files safe and it was pointed out that some countries have secure email servers for medical information – but as each country was different it would be up to the individual to look into what was available in their own area.

It was proposed that it is easy to give minimal information when the outcome of an assessment or supervision is positive, but when it is negative it is necessary to prove due process. The importance of discussing difficult situations and problematic cases in person during our meetings, or during the sponsors' visits, was extremely valued.

There was also concern about the detailed reports that candidates submit to Institutes when being assessed in their training. Although this is not an ING issue it was up to each Institute to ensure that there was a secure process for doing this – perhaps meeting personally with the candidates to carry out most of the assessment so there is no need for detailed clinical information to be circulated.

All the issues described about the culture of confidentiality illustrate the work to continue to develop and protect our mutual home, psychoanalysis and the IPA, in a changing world, with its continuous challenges and transformations. The current situation shows the process of transformation from the usual way of communicating and sharing information concerning colleagues and patients into a new way of conceptualizing and protecting the intimacy of analytic work and the delicate process of creating, and developing new analytic groups and societies.

Concluding remarks

In my view, psychoanalysis is a work in progress (Eizirik, 2006), and the ING illustrates very well this conviction. Each one of its previous chairs and cochairs contributed to developing procedures, rules, ways of relating to new groups, sponsors and liaisons, as well as ways of understanding better hopes, expectations, anxieties, frustrations, resistances, devotion, hard work and an overall commitment with the future of psychoanalysis. From the huge amount of activities, experiences, historical and cultural factors involved, conflicts and achievements, I hope I was able to put together some of the main aspects that constitute the vitality and the creativity of this so relevant activity. I hope, also, that I was able to demonstrate the main reasons that make it possible for the ING and all colleagues involved in the work to develop, hold and contain new psychoanalytic groups into the IPA.

What did I learn from the experience of chairing and working with ING?

In my view, the work of initiating and developing new groups into the IPA is possibly one of the most challenging tasks of the association. The selection and monitoring of Sponsoring Committees is greatly related to what kind of future society will be constituted. The proper and continuous work involving sponsors and the leaders and members of new groups, at each stage of their development, jointly with the ING, can enhance or undermine the construction of a society both scientifically solid and able to have a stimulating training program. The same holds true concerning ethical issues and ethical problems. That's why I need to emphasize how important it is to pay continuous attention to the procedural as well as to the emotional aspects involved throughout the development of a new component society.

My experience with the ING taught me the importance of meetings in person (or at least online, these days) both with sponsors and liaisons and group leaders and members. These meetings should be continued, because they allow us to listen to other colleagues, their feelings, anxieties and concerns, thus being able to help them to face them and to move forward. Maybe another important point would be a more structured training for new sponsors, to better prepare them for the work they are about to begin. Another project could be to include more systematically publications and research on the various issues that I presented in this chapter. I understand and described current concerns about confidentiality, but even considering them, it would be possible to develop ING activities further.

Reflecting on holding and containing, Ogden (2005, p.108) stresses that:

> Winnicott's holding and Bion's container-contained represent different analytic vertices from which to view the same analytic experience. Holding is concerned primarily with being and its relationship to time; the container-contained is centrality, concerned with the processing (dreaming) of thoughts derived from lived emotional experience. Together they afford 'stereoscopic' depth to the understanding of the emotional experiences that occur in the analytic setting.

In my view, after this immersion into the ING community, it became clear to me that both processes – holding and containing – are at the very core of the activity involved in developing new analytic groups.

As I described in this chapter, several procedural requirements need to be acquired along the duration of the whole process of developing a psychoanalytic society, but what is essential is the acquisition of a psychoanalytic identity, a feeling of intimacy with psychoanalytic theories and techniques and the ability to live this experience and becoming able to live it again and again with each patient as well as with the institution that was formed and needs to be protected, held and contained from now on.

Last but not least, the experience with the ING was an extremely lively one that produced in me a great admiration, respect and affection for most of the colleagues involved in this task, and for their love for psychoanalysis and the IPA. In such a challenging period of our culture, with so much fear, hatred, corrupt leadership, uncertainty about the future and lack of trust in so many national and international institutions, I witnessed and I feel proud to be part of a group of psychoanalysts who keep our work in progress full of vitality and creativity.

Acknowledgements

I am grateful to Drs. Harriet Basseches, Marilia Aisenstein and Silvia Flechner, ING Co-Chairs for North America, Europe and Latin America, for our joint work and for their continuous support and creative ideas, and to Drs. Gabor Szönyi and Maria Teresa Calabrese, liaisons with EPI and FEPAL. This chapter could not have been written, as well as my work as ING Chair could not have been done without the continuous, friendly, efficient, dedicated and affectionate presence of Joanne Beavis, Head of International New Groups. She is the person who makes all our huge work possible, as she is the real soul of the ING. I am also grateful to Sebastian Montes. I am indebted to Dr. Gabriele Junkers for her careful reading and relevant comments and suggestions.

Note

1   Sponsors are those two–three training analysts selected by ING who accompany the new group until the end of its status as 'Study group'; from 'Provisional Society' status onwards, two liaisons accompany the group until it is recognized as a constituent IPA Society.

References

Aisenstein, M. (2019a) *Splitting in Psychoanalysis, Splits in Psychoanalytic Societies*. Madrid: ING European Study Day Meeting.

Aisenstein, M. (2019b) *Challenges and Difficulties in Establishing and Following New Groups*. London: ING Panel, IPA Congress.

Basseches, H. (2019) *The Challenge of Developing New IPA Psychoanalytic Groups*. London: ING Panel, IPA Congress.

Bion, D.W. (1961) *Experiences in groups*. London: Tavistock.

Eizirik, C.L. (2006) Psychoanalysis as a work in progress. *Int J Psychoanal*: 87, 3:645–50.

Eizirik, C.L. (2011) The IPA administration from 2005 to 2009. In Loewenberg, P and Thompson, N. *100 Years of the IPA*. London: Karnac.

Eizirik, C.L. (2018) Contemporary developments and challenges of analytic training and practice. In Tylim, I. and Harris, A. *Reconsidering the Moveable Frame in Psychoanalysis*. London and New York: Routledge.

Eizirik, C.L. (2019a) *Splits in Psychoanalytic Institutions*. Madrid: ING European Study Day Meeting.

Eizirik, C.L. (2019b) *Fostering a Culture of Confidentiality in IPA Study Groups and Provisional Societies*. London: IPA International Congress.

Eizirik, C.L. and Foresti, G. (2019) *Psychoanalysis and Psychiatry – Partners and Competitors in the Mental Health Field*. London and New York: Routledge.

Erikson, E. (1963) *Childhood and Society*. New York: W.W. Norton.

Figueiredo, L.C. (1995) Foucault e Heidegger. A ética e as formas históricas do habitar (e do não habitar). *Tempo soc.* (online). Vol 7, n.1–2: 136–149.

Flechner, S. (2019) *The Challenges of Developing New Psychoanalytic Groups.* London: ING Panel, IPA Congress.

Freud, S. (1913) Totem and taboo. *S.E.*, 13:69–102.

Freud, S. (1921) Group psychology and the analysis of the ego. *S.E.*, 18:65–143.

Green, A. (2001) *Life Narcissism, Death Narcissism.* Free Association Books.

Jaques, E. (1976) *A General Theory of Bureaucracy.* New York: Halsted.

Kernberg, O. (1998) *Ideology, Conflict and Leadership in Groups and Organizations.* New Haven and London: Yale University Press.

Ogden, T. (2005) On holding and containing, being and dreaming. In: *This Art of Psychoanalysis.* London and New York: Routledge Report from the IPA Confidentiality Committee, November, 2018.

Utrilla, M. (2013) *Fanaticism in Psychoanalysis Upheavals in the Institutions.* London: Karnac.

Looking ahead

Gabriele Junkers

How can we psychoanalysts respond to the complex changes going on in the world? How can we prevail against the regressive forces operative in society and the tendencies they encourage to shun reflection, settle conflicts by means of hatred and violence, and evade genuine encounters, especially at a time when constant contact and immediate gratification serve as a substitute for contemplation and self-reflection? How can psychoanalysis weather these storms and preserve its legacy as a living and thriving science?

There is no panacea for these global troubles, nor yet for the specific conflicts in our analytic groups. We presumably consider analytic training to be the prime task of our institutions, but I believe that we cannot really live up to that claim unless we do everything in our power to improve cooperation and co-existence in our analytic groups.

This volume sets out to cast light on selected aspects of our analytic institutions and thus provide food for thought about the discontent and disaffection that bedevil communication and collaboration in our psycho-analytic groupings. Every author uses writing as a form of self-expression, and the colleagues assembled here will very likely reveal more about themselves as individuals and as group members than they may be aware of. They have assembled their material and carefully worked through the topics they address. In a process of mourning, all of them will have come to accept the fact that we will never find what we seek – consciously and unconsciously – and that our quest will always come up against limits and barriers. At the same time, writing is an engagement with the potential reader within and the reactions we expect from our audience. In this constant bid to regain the (objectivity of an) external gaze trained on our own selves, to see ourselves from the outside, we are greatly assisted by the presence of our readers.

As I worked on this volume and became increasingly convinced that our reflections should center around the concept of "containing," I gained the impression that ultimately the laments about our difficult and hurtful dealings with one another signify one thing: In our organizations we are dealing with

DOI: 10.4324/9781003301936-11

a damaged – and temporarily even broken – container. When we say that an event is "not good" or behavior is "unprofessional and uncollegial," then this judgment is almost always based on an a priori agreement. There is an implicit code, a list of unspoken rules that we know we should abide by but which are regularly violated. This implicitly shared feeling is something that we all have different ideas about, and it looks very much as if it must on no account be exposed to the light of day and never be made explicit.

If we run our minds over the quoted examples of inappropriate behavior displayed by colleagues, the conclusion I believe we will arrive at is that we are dealing here with aspects of a *collegial ethics*. My impression is that, for all our efforts to uphold the standards of professionalism and ethical probity required by psychoanalytic treatment, we have neglected to train an equally searching gaze on our professional conduct as colleagues. I am thinking of those instances where, either temporarily or more permanently, the concern to relate to one another and the capacity for reconciliation between the colleagues involved and for peaceable intervention by the onlooking group are conspicuous by their absence. Defined thus, the problem is indeed an ethical one.

When we analysts refer to ethical failings, we normally mean serious misdemeanors in the relationship between analyst and analysand (sexual exploitation, financial misconduct, etc.). In my experience, members of psychoanalytic organizations display major fear, not to say panic, at the thought of getting even remotely associated with "ethical proceedings" of some kind, let alone actually being involved in such proceedings. I have frequently observed that attempts by fellow analysts to preserve colleagues from such proceedings may go too far and prevent difficult topics from being broached and cleared up. It is not difficult to discern behind such conduct the omnipotent claim that we should, and indeed can, get everything right. Strictly speaking, this is incompatible with the basic assumption of our profession that we are not "lords of all we survey," particularly as we know how powerful unconscious undercurrents can be in the lives of institutions. The difficulties we have with the strictures of our superego are another factor preventing us from taking the liberty of contemplating the many "little" things that happen or the injuries and disappointments we inflict on others as part and parcel of a collegial ethic. But that means that when we are faced by instances of colleagues "ganging up" on some unfortunate victim or scapegoat, we have nothing to fall back on in our attempts to come to terms with the situation.

In our dealings with patients, we are accustomed to making the rules and regulations of such a relationship very clear from the outset and defining the setting accordingly. At the end of training, we more or less *grow into* membership of a psychoanalytic society or institution by submitting an application to be admitted to the organization in question. As far as I know, there is no explicit "beginning" to this procedure, no expression of mutual consent, nor are there initiation rites informing newcomers not only of their rights as members, but also of their obligations. Colleagues I have asked about this all say that they were told they had passed their exams, welcomed and admitted by their societies, and then officially informed about their induction as members of the IPA. But there was never any mention or open discussion of what this membership involved. This squares with my conjecture that we are very glad to join such an organization but equally reluctant to inform others or be informed ourselves about what this *explicitly* means.

In Chapter 3, I strongly advocate clearly defined structures and rules for institutional co-existence. In so doing, I run the risk of being seriously misunderstood. In no way do I believe that rules and structures alone are a guarantee for successful co-existence. They are just one of many resources that make life in complex relationships easier. I have recommended ongoing work-related reflection on how psychoanalytic organizations should function. Just as essential is caring concern for the quality of co-existence therein. By this I mean not only the specific delineation of the rights and duties of members, but also the necessity of breathing life into them in a dynamic discussion process. *Collegial ethics* should be something we are at pains to uphold in our everyday dealings with one another so that we can pass it on to our training candidates in a credible manner. This can only work if we are readily able to step outside the intensity of our dyadic relations with our patients and reflect on what is actually going on at the moment, in other words to take up a third-person perspective. If an individual or a group has problems to cope with, this requirement may be admittedly too much. But at given moments, the task is one that every member of the group is confronted with. With Philip Stokoe (Chapter 6) we might see the ability to uphold ongoing dynamic communication within the group as a secondary protective container that could afford and encourage benevolent inquiry via an external perspective on the group.

Whenever the group is diverted from its task, no matter how small the diversion may be, at that moment no functioning container is available. The same is true of splits in the group. This is a situation that causes anxiety and pressurizes participants into a position characterized by the quest for pleasure, certainty, and omnipotence, in which all that the participants want to do is survive without shame and ultimately act in terms of a dichotomy between right/wrong and just/unjust. This process is the mirror image of an inner setting in every individual as "member of the group." Under the influence of anxiety, we frequently seek an external solution because the inner capacity to assure adequate space for ourselves in the presence of the group is no longer stable, and we need this space to ask ourselves what is actually happening. This stasis can be so all-pervasive that the only solution appears to be the establishment of another analytic society. Instead of regarding a potential derailment as a severe reprehensible personal error with serious consequences, we need first of all to bear in mind that for group crises to register, they must avail themselves of the voices of individual members. It would hence be helpful and supportive for the group to use direct mediation wherever possible in dealing with patently inappropriate behavior.

Thinking about this book, I was reminded of my earlier work in the ethics committee of the German Psychoanalytic Association (DPV) that Raimar Schilling and I reported on in an article for the *IPA Newsletter*.[1] At the time, Schilling's approach to the *mediation* of ethical problems between analyst and patient (candidate) was praised by many colleagues as a very helpful standardized procedure. The approach was geared to the relationship between the practicing analyst and his/her analysand.

Dare we conceive of a comparable, analytically defined structure for the purposes of mediation between two analyst *colleagues* in conflict with one another? One thing this would do would be to demonstrate that "aberrant behavior" can be talked about and worked upon and is one of the things that happens in groups of whatever kind. In addition, it would be a way of imposing limits on the proliferation of destructive defense processes.

These ideas prompted me to contact the IPA and inquire whether existing codes of ethics in psychoanalytic societies were drawn upon primarily in dealing with complaints or accusations from patients and candidates, or whether they also held out the prospect of mediation in dealing with dissension between two analysts. I received the following answer:

"As far as is known, no IPA society has included mediation in its code of ethics. Mediation is not considered to be one of the purposes of an ethics code. These purposes are defined as follows:

1) the code of ethics exists to set down standards for acceptable behavior that all IPA members have to comply with;
2) a patient (or colleague) *can* submit a formal complaint if he/she believes that a colleague has infringed (acted against) one or more of those standards;
3) the purpose of the procedure is to establish as fairly as possible whether such an infringement has taken place or not. This is not a subject for negotiation or mediation but a question of fact;
4) once the facts have been established, there may be scope for mediation, although the IPA's own code, which defines the minimum standards to be complied with, does not provide for such an option."

A clear distinction is made here between right and wrong, retention and exclusion. I found the tenor of the remarks quite harsh, or at least not very friendly, which makes it easier to understand why I have encountered such major anxiety in discussions on ethics and ethical procedure in various societies. It is as if analysts feared ethics as a sadistic object that it is better to give a wide berth to, which in its turn may be the unconscious reason why we so often "forget" to offer regular seminars on professional psychoanalytic ethics. It may also be an explanation for why we repeatedly go to such lengths to protect a colleague from the prospect of ethical proceedings, even if we sometimes have to sacrifice the truth of the matter in order to do so. One product of this attitude is the frequency with which problematic behavior vis-à-vis patients, candidates, or colleagues is passed over in silence.

Thus, we witness how the inherent problems psychoanalysts have with their superegos are outwardly deplored for the impact they have on group members' dealings with one another and yet manage to find their way into the collective voice of the institution. The attitude operative within the group then appears to be geared at smothering any attempt to support or mediation, though frequently one of the reasons for this is that no one has any idea of how such issues might be addressed and tackled.

Accordingly, I shall attempt to transfer the framework for mediation between analyst and analysand to situations arising between one analyst and another and to outline what that framework might look like. A prerequisite would be to make such an offer of mediation part of the institutional regulations so that it can take place within a defined setting and in the form of an official procedure. In my view, it would be better *not* to make it subject to a code of ethics but rather to a separate support-providing body, perhaps along the lines of the Psychoanalyst Assistance Committees that some American societies have set up. This body would need to be made up of colleagues not only known for their allegiance to the analytic attitude, their absolute discretion, and their tact and empathy, but also obliged to avail themselves of a clearly defined set of regulations. A "mere" group of friends acting as go-betweens on an ad-hoc basis would be operating without such a clearly defined institutional framework, and there would be a risk of their efforts being misunderstood in one way or another. But this requirement again confronts us head-on with a major problem: many psychoanalysts would prefer to forgo such support, presumably for fear of revealing themselves to their colleagues as in need of help, a state of affairs very often fraught with insuperable shame.

In the following, I shall attempt to adapt the existing four-stage procedure to cases requiring mediation between colleagues. This attempt is designed to demonstrate that mediation between psychoanalysts is conceivable. The main concern is to create a formalized, clearly defined, transparent setting for this instrument that would be known to all members of a society. The name for such an instrument and the way it should be incorporated into the regulations is something best left to those psychoanalytic societies that find the idea helpful. The purpose of setting down this process in writing is to facilitate a reality-oriented working-through of the much-lamented difficulties we are laboring under. Naturally, documents materializing in the course of the process would have to be reliably destroyed after the termination of mediation.

1. *Preliminary stage*: The process sets in with a *preliminary telephone conversation* with the person who has a complaint to bring forward or with the

person who feels accused, provided that both are interested in settling the matter. This (anonymous) offer of contact in a protected setting opens up space for an initial description of the matter in hand. The attitude of the person conducting the conversation is abstinent, and a record is made of the exchange. At the end of the preliminary conversation, the modalities of the procedure should be explained and formal aspects clarified. The "plaintiff" is asked to describe the problems in a written report, which is then made accessible to the "accused," who is then also asked to present his/her view of the matter in writing. Once both parties have submitted a written account, the mediation process can commence.

Every member of a small pre-ordained group of mediators, all of whom have undertaken to maintain a fundamentally analytic attitude, receives a copy of the two written accounts.

2. *Conversation stage*: Two analysts from the mediation committee (m and f) who are familiar with the accounts speak first with one and then the other of the parties involved about the difficulties they are having, preferably on the same day and at the same place, and maintaining a psychoanalytic attitude. The time-frame should not exceed two hours. The reactivation of the difficulties may set off a highly emotional dynamic possibly providing initial indications of the way the misdemeanor/misconduct/bone of contention in question came about.

3. *Clarification stage*: The members of the mediation committee conducting the conversations document the course and the outcome of the exchanges and summarize their thoughts on the complaint(s) in an initial confidential *internal report*. On the basis of these documents and with knowledge of the written accounts submitted by the two parties, all the other mediation members who have had no contact with the disputing parties arrive at an opinion of their own on the problems at issue and set it down in writing. An opinion-forming process of a more profound nature then takes place in the framework of a group discussion.

4. *Concluding stage*: On the basis of the available documents and the group discussion, the head of the group formulates a final *summing-up* which is placed at the disposal of the two disputing parties. This comes with an offer for the two parties to discuss their dispute in a joint mediatory conversation conducted in the presence of two mediators.

In all cases I know of, the offer of mediation in its original form (between *analyst* and *analysand*) has been gratefully welcomed, even in those instances where it was not actually taken advantage of. The possibility of availing oneself of such an offer of support was felt by all to indicate acceptance of their problem and hence perceived as a source of strength. In conclusion, I should like to propose a thought-experiment centering around an "internal mediation process." Could we imagine the stages described earlier as taking place in our own selves, representing a process of working-through achieved via reflection in our own minds?

I have voiced my conviction that the preservation of psychoanalysis can only be achieved by means of genuinely collegial cooperation with one another, always of course with due awareness of the fact that even when circumstances are favorable not every dispute can be settled. In line with the significance of a protective code of ethics for the work of analysts with their analysands, my wish is that it should be realistically possible for members of analytic groups and societies to tackle difficulties with colleagues by enlisting the help of third persons in a standardized setting. Implementing this idea is unthinkable without an inner setting, and a framework described in terms of external circumstances can certainly have an objectifying supportive function for that inner setting. My concern here has been to present this outline for an analytic form of mediation as food for thought.

Finally, I should like to recall Freud's concluding remark in *Beyond the Pleasure Principle*: "What we cannot reach flying we must reach limping... The Book tells us it is no sin to limp." Freud is quoting here from Friedrich Rückert's translation of the *Maqâmât* by the Persian poet Al-Hariri of Basra. The line Freud omitted runs: "It is far better to limp than to go under completely."[2]

Notes

1 Schilling, R.; Junkers, G. (2002). The Ethics–Mediating committee of the German Psychoanalytic Association. *IPA-Newsletter, 11*(2), 31–33.
2 Churcher, J. (2002). *Conversation and Interpretation*. www.academia.edu/12802911

Abbreviations

APA	American Psychoanalytic Association
APdeBA	Asociación Psicoanalitica de Buenos Aires
CFS	Contemporary Freudian Society, New York
EPCUS	European Psychoanalytic Conference for University Students of the European Psychoanalytic Federation
EPF	European Psychoanalytic Federation
EPI	European Psychoanalytic Institute
EVP	European Exchange Visit Programme
EXCOM	Executive Committee of IPA
FEPAL	Federación Psicoanalítica de América Latina
ILAP	Latin American Institute of Psychoanalysis
ING	International New Groups Committee of IPA
IPA/IPV	International Psychoanalytic Association
IPU	International Psychoanalytic University of Berlin
IUSAM	Buenos Aires University Institute for psychic health
KPSG	Korean Psychoanalytic Study Group
LAISPS	Los Angeles Institute and Society for Psychoanalytic Studies
NAPsaC	North American Psychoanalytic Confederation
PCPCS	Primary Care Psychotherapy Consultation Service
SBP	Societé Belge de Psicoanalise
SPI	Società Psicoanalitica Italiana
UCL	University College London
WP SPTT	Working Party on the Specificity of Psychoanalytic Treatment Today

Index

For Product Safety Concerns and Information please contact our EU
representative GPSR@taylorandfrancis.com
Taylor & Francis Verlag GmbH, Kaufingerstraße 24, 80331 München, Germany